DANGEROUS CHARISMA

The Political Psychology *of* Donald Trump *and* His Followers

JERROLD M. POST, MD
WITH STEPHANIE R. DOUCETTE

PEGASUS BOOKS
NEW YORK LONDON

DANGEROUS CHARISMA

Pegasus Books, Ltd.
148 West 37th Street, 13th Floor
New York, NY 10018

Copyright © 2019 by Jerrold M. Post with Stephanie R. Doucette

First Pegasus Books cloth edition November 2019

All rights reserved. No part of this book may be reproduced in whole or in part without written permission from the publisher, except by reviewers who may quote brief excerpts in connection with a review in a newspaper, magazine, or electronic publication; nor may any part of this book be reproduced, stored in a retrieval system, or transmitted in any form or by any means electronic, mechanical, photocopying, recording, or other, without written permission from the publisher.

Library of Congress Cataloging-in-Publication Data is available.

ISBN: 978-1-64313-775-9

Printed in the United States of America
www.pegasusbooks.com

*To my wonderful wife Carolyn, a full partner in life, who is always there.
And to my three daughters, Cindy, Merrie and Kirsten, of whom I am so proud.
And to my grandchildren, Emily, Rachel, Jack, Sam and Kate, with bright futures ahead.*
—*Jerrold*

To my mother and role model, Barbara, who continues to inspire me.
—*Stephanie*

CONTENTS

PREFACE   vii

INTRODUCTION: *Narcissism and the Charismatic Leader-Follower Relationship*   xv

PART I: THE CHARISMATIC LEADER   1

1: *The Quintessential Narcissist*   3

2: *Entrepreneurial Provenance*   12

3: *Seeking the Spotlight*   30

4: *The Relationships of a Narcissist*   40

5: *King Donald*   55

6: *Political Personality*   64

PART II: THE POLITICAL PSYCHOLOGY OF TRUMP'S FOLLOWERS   77

7: *The Charismatic Leader-Follower Relationship*   79

8: *The Tea Party*   84

9: *A Divided Republican Party*   96

10: *The Working Class and Rural Areas*   121

11: *Permission to Hate*   135

12: *The Unexpected Followers*   165

PART III: TRUMP'S IMPACT   177

13: *The Mental Health of a Nation*   179

14: *The Left's Reaction*   187

15: *Foreign Affairs*   193

16: *What Does the Future Hold?*   221

EPILOGUE   225

ENDNOTES   231

INDEX   263

PREFACE
by Jerrold Post

As the founding father of political personality profiling, I am often asked about the route that took me to my unusual specialty. And like many life decisions, if the truth be known, it was really a matter of serendipity. I had long planned a career in academic psychiatry, and, to my delight, as my two-year research fellowship as a clinical associate at the National Institute of Mental Health was winding down, I had been accepted on the staff at the McLean Hospital, one of Harvard Medical School's premier psychiatric hospitals. My wife and I were already packing for our move to Belmont, Massachusetts. It was a promising beginning to my academic career.

And then came the call that was to transform my life. "Hi, Jerry, this is Herb." After I asked, "Herb who?," the caller identified himself as an acquaintance from medical school, someone two years ahead of me, who was really only a passing acquaintance. "I hear you don't have a job for next year," Herb said—a rather peculiar statement, given I had no idea where Herb had been for the past seven years. "Well, actually I do, Herb, but I'm always interested in talking," I responded, and we made arrangements to have lunch at a little restaurant in Georgetown, the Hickory Hearth. I remembered little about the restaurant other than that it had interior wooden shutters.

It was a very strange lunch. After about twenty minutes, I realized that Herb knew a great deal about me, which was rather peculiar, since (a) I knew nothing about Herb, (b) Herb was finding out more about me, and (c) he had not said word one about a job. "Herb, we were going to discuss a possible job, remember?" His teeth tightly clenched so as to prevent lip reading. Herb responded, "I'd rather not talk about it here." Well, that was kind of weird, I thought. Opening the interior wooden shutters, I sarcastically observed, "Look, there're no electronic bugs here." With a tight smile, Herb said, "Oh, you like that sort of thing, do you?" "Oh, sure," I responded. "I read all of Ian Fleming's James Bond novels in hardcover." Herb smiled mysteriously. "Why don't we take a drive, to someplace where we can talk more privately? Follow me in your car." Weird and weirder, I thought, but what the hell, in for a dime, in for a dollar, and I followed Herb, who was driving a beat-up Volvo, over the Key Bridge and onto the George Washington Memorial Parkway, where he pulled into the first parking overlook. Herb got out of his car and started walking toward me, as I got out of my car. Just as we met, a Park Police squad car drove in. "Oh, damn," Herb exclaimed, turning red in the face. "This happened to me once before. This could be embarrassing. I think we'd better drive on."

I got very anxious. What had I gotten myself into? All I could think of was that Herb was unaware that I was happily heterosexual, thank you very much, and he was about to make a homosexual pitch.

But I followed him to the next parking overlook, where Herb got out of his car, I got out of mine, and this time there was no Park Police squad car. After surveilling the area, Herb reached into his blazer pocket and pulled out a folded piece of paper. "Before I say anything, I want you to sign this." On official Central Intelligence Agency letterhead, it was labeled Secrecy Agreement. Intrigued, I signed, and Herb tightly smiled. He then declared, rather portentously, "Nothing I say can be discussed with anyone." He then proceeded to offer me a position starting a pilot project profiling world leaders at a distance, contingent of course on my getting through the security clearance process.

I obviously had to tell my wife, since we were about to move back to Boston. And I called Steve, my best friend from residency, since I wasn't sure I had the requisite skills for this important position. After all, I hadn't had a single course in international affairs as an undergraduate. Scott reassured me, observing that I was quite good at preliminary psychological profiles based on thin initial evidence, and, then, the clincher, "It sounds like a fantastic once-in-a-lifetime opportunity. What have you got to lose? After all, if you don't like it, you can always return to Mother Harvard after a few years."

PREFACE

That convinced me, but first I had to go through the security clearance process. I had sailed through the background security check, as I knew I would. My background was squeaky clean, boringly so. But on the polygraph, I was doing just fine, no drugs, alcoholism, financial problems, no problems with potentially compromising sexual inclinations, until the polygrapher asked me, "Have you ever given a classified document to an agent of a foreign power?"

"Of course not," I had replied indignantly, and the polygrapher, pointing an accusatory finger at me, said, "You're showing a deception response." Fortunately for me, the polygrapher was very experienced, quite sophisticated, and he burst out laughing so hard, he almost had to pull himself off the floor. He knew from my background that I would never have had access to classified documents and would not have known an agent of a foreign power if I stumbled over one. What he finally sorted out with me, after a series of carefully constructed questions, was that after having signed the secrecy agreement and agreeing to speak to no one, having spoken to my wife and my best friend from my psychiatric residency, I had subconsciously treated this as an act of treason, and so had reacted guiltily to the question about classified documents and foreign agents. So much for the infallibility of the "lie detector!"

◆

And then I began a twenty-one-year career at the CIA, which I can only characterize as a remarkable intellectual odyssey. I had the challenge of developing a method of constructing political personality profiles. Drawing on my undergraduate background in human culture and behavior, I brought together an interdisciplinary team, all at the doctorate level: a cultural anthropologist, a political sociologist, three psychologists with backgrounds in organizational psychology and social psychology, and political scientists with interests in leadership. Several other psychiatrists with an interest in international affairs filled out the team. Each project had a two-man team: a psychologist working with an anthropologist, a psychiatrist working with a political sociologist or a political scientist, etc. I also had the benefit of four consultants from academia with expertise in political psychology, all of whom went through a security clearance. The method we developed insisted upon accurately locating the leader under study in his political, historical, and cultural context. The method and those of several other profilers are described in detail in *The Psychological Assessment of Political Leaders*, a 2003 volume that I edited. Based on the case study method psychiatrists learn in their residency, it consisted of a longitudinal psychobiography coupled with a personality study, only the psychobiographic sketch, rather than emphasizing the life experiences that left the individual vulnerable to mental illness, described the life experiences that shaped the leadership of the political leader.

Assuredly, the highlight of my agency career was taking the lead on the Camp David profiles of Menachem Begin and Anwar Sadat, prepared for President Jimmy Carter at his request, and which he has credited with being of major assistance to him in preparing for the Camp David negotiations. This led to the institutionalization of the Center for the Analysis of Personality and Political Behavior regularly preparing political personality profiles for leaders with whom the president was having a summit meeting, as well as to assist in crisis situations.

After a twenty-one-year-long career with the CIA, I decided to move to academe and was appointed professor of psychiatry, political psychology, and international affairs at George Washington University, with the responsibility of developing a research and education political psychology center. It was from this base that I prepared a political personality profile of Saddam Hussein that led to testifying on two occasions before Congressional committees before the Gulf War and numerous media appearances. After this testimony was presented in a public forum, Ambassador Sam Lewis, then president of the U.S. Institute of Peace, cited the profile as a "contribution of the highest order to the national welfare." It assuredly was a career high point.[1]

The testimony was cited by several congressmen as having contributed to their decision-making during the crisis.

But my moment of pride was short-lived. And what was a career high point became a career low point when the chair of the American Psychiatric Association's Council of Psychiatry and International Affairs, on which I served, called indicating that he wished to speak to me about the profile. I was anticipating a compliment for my contribution to American psychiatry. You can only imagine my consternation when he dolefully intoned, "Jerry, the APA has received letters about your profile of Saddam, and there is reason to believe you may have violated the Canons of Ethics of the American Psychiatric Association." Apparently, as he went on to explain, a "profile of the profiler" article about personality profiling, one that drew on my Saddam Hussein profile, had appeared in the Science News section of the *New York Times*. This led to several letters complaining that

I had violated Section 7 of the Canons of Ethics of the APA, the so-called Goldwater Rule, because I had presented publicly a professional opinion about Hussein without interviewing him and without his authorization. I nearly exploded.

"Have you read the profile?" I asked.

"Well, no," he acknowledged.

"Then perhaps you should before rendering such judgments. The profile is not a psychiatric expert opinion. It is a political personality profile, an art form I have crafted, informed, to be sure, by my education as a psychiatrist, but concerned with such matters as leadership style, crisis reactions, negotiating style, relationship with leadership circle, etc." Moreover, I went on, "I think there is a duty to warn, involving a kind of Tarasoff principle,[2] because the assessments of Saddam's political personality and leadership that are guiding policy seem to me to be off"—he had been widely characterized as "the madman of the Middle East"—"and policy decisions are being made based on erroneous perceptions, which could lead to significant loss of life. In fact, he is a rational decision maker who, however, often miscalculates.

"Accordingly," I continued, "it would have been unethical to have withheld this assessment. I believed I had a duty to warn."

I faxed the profile to him and heard no more on the matter, but the conversation continued to trouble me. How can it be that a presentation deemed to be "a contribution of the highest order to the national welfare" could simultaneously raise questions concerning an ethical violation? Other academic specialists from the ranks of psychology, political science, and history regularly contribute to public discourse on political figures without having interviewed the subject, but for psychiatrists to do so is considered an ethical violation. The ethical principle seemed extreme and overdrawn.

Indeed, placing the Goldwater Rule[3] in the full context of Section 7 of the Canon of Ethics Particularly Applicable to Psychiatrists, it is also stated that psychiatrists "shall recognize a responsibility to participate in activities contributing to an improved community," "are encouraged to serve society," and "may interpret and share with the public their expertise in the various psychosocial issues that may affect mental health and illness."

Thus, beginning during the 2015 Republican Party primaries, continuing through the 2016 presidential campaign, and into his first year of presidency, there has been a rising chorus of opinions from journalists and other lay commentators about Donald Trump's psychology and mental stability. While there have been headlines calling Donald Trump delusional, crazy, psychopathic, narcissistic, manic-depressive, and mentally disturbed, there have been few psychiatrists who have offered opinions about his clinical psychology, inhibited by the Goldwater Rule.

Known for my contributions in profiling Saddam, I have been approached by journalists on forty to fifty occasions for interviews concerning my psychological profile of President Donald Trump, but have declined, citing the Goldwater Rule. But as concerns over the president's psychology and mental stability have risen, with reference to the full context of Section 7, I believe it is imperative, indeed an ethical obligation, to contribute my understandings of the complex psychology of our 45th president and his followers.

With the end of the Cold War, the relative balance in the international system characterized by the superpower rivalry has been replaced by an international arena populated by rogue leaders with widely differing individual agendas and psychologies. As concerns over nuclear proliferation mounted, the Carnegie Corporation Commission on Preventing Deadly Conflict was convened in the late 1990s with its report entitled *Preventing Deadly Conflict: The Critical Role of Leadership*, published in 1999. In the report, coauthor Alexander George emphasized the importance of what he called *actor-specific behavioral modeling* in undergirding coercive diplomacy as well as in managing crisis situations. Deterrence had to be tailored and based on actor-specific behavioral models.

Political Personality Profiling

I had the rich opportunity of frequent discussions with Professor George during the 1960s and 1970s as I was struggling to develop a method for systematically assessing leader personality and political behavior. Drawing on the anamnesis, the case study method I had been taught during my psychiatric residency, with my staff in the Center for the Analysis of Personality and Political Behavior, we systematically developed a practical method for assessing political leader personality profiling, with support from the Carnegie Corporation of New York, the Fund for the Improvement of Postsecondary Education (FIPSE), and the U.S. Department of Education.

The political personality profile was developed in order to provide policymakers with an understanding of psychological issues that affect a head of state's political leadership, decision-making, and negotiations. Thus, it embodies not only the conventional aspects of psychological assessment, but also such leadership considerations as strategic decision style, crisis decision style, negotiation style, and management style, as well as core attitudes. It typically consists of two major sections: a longitudinal section, the *psychobiography*, and a *personality study*, which is more cross-sectional and characterizes the predominant defense mechanisms and the basic personality structure. In addition, there are sections on world view and leadership style.

In creating a personality profile of a political leader, the psychobiography is designed to understand the key life experiences that shaped the individual developmentally and how they contributed to his becoming a leader, and to understand what kind of leader he becomes. It rests on the principle so eloquently summarized in William Wordsworth's epigram, "The child is father of the man." This longitudinal psychobiography is a central feature of the political personality profile.

The life events that an individual experienced which sensitized him/her and made him/her vulnerable to mental disorder were considered analogous to, but clearly different from, the life course events that shaped and influenced an individual's leadership.

To emphasize the importance of the life course, consider the Soviet adolescent who heard of Nikita Khrushchev's de–Stalinization speech at the 20th Congress of the Communist Party in 1956, decrying the cult of personality surrounding Stalin's rule at the very time when developmentally that adolescent was psychologically required to dethrone paternal authority. He would react very differently to it than a fifty-year-old who had long been conditioned to revere the Soviet dictator.

It is essential to accurately locate the subject in his historical/political/cultural context in order to understand the manner in which history, politics, and culture shape and constrain the leader. One simply cannot understand the power of Menachem Begin's vow, "Never again!"—with reference to the requirement for Israel to defend itself against aggression and always to be strong and on alert, never again yielding to nations out to destroy the Jewish people—without understanding his reaction to the chilling fact that most of his family had been killed in the Holocaust.

And how does this help us understand the political psychology of our 45th president, Donald Trump? As will be clarified in chapter two, "Entrepreneurial

Provenance," Trump comes from a long line of entrepreneurs, going back to his paternal grandfather Friedrich, who emigrated from Germany to the United States at age sixteen to participate in the Gold Rush in the West, earning a tidy fortune.

In developing political personality profiles, the two major sections are the psychobiography, the longitudinal description of the life course, which has just been described, and the personality study, the cross-sectional study of personality features. Included in this cross-sectional personality study are elements from the outside in, including appearance, emotional reactions, moods, impulses, cognitive style, intelligence, knowledge, judgment, interpersonal style, drives, and character structure. These elements systematically analyzed identify how leaders approach decision-making, both crisis and strategic decision-making, and the major influences on managing aggression and relationships. Putting this together with a detailed psychobiography can help one understand what makes this individual "tick." Such integrated profiles can provide strong assistance both in senior level negotiations and in crisis situations.

INTRODUCTION

Narcissism and the Charismatic Leader-Follower Relationship[1]

We write not of charismatic leaders but rather of charismatic leader-follower relationships. In this introductory chapter we shall be elaborating on the political psychology of this powerful tie between leaders and followers that will be an essential focus in this book, attempting to identify crucial aspects of the psychology of the leader which like a key, fit and unlock crucial aspects of the psychology of their followers. In delineating this lock and key relationship, we will draw upon emerging understandings of the psychology of narcissism.

When sociologist Max Weber first introduced the concept of charismatic authority, he addressed the psychology of the followers, but only in cursory fashion. He made it clear that he considered that the predominant determinant of the relationship between the charismatic leader and his followers was the compelling forcefulness of the leader's personality, in the face of which the followers were essentially choiceless and felt compelled to follow. Psychologist Irvine Schiffer has observed that later commentators on the phenomenon of charismatic authority have also focused disproportionately on the magnetism of the leader, failing to make the fundamental observations that all leaders—especially charismatic leaders—are at heart the creation of their followers.

A notable exception to this criticism is the corpus of work of D. Wilfred Abse and Richard Barrett Ulman. They give important attention to the psychological qualities of the followers which render them susceptible to the force of the charismatic leader and lead to collective regression, drawing on the remarkable case history of the collective Flavor Aid suicide at the Peoples Temple in Guyana. In so doing, they draw attention to the relationship between the psychological qualities of narcissistically wounded individuals and charismatic leader-follower relationships.

In *The Spellbinders*, her review of the subject of charisma, Ann Ruth Willner has observed that the concept of charisma has been much abused and watered down since Weber first introduced it. The media indeed often use charisma as synonymous with popular appeal, whereas Weber defined charismatic authority as a personal authority deriving from "devotion to the specific sanctity, heroism, or exemplary character of an individual person and of the normative patterns or order revealed or ordained by him." To operationalize the concept, Willner surveyed the vast (and often contradictory) literature bearing on charismatic leadership. She emerges with this definition: Charismatic leadership is a relationship between a leader and a group of followers that has the following properties:

1. The leader is perceived by the followers as somehow superhuman.
2. The followers blindly believe the leader's statements.
3. The followers unconditionally comply with the leader's directives for action.
4. The followers give the leader unqualified emotional support.

In fact, each of these properties relates to a perception, belief, or response of the followers. But Willner nevertheless devotes the majority of her scholarly energies to analyzing the leaders who elicit these responses, paying scant attention to the psychology of the followers. Thus Willner has committed the same sin of omission as the authors of the earlier reviews criticized by Schiffer. Indeed, she relegated Schiffer's pathbreaking psychoanalytic exploration of charisma and mass society to an extended footnote, where he shares the distinguished company of Erik Erikson and Sigmund Freud.

In particular, Willner dismisses an interesting—but unproven—hypotheses that "in times of crisis, individuals regress to a state of delegated omnipotence and demand a leader (who will rescue them, take care of them)" and that "individuals susceptible to (the hypnotic attraction of) charismatic leadership have themselves fragmented or weak ego structures."

In my judgment, there is indeed powerful support for these hypotheses. Clinical work with individuals with narcissistic personality disorders, the detailed studies of individuals who join charismatic religious groups, and psychodynamic observations of group phenomena all provide persuasive support for these hypotheses concerning the psychological makeup and responses of individuals susceptible to charismatic leadership—the lock of the follower for the key of the leader. In particular, these individuals emerge from the earliest developmental period narcissistically scarred, feeling incomplete unto themselves, searching for a powerful nurturing figure to whom to attach themselves.

The central features of the development and phenomenology of the narcissistic personality have significant implications for understanding the nature of charismatic leader-follower relationships. They are described in the first three chapters of this book, which especially delineate pathways to "the wounded self." Here we wish to describe the consequences of the wounded self on adult personality development and emphasize how narcissistically wounded individuals are attracted to charismatic leader-follower relationships, both as leaders and as followers.

Psychoanalyst Heinz Kohut's formulations of the mirroring and idealizing transferences are particularly elegant, and an elaboration of narcissistic transferences is essential to this examination of charismatic leader-follower relationships.[2] Formation of the "injured self" results in two personality patterns that have particular implications for our study of charismatic relationships: the "mirror-hungry" personality and the "ideal-hungry" personality:

> "In other words, we are dealing with either (a.) the wish of a self which feels enfeebled . . . to retain its cohesion by expanding temporarily into the psychic structure of others, by finding itself in others, or to be confirmed by the admiration of others (resembling one of the varieties of mirror transference) or (b.) the need to obtain strength from an idealized other (resembling an idealizing transference)."

The Mirror-Hungry Personality

The first personality pattern resulting from "the injured self" is the mirror-hungry personality. These individuals, whose basic psychological constellation is the grandiose self, hunger for confirming and admiring responses to counteract their inner sense of worthlessness and lack of self-esteem. To nourish their famished self, they are compelled to display themselves in order to evoke the attention of others. No matter how positive the response, they cannot be satisfied, but continue seeking new audiences from whom to elicit the attention and recognition they crave.

The Ideal-Hungry Personality

The second personality type resulting from "the wounded self" is the ideal-hungry personality. These individuals can experience themselves as worthwhile only so long as they can relate to individuals whom they can admire for their prestige, power, beauty, intelligence, or moral stature. They forever search for such idealized figures. Again, the inner void cannot be filled. Inevitably, the ideal-hungry individual finds that their god is merely human, that their hero has feet of clay. Disappointed by discovery of defects in their previously idealized object, they cast him aside and searches for a new hero, to whom they attach themself in the hope that they will not be disappointed again.

Narcissistic Transferences and the Charismatic Leader-Follower Relationship

The phenomenon of the charismatic leader-follower relationship is surely too complex to lend itself to a single overarching psychodynamic personality model. In addition to features of the leader, the followers, and their relationships, one must take into account complex socio-cultural, political, and historical factors. Nevertheless, we believe elements of the narcissistic transferences just described are present in all charismatic leader-follower relationships, and in some charismatic leader-follower relationships are critical determinants.

In certain of these cases, the complementarity between the two transference postures is so striking that it is extremely tempting to relate the two principal actors in this relationship—leaders and followers—to these postures. In the balance of this introductory chapter, we will yield to that temptation, and relate charismatic leaders to the narcissistically wounded mirror-hungry personality and charismatic followers to the narcissistically wounded ideal-hungry personality. In so doing, we wish to emphasize that this is in the service of illuminating certain elements of the psychology of charismatic leaders and their followers, and is not intended as an all-encompassing explanation of all charismatic leader-follower relationships.

The Charismatic Leader as Mirror-Hungry Personality

The mirror-hungry leader requires a continuing flow of admiration from his audience in order to nourish his famished self. Central to his ability to elicit that admiration is his ability to convey a sense of grandeur, omnipotence, and strength. These individuals who have had feelings of grandiose omnipotence awakened within them are particularly attractive to individuals seeking idealized sources of strength. They convey a sense of conviction and certainty to those who are consumed by doubt and uncertainty. This mask of certainty is no mere pose. In truth, so profound is the inner doubt that a wall of dogmatic certainty is necessary to ward it off. For them, preserving grandiose feelings of strength and omniscience does not allow acknowledgment of weakness and doubt.

For the mirror-hungry charismatic leader, the roar of the admiring crowd is music to his ears, a heady elixir. Especially early in his career Fidel Castro would deliver eight-hour perorations, and would seem to gain strength during these remarkable performances. There was an almost chemical connection between Castro and his adoring followers, and their energy seemed to flow into him. On these broiling days, they would be wilting, but he was apparently getting stronger. He required their shouts of approval.

The mechanism of splitting is of central importance in maintaining their illusion.

The Language of Splitting is the Rhetoric of Absolutism

There is the "me" and the "not me," good versus evil, strength versus weakness. Analysis of the speeches of charismatic leaders repeatedly reveals such all-or-nothing polar absolutism.

Either/or categorization, with the charismatic leaders on the side of the angels, is a regular characteristic of their evocative rhetoric. Consider these words of Maximilien Robespierre: "There are but two kinds of men, the kind that is corrupt and the kind that is virtuous." By the virtuous, as Gustav Bychowski notes in *Dictators and Disciples,* Robespierre means those who thought as he did; his main criterion for judging the morals of others became the extent to which they agreed with his ideas. Bychowski has observed the predominance of the theme of strength and weakness in Hitler's speeches: the emphasis upon the strength of the German people, the reviling of weakness, the need to purify the race of any contamination or sign of weakness. But what could be the barrier to the German people achieving its full measure of greatness? "If we Germans are the chosen of God, then they (the Jews) are the people of Satan." This is very similar to the rhetoric of Osama bin Laden. Here the polarity is between good and evil, between children of God and the people of Satan.

"Look at our splendid youth . . . I do not want anything weak or tender in them." Hitler invokes the cult of strength and reviles weakness. "One must defend the strong who are menaced by their inferiors," he asserts, and then indicates that "a state which, in a period of race pollution, devotes itself to caring for its best racial elements must someday become the lord of the earth." The fear of appearing weak is projected upon the nation with which he identifies.

Being on the side of God and identifying the enemy with Satan is a rhetorical device found regularly in the speeches of charismatic leaders. Ayatollah Khomeini continued to identify the United States as "the Great Satan" as did Saddam Hussein. Willner sees this as an identifying feature of the speeches of the charismatic leader that heightens his identity as a leader with supernatural force.

The invocation of divine guidance and use of Biblical references are surely the currency of American political rhetoric, and no politician worth his salt would ignore them. What is the difference between the politician whose use of such rhetoric rings false, as hollow posturing, and the politician whose religious words inspire? Is this related to Rudolf Wildenmann's distinction between charisma and pseudo-charisma? We would suggest that the narcissistic individual who does indeed consciously believe that he has special leadership gifts and accordingly has a special role to play may utilize religious rhetoric much more convincingly. Most convincing of all is its use by leaders like Ayatollah Khomeini and Osama bin Laden, who were indeed genuinely convinced they had a religious mission to perform.

While the ability to convey belief is an important asset, real belief is most convincing. This is also true of the polarization of good and evil, *we* versus

INTRODUCTION

them. Again, while it is a common political tactic to attempt to unify the populace against the outside enemy, the rhetoric of polarization is most effective when, as in the case of Hitler, *they* are absolutely believed to be the source of the problem, *they* are evil, and to eliminate *them* is to eliminate *our* problems. Phyllis Greenacre observed that in order to be effectively charismatic it is a great asset to possess paranoid conviction. While there is no necessary relation between charisma and paranoia, when the two are linked some of the most fearful excesses of human violence in history have occurred.

As will be observed later in discussing the ideal-hungry follower, the posture of total certainty, of total conviction on the part of the leader, is very attractive to one besieged by doubt. Indeed, this posture is necessary to ward off the inner doubt of the leader too. In one of his last essays, Kohut began to consider implications of self-psychology for group psychology and historical phenomena. He summarizes the characteristics of the individual who is especially suitable to become the admired omnipotent model, observing that:

> Certain types of narcissistically fixated persons (even bordering on the paranoid) . . . display an apparently unshakeable self-confidence and voice their opinions with absolute certainty . . . Such individuals' maintenance of their self-esteem depends on the incessant use of certain mental functions . . . they are continually judging others—usually pointing up the moral flaws in other people's personality and behavior—and, without shame or hesitation, they set themselves up as the guides and leaders and gods of those who are in need of guidance, of leadership, and of a target for their reverence.

Indeed, the degree of moral righteousness is often quite extraordinary. Kohut goes on to observe that the psychological equilibrium of such charismatic leaders is of "an all or nothing type: there are no survival potentialities between the extremes of utter firmness and strength on the one hand, and utter destruction on the other."

It is important to reemphasize that such individuals have disowned and projected upon the environment all of the unacceptable weakness and imperfection within themselves. Psychologically they cannot permit themselves to recognize that the source of their feared destruction is not from without but from within. The mirror-hungry personality is held together by this rigid shell of apparent total self-confidence to keep profound inner doubt from breaking through. For the charismatic leader with paranoid characteristics who is projecting his inner aggression, the rhetoric becomes the basis for justifying attacking the outside enemy. "We are (I am) not weak. The problem is out there, with them. By destroying them, by expelling them (the weakness within me) from our midst, we (I) will be the strong people we want to be." And each time the admiring crowd shouts its approval in response to his externalizing rhetoric, the leader's facade of certainty is strengthened and his inner doubts assuaged.

Charismatic Leader-Follower Relationships as a Form of Mass Hypnosis

There is a quality of mutual intoxication in the leader's reassuring his followers who in turn reassure him. One is reminded of the relationship between hypnotist and subject. Manifesting total confidence, the hypnotist instructs his subject to yield control to him and to suspend volition and judgment. To watch the films of Hitler's rallies and focus on his hypnotic use of language—the repetition of simple phrases, building to a crescendo, the crowd echoing his phrases—is to watch hypnosis on a large scale. Observers of the powerful mesmerizing effect of Hitler on his followers at the mass rallies have likened him to a hypnotist who placed his entire audience into a trance. Even those present at the rallies who have not understood a word of German have described themselves as coming under his hypnotic sway and, most striking of all, it is also autohypnosis, as Hitler himself apparently enters a trance state, mesmerized by the enraptured responses of his mesmerized followers.[3]

But the power of the hypnotist ultimately depends upon the eagerness of his subjects to yield to his authority, to cede control of their autonomy, to surrender their will to the hypnotist's authority.

The Followers as Ideal-Hungry Personalities as Well as Temporarily Overwhelmed Individuals

Let us turn now to an examination of the psychology of the admiring crowd of hypnotic subjects—the ideal-hungry followers without whose uncritical response the charismatic leader would be but an empty shell, "full of sound and fury, signifying nothing." We should like first to make a distinction between those who, by virtue of external circumstances, are rendered temporarily susceptible to enter into a charismatic leader-follower relationship, and those narcissistically injured personalities who are permanently prone to enter such relationships.

Societal Crisis Produces Temporarily Overwhelmed Followers

At moments of societal crisis, otherwise mature and psychologically healthy individuals may temporarily come to feel overwhelmed and in need of a strong and self-assured leader. But when the historical moment passes, so too does the need. Few would omit Winston Churchill from the pantheon of charismatic leaders. The sense of conviction and assuredness he conveyed provided a rallying point to Great Britain and the Western Alliance during their darkest hours. During the crisis, Churchill's virtues were exalted and idealized. But when it passed and the need for a strong leader abated, how quickly the British people demystified the previously revered Churchill, focused on his leadership faults, and cast him out of office!

Indeed, the process of idealization carries within it the seeds of disillusion. And the intensity of disengagement from the charismatic leader can be every bit as powerful as the attraction, a reflection of the cyclic course of history and the changing needs of the populace.

This demonstrates that charismatic leader-follower relationships require not only the congruence of a particular leader with a particular followership, but also a special historical moment. Weber characterized a time of societal readiness for revolutionary change and a charismatic revolutionary leader. Through the years of exile in Iraq and France, Ayatollah Khomeini retained a loyal following. His basic personality, leadership style, and rhetoric were consistent over the years. But it was only when the Shah hastened the pace of societal change in hopes of achieving his White Revolution before he died, thereby creating massive societal dislocation and disruption of the social order, that the ideal-hungry followers and the special historical moment were also present, and the charismatic leader-follower relationship blossomed and grew.

We do not mean to imply that charismatic leader-follower relationships only develop at such historical moments. Rather we are suggesting that they are particularly apt to occur at those times, when the ranks of dependent followers will be swollen by normally self-sufficient individuals who have temporarily been rendered psychologically vulnerable by external events.

The Narcissistically Wounded Ideal-Hungry Followers

But even in the quietest of times, charismatic leader-follower relationships develop. What are the characteristics of the ideal-hungry followers? As has been suggested earlier, one of the possible vicissitudes of damage to the self-concept during early childhood development is to leave the individual permanently psychologically scarred, with an enduring need to attach himself to a powerful, caring other. Incomplete unto themselves, such individuals can only feel whole when in relationship with, when attached to, when merged with this idealized other. The charismatic leader comes to the psychological rescue of the ideal-hungry followers. Taking on heroic proportions and representing what the followers wish to be, he protects them from confronting themselves and their fundamental inadequacy and alienation. The leader's success becomes the follower's success, a succor to his self-esteem.

Charismatic Religious Cults

Marc Galanter's[4] studies of charismatic religious groups provide confirmation for the hypothesis that narcissistically wounded individuals are especially attracted to charismatic leader-follower relationships. He found that the more lonely and isolated the individual was before joining, the more apt he was to affiliate himself strongly with the Unification Church and stay through the entire recruitment process. There was a tendency to suspend individual judgment and follow unquestioningly the dictates of the leader. Moreover, the more psychological relief that was experienced on joining, the less likely the individual was to question the leader's requirement for actions and behavior which ran counter to his socialization.

INTRODUCTION

Repetitive Patterns of Group Behavior

Just as cult members seek the comfort of the group and seem to develop a "group mind," this is true of psychologically scarred individuals and individuals under stress who are particularly prone to act as if they have a group mind, as if they are acting under the same psychological assumptions, what the social psychiatrist Wilfred Bion has described as "basic assumption states."[5] For alienated and marginal individuals who tend to externalize the source of their own failures—for the narcissistically wounded ideal-hungry individuals described by Kohut—we believe the psychological attractiveness of these states is overwhelming.

We would go so far as to suggest that these basic assumption states regularly characterize the followers in charismatic leader-follower relationships and that the skillful charismatic leader intuitively shapes and induces these states in his followers. Some may be attracted to the charismatic religious cults described by Galanter, others to the path of terrorism, as we have noted elsewhere, and, especially in times of societal stress, some may be attracted to the banner of charismatic political leaders.

When one is feeling overwhelmed, besieged by fear and doubt, it is extremely attractive to be able to suspend individual judgment and repose one's faith in the leadership of someone who conveys his conviction and certainty that he has the answers, that he knows the way, be it Reverend Sun Myung Moon or Reverend Jim Jones, Adolf Hitler or Ayatollah Khomeini. Particularly through skillful use of rhetoric, the leader persuades his needy audience: "Follow me and I will take care of you. Together we can make a new beginning and create a new society. The fault is not within us but out there, and the only barrier to the happiness, peace, and prosperity we deserve is the outside enemy out to destroy us."

There is an additional bonus for the potential follower lured by the siren song of the leader's strength and conviction. Promised "Join my followers and you will no longer be alone," he then draws additional strength from sharing his allegiance with others. The identity of follower becomes a badge of honor, a statement of membership in a collective self. And in having merged his self with the collective other, the success of the followers becomes his success.

For isolated individuals with damaged self-esteem and weak ego boundaries, the sense of "we" creates and imparts a coherent sense of identity. For such individuals, the self and the "we" are fused so that the self is experienced *as* the relationship. This leads to a tendency to merge themselves with the group. In a figurative manner, as we have noted, we can speak of the development of a group mind or group ego. The group becomes idealized and the standards of the group, as articulated by the leader and his disciples, take over and become the norm. This helps explain the startling degree to which individuals can suspend their own standards and judgment and participate in the most violent of actions when under the sway of the psychology of the group, if persuaded that the cause of the group is served by their actions. Even that most basic of human needs—the drive for self-preservation—can be suspended in the service of the group, as was horrifyingly evidenced by the phenomenon of the collective suicide with Flavor Aid at the Peoples Temple in Jonestown, Guyana. The Branch Davidians is another example of a closed religious cult that ended tragically, in this case with the fiery conflagration that ended the fifty-one-day siege at Ranch Apocalypse in Waco, Texas.

Differentiating the Destructive Charismatic from the Reparative Charismatic

In citing the phenomena of Jonestown, Waco, and Germany under Hitler, we may falsely convey the impression that charismatic leader-follower relationships are only a force for human destructiveness. They will be if the narcissistically wounded leader rages at the world for depriving him of "mirroring" and enlists his followers in attacking it. This is the destructive charismatic, as exemplified by Hitler.

By contrast, charismatic leader-follower relationships can also catalyze a reshaping of society in a highly positive and creative fashion, what psychiatrist Vamik Volkan and historian Norman Itzkowitz have termed repartive charismatic leadership. They have persuasively demonstrated in their study of Mustafa Kemal Atatürk of Turkey that the narcissistically wounded mirror-hungry leader, in projecting his intrapsychic splits upon society, may be a force for healing. The reparative charismatic leader seeks a sense of wholeness through establishing a special relationship with his ideal-hungry followers. As he tries to heal his own narcissistic wounds through the vehicle of his leadership, he may indeed be resolving splits in a wounded society. Other examples of reparative charismatic leadership are Mohandas Gandhi and Dr. Martin Luther King, who modeled his nonviolent resistance on that of Gandhi.

Just as the temporarily needy person may attach himself to an idealized object at trying moments in his personal psychological development, so too a temporarily needy nation may need the leadership of an idealized object at trying moments in its historical development. And just as the object of individual veneration is inevitably dethroned as the overwhelming stress upon his followers is relieved and they no longer require rescuing, so too the idealized leader will be discarded when the moment of historical need passes, as evidenced by the rise and fall of Winston Churchill.

But whatever fluctuations in the external circumstances of whole populations, within them there will always be individuals whose internal needs lead them to seek out idealized leaders. And when these ideal-hungry followers find a mirror-hungry leader, we have the elements of a charismatic leader-follower relationship. These relationships can be looked upon as peculiar aberrations, as cults, during times of relative societal repose. Microscopic in scale at first, in times of social crisis these powerful relationships can become the nuclei for powerful transforming social movements, as was the case with the reparative charismatic leadership of Atatürk, Gandhi, King, and Nelson Mandela, and the destructive charismatic leadership of Adolf Hitler, Ayatollah Khomeini, and Osama bin Laden.

The adoration of the crowd sustains the "mirror-hungry" leader. He is incomplete without it. Similarly, he turns to those in his immediate surround for psychological stability, reassurance, and a sense of completeness; this includes both his wife and his inner circle. These special, albeit distorted, relationships, which are psychologically required by the narcissistic leader, are called self-object relationships.

PART I
The Charismatic Leader

1

The Quintessential Narcissist

If one were to strike from the ranks of political leaders all those with significant narcissistic personality traits, the ranks would be perilously impoverished. Indeed, in this age of the "selfie" and social media, the percentage of the population with narcissistic personality features has risen to the point where during the debates of the American Psychiatric Association committee reformulating the fifth edition of the *Diagnostic and Statistical Manual of Mental Disorders,* serious consideration was given to eliminating the narcissistic personality disorder from the diagnostic nosology because it was rapidly becoming the "new normal." The rise of the "me generation" and the social media generation is the subject of frequent social commentary. It has been estimated that upward of 10% of the American public have significant narcissistic personality features.

Most major psychoanalytic theorists see a continuity between normal narcissism and pathological narcissism. The extremity of the narcissistic personality disorder illuminates normal narcissism. In the *DSM IV,* 1994, the overall description of the Narcissistic Personality Disorder (NPD) is a "pervasive pattern of grandiosity (in fantasy or behavior), need for admiration and lack of empathy, beginning in early adulthood, and present in a variety of contexts." Including five (or more) of the following, the person with the NPD:

1. Has a grandiose sense of self-importance (e.g., exaggerates achievements and talents, expects to be recognized as superior without commensurate achievements).
2. Is preoccupied with fantasies of unlimited success, power, brilliance, beauty, or ideal love.
3. Believes that he or she is "special" and unique and can only be understood by, or should associate with, other special or high-status people (or institutions).
4. Requires excessive admiration.
5. Has a sense of entitlement (i.e., unreasonable expectations of especially favorable treatment or automatic compliance with his or her expectations).
   —American Psychiatric Association, 2013, p. 669

At the extremity of the above description, it would be difficult to sustain leadership of an organization or nation. But the combination of high self-confidence, ambition, talent, and opportunity are the ingredients of success. As the psychoanalyst Helen Tartakoff has written in her article on the Nobel Prize Complex, some individuals are driven from their earliest years to pursue the highest honors, consumed by the fantasy of having the Nobel gold medal draped around their necks at the ceremony in Stockholm, Sweden (or if animated by the quest for the Nobel Peace Prize, in Oslo, Norway). And some who reach for the stars will achieve them. Indeed, without reaching for glory, it will rarely be achieved.

There is a continuum of narcissism from normal to the extremity of malignant narcissism (Kohut) and pathological narcissism (Kernberg) at the very end of the continuum, the most dangerous personality disorder. This personality is characterized by such extreme grandiosity and self-absorption that:

There is no capacity to empathize with others. This in political leaders will be reflected not only in an incapacity to empathize with one's own people, but also to have extreme difficulty empathizing with one's adversary, a very dangerous difficulty in this nuclear age. At the moment of this writing, Kim Jong-un, the president of the Democratic People's Republic of Korea (DPRK) is involved in a mutually threatening war of words with President Donald Trump, a situation fraught with the possibility of miscalculation.

Donald Trump has continuously over the years demonstrated an incapacity to empathize with others, including his own family. Following his father's death in 1999, Trump found himself at odds with the children of his eldest brother over Fred Trump Sr.'s will. Fred Trump Jr.'s two children, Fred III and Mary, were seeking a portion of what would have been their late father's estate, as well as continued medical coverage under Fred Trump Sr.'s company Apartment Management Associates. Fred III at the time was struggling with paying medical bills amounting to nearly a third of a million dollars for his newborn son William Trump, who suffered from seizures. Donald Trump, as well as his other brother and two sisters, fought Fred III and Mary over receiving any more money from Fred Trump Sr.'s estate and denied them, including Fred III's sick newborn son, medical coverage. When questioned over this matter and the lawsuit, Trump stated, "Why should we give him medical coverage?" Donald Trump showed no empathy for his nephew's situation nor any remorse for leaving his ill newborn grandnephew without medical insurance.

Trump has continued to demonstrate his inability to empathize with others. In June 2018, he made another derisive comment about Senator McCain, concerning his key vote against killing the Affordable Care Act (Obamacare). To attack McCain when he was dying of terminal brain cancer is an exemplar of Trump's lack of empathy and cruelty. Early in the campaign (July 2015), Trump attacked McCain's heroic stature, questioning whether being a prisoner of war deserved his reputation for heroism, stating:

> "He's not a war hero. He was a war hero because he was captured. I like people who weren't captured."

Trump continued to lash out at Senator McCain, even after the announcement of his terminal cancer diagnosis, and was criticized for his tweet about the diagnoses where he wrote, "Get well soon." While former president Barack Obama tweeted, "John McCain is an American hero and one of the bravest fighters I've ever known. Cancer doesn't know what it's up against. Give it hell, John," and former president Bill Clinton tweeted, "As he's shown his entire life, don't bet against John McCain. Best wishes to him for a swift recovery."[1]

When McCain's brain cancer was diagnosed, an aide of Trump, commenting on a forthcoming vote, offhandedly remarked, "Well, he's dying anyhow."[2] McCain died on August 25, 2018, and specifically had instructed that President Trump not attend or participate in his funeral. He also asked that both former presidents Bush and Obama, both critics of Trump, deliver eulogies. Despite McCain's passing, he has continued to mount attacks on the late senator, even complaining that he "didn't get a thank you" for McCain's funeral. Despite the fact that it was Congress who approved giving the late senator the honor of lying in the state, Trump only approved of the military flight of McCain's remains from Arizona to Washington. Trump's disdain of McCain is so intense that during Trump's visit to Japan in May 2019, the White House requested that the USS *McCain*, which is stationed in Japan, be moved out of sight. In addition, the sailors of the USS *McCain* were not invited to Trump's speech on another naval ship. While Trump claims he was not a part of the request to obscure the USS *McCain* from sight during his visit, he did defend the request: "They thought they were doing me a favor because they know I'm not a fan of John McCain."

Trump has lashed out at the Gold Star parents of a heroic Muslim American solider, Army Captain Humayun Khan, who died in Iraq in 2004. Khan's father, Khizr Khan, spoke out against Trump's comments on the Muslim community in the United States at the Democratic National Convention in July 2016. A week later, during an interview with George Stephanopoulos, Trump commented that Khizr was "very emotional" in his speech and questioned why Mrs. Khan had not spoken during the speech, stating, "If you look at his wife, she was standing there. She had nothing to say. She probably—maybe she wasn't allowed to have anything to say. You tell me." Further on during the interview, Stephanopoulos questioned what sacrifices Trump had made for his country, to which Trump replied, "I think I've made a lot of sacrifices. I work very, very hard. I've created thousands and thousands of jobs, tens of thousands of jobs, built great structures. I've had tremendous success. I think I've done a lot."[3] Trump was also heavily criticized for mocking a journalist with a disability during one of his campaign rallies. While criticizing some of Serge Kovaleski's writings, Trump started flailing his arms about, mocking the journalist. (Kovaleski has arthrogryposis, a congenital condition affecting the joints.)

One of the most dramatic examples of Trump's incapacity to empathize with the American people as a whole occurred on his visit to Texas during Hurricane Harvey. While he knew it was important to be "presidential," his major focus seemed to be on the size of the crowd at his rally, without mentioning the overwhelming disaster affecting Texas. Quite remarkably, Jenna Johnson, who traveled with him on his trip to Texas, pointedly noted in her article in the *Washington Post* that Trump continuously managed to turn attention on himself with comments such as, "What a crowd! What a turnout!" He had little to say about the millions of "Texans whose lives have been dramatically altered by the floodwaters."[4] He had not a word to say about the hardships of the tens of thousands of citizens who had lost their homes—demonstrating a remarkable inability to convey empathy. This was a vivid contrast with Lyndon Johnson participating in response efforts for Hurricane Betsy in 1965. Trump seemed to be consumed with admiration for himself. Thus, under that arrogant façade is deep-seated insecurity.

The secret policy of separating children as young as five months old from their illegal immigrant parents at the U.S. border—to serve as a deterrent—produced a firestorm of protest, including 750 protests led by women on June 30, 2018. Trump initially tried to blame the uproar on the Democrats. But his inability to understand the traumatizing effect of such actions, with no plans to reunite the families again, evidenced his impaired empathic capacity.

No constraint of conscience. The only loyalty a person with his malignant or pathological narcissism has is to himself and his own survival. With loyalty being a one-way street, there is a tendency to produce a sycophantic leadership circle, reluctant to challenge the leader, for this will be interpreted as disloyalty. Trump has no constraint of conscience as viewed by his continuous and vicious attacks on individuals, including journalists and politicians, who do not agree with him. Trump continues to attack various news sources, including CNN, MSNBC, ABC, NBC, the *New York Times*, and the *Washington Post*, as well as specific journalists. On June 29, 2017, Trump tweeted, "I heard poorly rated 'Morning_Joe' speaks badly of me (don't watch anymore). Then how come low I.Q. Crazy Mika, along with Psycho Joe, came . . . to Mar-a-Lago 3 nights in a row around New Year's Eve, and insisted on joining me. She was bleeding badly from a face-lift. I said no!"[5] Trump has been persistent in attacking members of the Democratic Party, including Connecticut senator Richard Blumenthal, who he called "a phony Vietnam con artist."[6]

Paranoid orientation. Not paranoid in the sense of being psychotic, out of touch with reality, but rather a readiness to be betrayed, and a tendency to scapegoat. Donald Trump has often placed a strong value on his paranoia as being one of his keys to success. In his book *Trump: The Art of the Comeback*, he lists his "Top Ten Comeback Tips," the third tip being "Be Paranoid," where he writes:

> I have noticed over the years that people who are guarded or, to put it coldly, slightly paranoid, end up being the most successful. Let

some paranoia reign! You've got to realize that you have something other people want. Don't let them take it away.[7]

For years Trump has used the media as a scapegoat, citing any negative publicity as being the media "out to get him" or as "fake news." In his 2015 book, *Crippled America: How to Make America Great Again*, Trump wrote:

> For a long time, I've been the man the media loves to hate. It hasn't taken me long to learn how truly dishonest the political media can be. At the first Republican debate, Fox journalist Megyn Kelly was clearly out to get me. And of course, the second debate, virtually everyone was attacking me because most of their poll numbers were sinking while mine were surging.[8]

Trump has discussed the coverage of the Russia investigation by the media in a similar manner, tweeting on June 15, 2017, "You are witnessing the single greatest WITCH HUNT in American political history—led by some very bad and conflicted people! #MAGA."[9] Trump had made a similar tweet in January 2017, "Intelligence agencies should never have allowed this fake news to 'leak' into the public. One last shot at me. Are we living in Nazi Germany?"[10] Rather than addressing why this investigation is taking place, Trump consistently uses the media as a scapegoat, saying they are fabricating everything to "get him."

Unconstrained aggression. Such a person will use whatever aggression is necessary to achieve his goal, whether it is to kill a potential rival or to eliminate a group. Consider as an example Kim Jong-un's assassination of his uncle, who had been serving as his regent and mentor. Trump has also been proud of his aggression, with his ninth comeback tip in *The Art of the Comeback* being "Get Even," where he states:

> During the bad times, I learned who was loyal and who wasn't. I believe in an eye for an eye. A couple of people who betrayed me need my help now, and I am screwing them against the wall! I am doing a number . . . and I'm having so much fun."[11]

In 2014, Donald Trump tweeted a quote from Alfred Hitchcock, stating, "Revenge is sweet and not fattening."[12] In an interview on Fox News with Sean Hannity on November 2015, Trump stated of his fellow GOP candidates, "Anybody who hits me, we're gonna hit them ten times harder."[13] There have been countless instances where Trump has displayed unconstrained aggression, instances he has often boasted about. In his 2007 book *Think Big and Kick Ass: In Business and in Life*, Trump discusses attacking Rosie O'Donnell after she criticized him on the TV show *The View*. He writes:

> Now I had a choice; I could attack back, or I could let it pass. I chose to attack her so hard she would rue the day she decided to attack me. The media was very interested in my response. I gave them an earful! I got calls from *Entertainment Tonight*, *Inside Edition*, *Access Hollywood*, *Extra*, and others asking, "Do you have a response?" Yes, I had a response. I said, "Rosie O'Donnell is disgusting, both inside and out. Take a look at her, she's a slob. She talks like a truck driver, her show failed, her magazine was a total catastrophe, she got sued. So, I'll probably sue her, because it would be fun. I'd like to take some money out of her pockets." I said, "Rosie is a very unattractive woman who is a bully. Rosie is a loser and ultimately *The View* will fail because of Rosie. Barbara Walters made a mistake in hiring her." Barbara told me, "Donald, don't get into the mud with pigs."[14]

Underlying insecurity. Under this grandiose façade is significant insecurity. Thus, the grandiosity is an illusion, fragile, and easily pierced. Psychiatrist Harry Stack Sullivan observes that the grandiosity defends against the profound underlying insecurity. Donald Trump's façade is extremely fragile, a façade that he attempts to defend by acting out with aggression, as well as attempting to draw attention away from any insecurity. This has been particularly evident with the ongoing Russia investigation. Trump's slavish idolatry of Vladimir Putin suggests that he has something to hide. He has continuously attempted to deflect media attention away from the Russia investigation, for instance with his focus on Venezuela. On August 11, 2017, Trump stated:

> This is our neighbor . . . You know, we are all over the world and we have troops all over the world in places that are very, very far away. Venezuela is not very far away and the people are suffering, and they are dying. We have many options for Venezuela, including a possible military option if necessary.

Trump's attempt to rapidly switch gears from Russia to Venezuela further adds to the impression that Trump is attempting to hide something regarding the Russia investigation, highlighting his own insecurities about it, as well as his attempt to protect his own grandiose façade.

Extreme sensitivity to slight. The leader with this personality configuration is extremely sensitive to slight, when the façade is pierced. A prominent example of Trump's extreme sensitivity to slight has been his obsession with the election, specifically with the popular vote, as well as his preoccupation with the turnout for his inauguration. It was insufficient that Trump won the election, for Trump had to have the greatest victory in American history, including by winning the popular vote. In an effort to remove the discomfort he feels of losing the popular vote to Hillary Clinton, Trump has deemed this to be "electoral fraud." On November 27, 2016, Trump had a Twitter storm, tweeting roughly twelve times regarding the election, including the tweet, "In addition to winning the Electoral College in a landslide, I won the popular vote if you deduct the millions of people who voted illegally."[15] Even following his inauguration, Trump has continued to be preoccupied with the popular vote, tweeting on April 23, 2017, "New polls out today are very good considering that much of the media is FAKE and almost always negative. Would still beat Hillary in . . . popular vote. ABC News/Washington Post Poll said almost all stand by their vote on me and 53% said strong leader."[16] Trump has also claimed that he had the largest turnout for his inauguration in American history, as well as the highest TV viewership, tweeting on January 22, 2017, "Wow, television ratings just out: 31 million people watched the Inauguration, 11 million more than the very good ratings from 4 years ago!"[17] In order to maintain his grandiose façade, Trump has to view his presidential win as being the greatest in American history, despite all evidence to the contrary.

Citizen Trump[18]

Inadvertently, Trump has self-identified as a narcissist. Interviewed in 1992, around the end of his stormy divorce from Ivana, Trump stated that his "all-time favorite movie" was *Citizen Kane*. *Citizen Kane*, which is loosely based on publishing mogul William Randolph Hearst, is a flashback of character Charles Foster Kane, a publishing tycoon, who despite surrounding himself with material luxury fails to find happiness. In the interview, Trump stated: "I think you learn in *Citizen Kane* that maybe wealth isn't everything. Because he had the wealth, but he didn't have the happiness. The table getting larger, and larger, and larger, with he and his wife getting further and further apart as he got wealthier and wealthier—perhaps I can understand that." Trump's self-identification with the character Kane is somewhat ironic, as Kane, like Trump, is a quintessential narcissist. And in fact, Trump has quite a bit in common with the fictional character of his "all-time favorite movie." Both became successful and wealthy in their respective careers, Kane in publishing and Trump in real estate. Both came from wealthy families who financially helped them get their start in their careers. Following creating their subsequent empires, both created an estate in Florida. For Trump it is Mar-a-Lago and for Kane it was Xanadu. In addition, both went through two divorces. And lastly, both in some way are unfulfilled. Kane at the end of his life yearns for his simpler childhood, as represented by his sleigh "Rosebud," and Trump is still attempting to fulfill his dreams of glory.

Profusion of Psychiatric Diagnoses

There has been a profusion of psychiatric diagnoses offered by distinguished journalists by checking behavioral boxes in the *Diagnostic and Statistical Manual V (DSM)* of the American Psychiatric Association. Many have chosen variants of narcissism, many others have selected the psychopathic personality, and still others such as *New York Times* columnist David Brooks are struck by manic aspects of his reactions, such as the early morning Twitter storms, suggesting that he is suffering from something in the bipolar spectrum.

There is a notable absence of psychiatrists offering commentary on Donald Trump's psychological reactions. Constrained by the canon of ethics pertaining to psychiatrists, colloquially referred to as the Goldwater Rule, it indicates psychiatrists should not offer a professional opinion about a figure in the light of public day unless they have personally evaluated the subject and have his/her permission.

There is a hazard in terms of columnists focusing on the surface grandiose behavior that they will neglect the underlying insecurity. Moreover, in trying to solve the conundrum of narcissism versus the psychopathic personality, the extremity of the narcissistic personality spectrum represented by malignant/psychopathological narcissism contains weak or absent conscience.

2

Entrepreneurial Provenance

Entrepreneurial Grandfather and Father[1]

To understand the roots of Donald Trump's entrepreneurial capacities, we must look to his remarkable paternal grandfather Friedrich and his millionaire real estate developer father Fred. While Donald did not know his grandfather, who died in the flu epidemic when Fred was twelve, there can be little doubt that his father was strongly influenced by Friedrich's successful business career, an admiration he would have passed on to his son Donald.

Friedrich Trump

The family lived and worked on a vineyard in Kallstadt, in southwestern Germany. When his father Johannes died at age forty-eight of chronic obstructive pulmonary disease, he left his family saddled with heavy debt. Friedrich was eight. He was apprenticed to a barber at age fourteen in nearby Frankenthal. In 1885, at the age of sixteen, facing years of military service and a dreary future,

Friedrich decided to pursue his dream of emigrating to the United States to join his sister Katherine. Sneaking off in the middle of the night, informing his mother of his decision by leaving a note on the kitchen table, Friedrich made his way to the port city of Bremen. He then spent eight days traveling in steerage from Bremen to America, an act of extreme self-confidence and/or adolescent rebellion. He had concluded that America was the land in which to become wealthy.

On arriving in the émigré reception center, his name was transcribed as Trumpf, but Friedrich was soon to remove the terminal *f*. Having apprenticed as a barber in Germany, he quickly found a German-speaking barber in the Labor Exchange (which was part of the emigration facility), for whom he would be working seven days a week. Acquiring a job within hours of arriving in New York, he quickly became infected with the dream of instant wealth. Initially staying with his sister Katherine and her husband Fred Schuster, he was restless and moved from neighborhood to neighborhood.

Being a barber was not a rapid path to wealth, however. With the rumors of the gold rush, Friedrich moved to Seattle at age twenty-one and with his savings started the Dairy Restaurant in a bawdy section of the burgeoning town named Whitechapel, after the red-light district in London. In addition to the busy trade in meals and ale, the back section was advertised as having "private rooms for ladies," code for prostitutes. For this service, Friedrich charged hard cash and prospered. This, however, is something that Donald Trump continues to deny, saying that evidence of his grandfather profiting from prostitution is "totally false."

Then in 1894, he heard that John D. Rockefeller was bankrolling a mining operation outside of Seattle. So Friedrich sold his restaurant/bordello, filed a bogus mineral claim, and with money from his mother established a new business thirty miles north on land he did not own (one of those legal niceties Trump did not let stand in his way). However, in 1887, with business slow, Friedrich decided to cash out, later opening a new establishment in the new town of Bennett, British Columbia, in 1898. It was a hotel that he named the New Arctic, specializing in short stays where the "sporting ladies" congregated. He even installed a scale to weigh gold dust, for the miners to pay for their services. One newspaper at the time reported that it "would not advise respectable women to go there to sleep as they are liable to hear that which would be repugnant to their feelings and uttered, too, by the depraved of their own sex." It was a rich profit center for Trump.

Friedrich (by now Frederick) then heard of the gold rush in the Yukon. Having devised the winning formula, he did not go north to pan for gold, but to supply the miners with a broad spectrum of their needs, including sexual needs. Trump continued to cater, profiting richly, from providing "sporting ladies" to miners. He managed to leave with his haul just ahead of the local authorities, and the now wealthy son returned to Germany at age thirty-two in 1901.

There his mother arranged for her son to meet a bevy of eligible young ladies, but Trump became engaged to the twenty-year-old girl next door, Elizabeth Christ, who had been only five years old when he left for America. The couple then returned to New York City, where Frederick started over, working as both a barber and a hotel and restaurant manager.

When his wife, homesick and not feeling accepted in the United States, persuaded Frederick to return to Kallstadt, he decided to make that return permanent. But Frederick had not served his military obligation, absent in America during the window of required service. Despite his ardent pleading with German officials, he looked like a draft dodger. They denied his application for restoration of citizenship and required Frederick and the pregnant Elizabeth Trump to return to the United States, where they settled in a German neighborhood in New York. Frederick Trump began acquiring vacant lots, revealing a keen sense of property values. There, Frederick Christ Trump, their first son, and the father of Donald Trump, was born on October 11, 1905.

Fred Trump

Frederick Trump died of the flu in the 1918 epidemic, when his son Fred was only twelve. As his father's death occurred at the cusp of Fred's adolescence, he would likely have idealized his father. Fred picked up his father's entrepreneurial mantle and began working at the age of ten as a butcher's delivery boy. Throughout high school, Fred continued to work part-time jobs.

Fred Trump rarely spoke of his mother, but she too encouraged his entrepreneurial side, urging him to start his construction company before he was twenty-one. The company was named Elizabeth Trump & Sons, because Fred was not old enough to sign the checks for the business. Thus, despite his mother's encouragement, depictions of the family dynamics uniformly describe Fred standing in awe of his father and being detached from his mother. Similarly, Donald Trump would rarely speak of his mother, Mary. When Donald has described her it is often as "a homemaker" who "loved it" and "a great beauty."

Fred was arrested at age twenty-one for participating in a clash between one thousand Ku Klux Klansmen and one hundred policemen. The articles stated that the protesters arrested were "berobed."[2] This was an interesting predictor of Donald Trump's provocative reaction to the Klan/neo–Nazis' fatal riot with counterprotesters in Charlottesville, Virginia, in August 2017, when Donald Trump opined that "there were fine people on both sides."

During World War II, Fred was said to be the first in line for Federal Housing Authority loans to build subsidized housing near navy shipyards in Virginia and Pennsylvania. Fred did not acquire a reputation for quality building but rather for using the cheapest supplies. The Trump family continues to collect rents on some of these properties to this day.

Over the years many of Fred Trump's competitors were facing work stoppage by the mob-controlled unions. Not Fred Trump! With the assistance of the aggressive attorney Roy Cohn he partnered with the well-connected Willie Tomasello, reported by the New York State Organized Crime Task Force to be an associate of the Genovese and Gambino organized crime families. It helps to have good friends! In addition, Fred Trump created a well-developed web of political connections. He often used these political connections to access government programs, specifically to receive subsidized funding for his apartment building projects. Recently, the FBI also released their records concerning Fred Trump, demonstrating that they had had a brief interest into his possible criminal connections, as well as his political donations. However, due to the file's short length (being only eight pages), it is clear that Fred Trump never faced any major scrutiny from the Bureau.

Fred Trump was never ashamed of the measures he took in his business. When he was investigated for housing abuse by a U.S. Senate committee, Fred admitted to his manipulation of the program, but that he saw no issue with doing so. Trump would complain about the committee's investigation as being "very wrong, and it hurt me," and complaining that it did "untold damage to my standing and reputation."

Donald's father Fred was not only a model of the real estate entrepreneur. He also thrived on being in the limelight, and had a knack for capturing headlines. Well before Donald Trump christened his buildings and hotels with TRUMP, Fred Trump opened a grocery store in Woodhaven, Queens, named Trump

Market and a Coney Island, Brooklyn, apartment complex named Trump Village. Trump Village is a complex of seven twenty-three-story high-rise apartment buildings near the site of Coney Island's famous Parachute Jump. Fred instructed for the buildings, like his others, to be built as cheaply as possible, with the least expensive brick. The construction of the complex was supported by the New York State Housing Finance Agency through public bonds, for which Fred also received tax exemptions.

Donald's Early Years

Fred Trump's boys would accompany him on his rounds at his projects, as he groomed them for leadership in the family real estate empire. His eldest son, Fred Jr., was often the target of his father's critical eye, which he did not appreciate. When his father publicly criticized him as not being cost conscious for ordering new windows rather than refurbished ones, he was humiliated and decided that life under his father's barrage of criticism would not be pleasant. He turned to alcohol to help with the tense relationship with his father. Moreover, he apparently did not approve of his father's business methods and trained to be an airline pilot.

But Donald, who accompanied his father on his Saturday rounds, greatly admired him and was to be designated his successor. Taking these rounds with his father had a great impact on Donald. He wrote in his book *Crippled America: How to Make America Great Again*:

> Fred Trump, my wonderful, tough but loving father, built, owned, and managed buildings in Queens and Brooklyn. He made enough money to just sit back and relax, but that wasn't who he was. Even on the weekends he'd be walking through a building, a house or a construction site. If the halls were dirty or a bulb was out, the people working there would know about it. My father wasn't overly concerned with hurting someone's feelings—he wanted the floors to be cleaned or, as he would often say, in "mint condition." If the person responsible couldn't keep them clean, he was gone. My father believed he had an obligation to his tenants. His motto was simple: "You do your job, you keep your job. Do it well, you get a better job." That always made sense to me.

On these rounds, Fred was presumably conveying to his son and designated successor Donald how to make it in the tough and highly competitive real estate world of Brooklyn and Queens. Trump often states that his father taught him to "be a killer," and told him that "you are a king." Indeed, to be discussed, will be the manner in which Trump viewed the presidency as being king of the United States, frustrated with the checks and balances of constitutional government.

The loving admiration for his father, whose positive model is credited again and again in his writings as the basis for success, is dramatic. But it begs the question, what about his mother?

The Shaping Roles of Mothers in the Development of Their Sons, the Future Leaders

In Dr. Post's political personality profiles of world leaders, he was regularly struck by the important shaping role of the mother. Let me mention in summary form four dominating mothers who assuredly can be credited with powerfully shaping the political personalities and leadership of their sons: President Woodrow Wilson, President Franklin Delano Roosevelt (FDR), General Douglas MacArthur, and Australian Prime Minister Robert Hawke.

Woodrow Wilson's Mother and Her Special Son

In Alexander and Juliette George's influential 1964 psychobiography *Woodrow Wilson and Colonel House: A Personality Study*, the authors emphasize the powerful shaping effect of Wilson's father's demanding perfectionistic parenting on the emerging political personality of young Woodrow. But this was in many ways softened by the special parenting of his mother, which was almost designed to produce a highly narcissistic son. The letters between mother and son when he was away at college demonstrate the powerful feelings between them. Consider the following, which sounds more like the letter of a mother to a homesick boy attending sleepaway camp for the first time:

> My darling Boy, I am so anxious about that cold of yours. How did you take it? Surely you have not laid aside your winter clothing?

> Another danger is sitting without fire these cool nights. Do be careful, my dear boy, for my sake. You seem depressed, but that is because you are not well. You need not imagine that you are not a favorite. Everybody here likes and admires you. I could not begin to tell you the kind and flattering things that are said about you by everybody that knows you. Yes, you will have no lack of friends in Wilmington—of the warmest sort. There seem to be an unusual number of young people about your age there—and of a superior kind—and they are prepared to take an unusual interest in you particularly. Why, my darling boy, nobody could help loving you, if they were to try. I have a bad headache, this morning, dear—won't attempt to write you a letter. My chief object in writing is to tell you that I love my absent boy—oh so dearly.[3]

Similar in tone to the poem by MacArthur's mother, this scarcely needs a psychiatrist to interpret. As Post observed in his book *Narcissism and Politics: Dreams of Glory*:

> Heady yeast, that! This is the stuff of which narcissistic personalities are brewed. In this brief missive, Mrs. Wilson communicates to her son . . . that she and he are one and inseparable and that her well-being depends on him. She conveys to him that among superior people he is especially admired. The perceptions and urgings of such mothers are not designed to produce sons and daughters of modest ambitions. Indeed, these early perceptions and the continual psychological shaping undoubtedly play a major role in leading their "beneficiaries" to reach for—and achieve—the stars.

The Dominating Role of Franklin Delano Roosevelt's Mother Sara

In James MacGregor Burns's 1956 Pulitzer Prize–winning biography of FDR, he emphasizes the overlarge presence of his mother Sara. When Franklin and his cousin Eleanor announced their engagement, his mother Sara was outspoken in her objections, stating to him that they were much too young. Young Roosevelt wrote to her, "I know my mind," and then attempted to reassure her:

And for you dear Mommy, you know that nothing can ever change what we have always been & always will be to each other, only now you have two children to love and to love you.

Eleanor reached out to her dominating future mother-in-law to soften her objections with a letter:

I do so want you to learn to love me a little. You must know that I will always try to do what you wish, for I have grown to love you very dearly during the past summer.

Roosevelt was not persuaded by his mother's objections, but undeterred by his steadfast objections and her future daughter-in-law's professions of love, she took her son on a Caribbean cruise where she had an audience of one for her concerns. To her dismay, his love for Eleanor prevailed. But she would not easily give up her close involvement in Franklin's life and continued to encroach on Eleanor's territory as new wife. When the couple returned from an extended European honeymoon, they returned to an apartment on Manhattan's East Side which Sara had rented and furnished in their absence. And while the newlywed couple lived in their new furnished apartment, Sara built two adjoining houses on 65th Street, one for the newlywed couple, and one for her. The houses were connected by a passageway on the second floor, which led to the master bedroom in the couple's house.

As intrusive and influential as the mother of Franklin Delano Roosevelt was in the life and personality development of her special son, so too was Douglas MacArthur's mother for her very special son.

Douglas MacArthur's Mother Pinky Measures Her Success by Her Son's Success

In his 1964 autobiography, MacArthur includes this poem by his mother, identifying the powerful relationship between mother and son:

Like mother, like son, is saying so true
The world will judge largely of mother by you
This then your task, if task it shall be

> *To force this proud world to do homage to me*
> *Be sure it will say when its verdict you've won*
> *She reaps as she sowed, "This man is her son!"*

This says it all. As this verse makes clear, she viewed her son's success in this world as the measure of her success. He was, after all, from a long line of military leaders; his father, Lieutenant General Arthur MacArthur won the Congressional Medal of Honor at age eighteen by flouting the order to retreat.

Knowing that youth often did not tend to their studies, Douglas's mother took an apartment within easy distance of the West Point campus to ensure that her son achieved academic honors, which he did. She also supervised his social life and was upset that he did not clear his first wife with her. She supported his decision to divorce his first wife when she was insufficiently supportive of his military career. His mother carefully chose his second wife, Jean Faircloth, and in her terminal illness told Jean, "Don't worry. He is going to love you very much."

The Mother of Prime Minister Hawke and Her Special Son

In her memoir, the mother of Australian prime minister Robert Hawke vividly documents that she meets the criteria to join this sorority of mothers of presidents, generals, and prime ministers who shaped the leadership and narcissism of their sons. When she looked into the crib and first saw her newborn son, she indicated she realized that something very important had happened and that one day her son would be prime minister. Indeed, she was later to reflect that the special event was not the moment of birth, but nine months earlier, at the moment of conception. This is not to say that she was prescient but is evidence that she raised her son to be special.

Donald Trump's Mother, Mary Trump

Mary Anne MacLeod, the tenth of ten children of the daughter of a fisherman, had difficult early years in Stornoway in the Outer Hebrides. It was a gloomy, isolated environment. She attended school there through the eighth grade, and then followed her three sisters to the United States.

The special role of the mother in shaping her son's dreams of glory, reflected in the cameos of Wilson's, Roosevelt's, MacArthur's, and Hawke's mothers, and their roles in shaping their sons' political narcissism is distinctly absent from the description by Trump of the parental shaping role of his parents. Trump regularly credits "Fred Trump, my wonderful, tough but loving father" for his success, only having perfunctory kind words for his mother when asked in press interviews. In a thoughtful exploration of "The Mystery of Mary Trump," the authors sensitively observe the discrepancy between the prominently placed photograph of his father, which was always on his desk in Trump Tower, and later on his desk in the oval office, and, as prominent, in the words of a former staffer, the "noticeably absent photograph of his mother Mary."[4] This disparity in photographic images was reflected in the gap in the verbal record of credits given to his father for the influence in shaping him, versus the limited credit given to his mother. This is in vivid contrast to President Obama, who, asked about his mother in an interview, described her as "an almost elemental force. For all the ups and downs of our lives, there was never a moment when I didn't feel as if I was *special*."

In speaking of this specialness, in *Narcissism and Politics* Post observes:

> In likening the blinding infatuation of the lover to the doting adulation of the parents for their newborn, Freud found the element in common to be "over-valuation." Whether in oneself or another, the element being considered is "magnified in importance, is overvalued, its unique perfection extolled."

This adulation and overvaluation is particularly apt to be the case for the firstborn child, especially the firstborn son. There are no observations that indicate Mary Trump had the kind of special adulation when her fifth child and second son Donald was born in an emergency medical situation, with severe hemorrhaging, requiring an emergency hysterectomy.

When Mary died in 2000, on her deathbed she expressed regret for the son that emerged from her womb and the way he had turned out. She certainly did not impart to him, as did the mothers of President Wilson, President Roosevelt, General MacArthur, and Prime Minister Hawke, a sense of specialness and entitlement. But being behind Freddy Jr. in the family ranking and being groomed by his father Fred to succeed him certainly did endow young

Donald with a sense of ambition and specialness. Yet watching the failure of Fred Jr.'s life, it was resting on a very insecure foundation.

It is the mothers who sing to their infant sons and daughters in the crib, "I'm special, look at me," producing, in the words of the authors and social psychologists Jean Twenge and W. Keith Campbell, the provocatively titled book about a growing trend in American society, *The Narcissism Epidemic: Living in the Age of Entitlement*.

As Donald was becoming more and more prominent, the question was often asked, "Who was Donald Trump's mother?" And the answers to this provocative question emphasized that she was "conservative," "tight-lipped," "nice," "friendly," "pleasant," "polished, "proper," and "unassuming." Friends from his boyhood recalled little about his mother, who was hardly in evidence about the house. Rather it was his father whom they remembered. One of his boyhood friends recalled, "We hardly ever saw Mrs. Trump, Donald stood in awe of his father." This was a patriarchal house, dominated by his father, and the special attention bestowed on young Donald was mainly from his father. Donald was described by friends as being detached from his mother.

Mary, as the tenth of ten children, probably received little nurturing from her mother, who probably delegated to her older sisters much of Mary's caretaking. That his discussions of influences of his father on his development are so frequent, and the references to the influences of his mother so infrequent, is in and of itself telling. As a former president of the American Psychoanalytic Association, Prudence Gourguechon, indicated:

> A solid relationship with an ordinary devoted mother is the basis for a foundation of trust. Knowing what's real and what's not real. A sense of security versus insecurity. Empathy develops through your maternal relationship.

And so, given the apparent lack of a solid maternal relationship with his mother, the foundation would be laid for problems with trust, underlying insecurity, difficulties with appraising reality, and problems with empathy.

Friends recall that Donald spoke frequently about his father's advice, of his telling him "to be a king, to be a killer." But he rarely spoke about his mother and her advice to him. "He didn't say anything about her. Not a word." She was like a shadow in his life.

It will be noted that Fred Trump confined his real estate dealings mainly to Brooklyn and Queens. Manhattan was another story. That was where "the big boys played." That was a limit to be placed on Donald's sights, and Fred repeatedly warned his son of the dangers of Manhattan. There is reason to believe that the adolescent Donald took this warning as a challenge, as an incentive. He would sneak into Manhattan on weekends with his best friend Peter Brant. This was to become the incubation of his dream of becoming a major player in the heady world of Manhattan real estate. While his father might be wary of the Manhattan real estate world, Donald was gutsy, and now was motivated someday to build shiny landmark buildings in Manhattan.

While this experience was important, at the same time, Donald was a tough kid who was always getting into trouble in the private elementary school, Kew-Forest, where his father served on the board of trustees. Fred was quietly pleased with the image of his tough son, the troublemaker. On one occasion, displeased with the ignorance of music shown by a music teacher, he punched him in the eye. Young Donald got so many detention hours that they were nicknamed DT's—short for "Donny Trumps." Donald and his crew resisted teachers from the start. It was as though he confined his rebelliousness to school, while positively modeling himself after his father.

Crown Prince Donald

Thus, Donald was raised from boyhood on as a Crown Prince to succeed his father, the real estate Emperor-King of Brooklyn and Queens. When Donald's older brother Fred Jr., who was exposed to a constant barrage of controlling criticism and did not approve of the way his father conducted business, chose to pursue a career in aviation, Donald's father, stung by the defection of his firstborn, designated Donald as successor and tended closely to shaping his development. It is not difficult to imagine Fred saying to his son when he took him on his Saturday rounds, "Someday, this will all be yours." Donald's ambition was not only to follow in his father's path but to go on to the next level.

Having been rebuffed by Fred Jr., Fred Trump especially invested in shaping his son Donald to succeed him as real estate king. The lack of interest Fred Jr. had in entering the world of major real estate development must have been very painful for his father, and added emphasis to the importance of shaping Donald early on to assume that role.

This is reminiscent of the abdication crisis of King Edward VIII. When his father George V died, his son Edward, the next in line for the throne, was crowned King Edward VIII on January 20, 1936. But by now he was hopelessly in love with a commoner, the American socialite Wallis Simpson, divorced once and on the verge of her second, and unsuitable for a royal bride. And several months into his monarchy, he caused a scandal by proposing marriage to her. He invited Prime Minister Stanley Baldwin to Buckingham Palace to inform him of his decision, and Baldwin threatened to resign. Ultimately, Edward, who was "besotted with love," decided:

> I have found it impossible to carry the heavy burden of responsibility, and to discharge my duties as King as I would wish to do, without the help and support of the woman I love.

And on December 10, 1936, he signed the Instruments of Abdication, one of the shortest reigns in British history. He was unable to join Simpson until her divorce became absolute several months later. His younger brother, George VI, who had a significant stammer, was required to step into the breach when Edward put his own desires ahead of his obligation to serve as king. (George VI's speech therapy and need to win the nation's approval as it faced the gathering storm of Hitler's aggression is sensitively depicted in the film *The King's Speech*.)

But the heroic older brother and "second choice son" dynamic that has been cited did not reflect the relationship of Fred to his sons. The firstborn son and elder brother Fred Jr. served as his father's crown prince, but he made it clear he did not wish to follow in his father's real estate path, did not approve of his father's business practices, and sought to establish his own identity and career in aviation. The abandonment of a career in the family business stung Fred, and in appointing Donald as his successor, the father resolved to watch especially closely over his son's development. This book will attempt to provide a pathway through past influences on him. The position of second son is reminiscent of a pattern identified in *Narcissism and Politics*, in the chapter titled "Leader by Default: Second Choice Sons." (This chapter was coauthored by Ruthie Pertsis.) There are cameos of four leaders who fit this pattern: President John F. Kennedy, Prime Minister Benjamin Netanyahu of Israel, Prime Minister Rajiv Gandhi of India, and President Bashar al-Assad of Syria.

John F. Kennedy

JFK had planned a career in journalism. His older brother Joe had been identified as the political star of the family, designated to enshrine the family in American history. Joe died in World War II on a bombing mission on the North Sea coast. His father, Ambassador Joseph Kennedy, told Jack that Joe was dead, and that it was therefore Jack's responsibility to run for Congress and start to climb the political ladder.

Benjamin Netanyahu

Similarly, Yonatan Netanyahu was identified as the rising political star of the Netanyahu family. The commander of the heroic rescue mission in Entebbe, Uganda, to rescue hijacked Israeli air passengers, Jonathan was the one fatality during the rescue mission. This placed Benjamin in his shoes as a political hero, as the iconic image of Yonatan loomed over them. In April 2019 Benjamin was elected to his fifth term as prime minister.

Rajiv Gandhi

Rajiv Gandhi did not have a taste for politics, and early on sought a career in aviation, where he could rise by his own abilities, not by his family reputation. Sanjay, his younger brother, was charismatic, macho, and enjoyed fast cars and physically demanding sports. He was a natural fit for successor to Indira Gandhi. But when Sanjay died in a flying accident, it fell to Rajiv to succeed his mother. And Rajiv's assassination for the first time left India's National Congress party without a Gandhi as a natural successor.

Bashar al-Assad

Perhaps the most dramatic "second choice son" was Bashar al-Assad. Hafez al-Assad had ruled Syria with an iron fist for three decades. He had originally designated his oldest son Bassel as his successor. Macho and competitive, Bassel was a competitive horse rider, an aficionado of fast cars, and was popular with women. His younger brother Bashar grew up in Bassel's shadow and aspired to a career in medicine, an ambition to which his father once aspired. He entered the specialty of ophthalmology and undertook fellowship training in London. There he met a Syrian investment banker, Asma, and they were married in 2000.

On January 21, 1994, while Bashar was having a routine day at the eye clinic at Western Eye Hospital in London, he was summoned back to Syria because his older brother Bassel had been killed in a high-speed car accident. Hafez named his son Bashar as his successor. Initially there was speculation (or a wish) that because of his training in London, and his marriage to an investment banker, that Bashar would be a modernizing force. But this was not to be.

It would seem that Hafez appointed Bashar to be the dignified face of the regime, and his younger brother Maher, who was very similar in personality to Bassel, as the enforcer. Indeed, in a revealing interview with Barbara Walters in 2011, when Walters asked Bashar whether his forces had cracked down too hard on the protesters, Bashar responded:

> These are not my forces, they are military forces belonging to the government. . . . I don't own them. I am president. I don't own the country.

Idolized Father, Yet Rebellious Adolescent

But the heroic older brother and "second choice son" dynamic that has been described does not really apply to Fred Trump's sons. Initially, his firstborn son, Fred Jr., served as his crown prince. In response to the stress of working for his critical and demanding father, Fred Jr. started abusing alcohol, and died of of a heart attack related to alcoholism at age forty-one.

While Donald dutifully went on rounds with his father every Saturday, he was also a tough kid who was always getting into trouble in school. His father grudgingly admired his toughness, but when he started getting letters from the principal, he decided to send him at age thirteen to the New York Military Academy, a prep school, to get his behavior under control. Trump has even admitted to this stage of his early years, writing in *Crippled America*:

Growing up in Queens, I was a pretty tough kid. I wanted to be the toughest kid in the neighborhood and had a habit of mouthing off to everybody while backing down to no one. Honestly, I was a bit of a troublemaker. My parents finally took me out of school and sent me upstate to the New York Military Academy. I had my share of run-ins there as well.

The discipline at the New York Military Academy was extreme. As soon as students arrived, they were immersed in "marching, saluting and military disciplines." He was particularly close to Major Theodore R. Dobias (known to the students as Coach Doby), according to whom Donald was particularly coachable. Interestingly, Donald thrived on the military discipline.

Thrives at Military Academy

Donald flourished in this environment. He loved the spit and polish; he received medals for neatness. And he was a star athletically, especially in baseball, and made the varsity squad in football as well.

And somehow he managed to convince himself that a military prep school was the equivalent of military service. Trump even stated that at the New York Military Academy he received "more training than a lot of the guys that go into the military." When discussing his time there, Donald Trump wrote in *Crippled America*:

> I went to a military school, New York Military Academy. It was a tough, tough place. There were ex–drill sergeants all over the place. And these people liked to scream and, above all, they liked to fight! Our instructors were demanding about everything from academics to personal hygiene. I learned American history and I learned how to neatly fold my clothing so it could be stacked. That might not be a skill that has had much application in my life, but it was part of teaching my fellow cadets and me discipline, focus, and self-reliance. The main rule was simple: do it right or do it again.
>
> One of my roommates from school told a reporter recently, "The school taught you how to be a leader. It taught you, 'Show me a sore loser, and I'll show you a loser.' . . . Honesty and

straightforwardness were the rule of law. It got ingrained in us that you don't lie, cheat, or steal, or tolerate those who do." This may be why I never became a politician (until now)![5]

Trump fully absorbed the military culture. He was named captain for his senior year and ordered officers under his command to keep strict discipline. A sergeant under his command took this direction too literally and enthusiastically, and after three months, when a freshman's family complained concerning the severity of hazing, Trump, as the commanding officer, was transferred from his position. This was not the only instance when Trump was described as enjoying "wielding authority" and showing "aggression" toward other cadets. Trump was accused of ordering another cadet to be hit in the back with a broomstick for breaking formation and also of trying to push another cadet out of a second story window. During his time at military school he was also known as a "Ladies' Man," which was the caption for his yearbook photo.[6]

Trump, during his time at the New York Military Academy, was viewed as "a conniver" by his mentor (and coach) Theodore Dobias. Dobias recalls one Columbus Day in New York City, when Trump and his classmates were set to march in the parade, only to find that a group of Catholic schoolgirls were to walk ahead of them. Trump then announced he would take care of the problem, heading over to the group to negotiate that he his fellow cadets be put at the front of the parade. Dobias claims that Trump "just wanted to be first, in everything, and he wanted people to know he was first."

As this was during the height of the Vietnam War, there was an expectation that graduates would enlist. Trump was able to get four student deferments during his college years, first at Fordham University and then finishing his undergraduate degree at the University of Pennsylvania's Wharton School. He then, on the basis of "bone spurs," was able permanently to avoid military service.

However, despite Trump's claims that attending the New York Military Academy was equivalent to actual military service, he lacks actual military knowledge. While he may have practiced military drills in school, he does not possess knowledge on the laws of war. In an interview with ABC's David Muir, when responding to a question regarding the use of waterboarding by the military, Trump responded by stating he wanted to do everything "within the bounds of what you're allowed to do legally" to "fight fire with fire." As pointed out by Jane Mayer of the *New Yorker*, Trump does not know the basics of:

> The Geneva Conventions and the Convention Against Torture, which impose absolute, unconditional bans on torture and other forms of cruel and inhumane treatment of enemy combatants, categorizing such conduct, under any and all circumstances, as a war crime.

3

Seeking the Spotlight

Business as a Formative Experience

While Trump has continuously portrayed himself as a successful businessman, his career has been a rollercoaster of successes and failures. While as a real estate tycoon Trump had numerous successes including the Grand Hyatt hotel, Trump Place, Trump Tower, 40 Wall Street, and Trump International Hotel and Tower in Chicago, a number of his other business ventures were failures. This includes Trump Airlines, Trump Vodka, Trump Magazine, GoTrump.com, Trump Steaks, Trump University, Trump Ice, Trump Mortgage, and his casinos. Trump Airlines, for which he took out a $245 million loan in 1988, focused on commuter flights between New York, Boston, and Washington, DC. The planes, which featured gold bathroom fixtures, were not successful and eventually he could not earn even enough profit to cover the monthly $1 million interest payments on his loan. He eventually defaulted on his loans and surrendered the business to his creditors. Trump University, which was open from 2005 to 2010, ended up with two federal class-action lawsuits: one against Trump himself and one against the university and its managers, plus an additional suit in New York State. The lawsuits alleged that Trump University engaged in such illegal business activities as false claims and racketeering. In 2016, Trump agreed to pay $25 million to settle all three cases. As for Trump's casinos in Atlantic City, he filed for bankruptcy three separate times. The first time was in 1991 for the Trump Taj Mahal, which faced roughly $3 billion in debt after being open for only one year. Then in 2004, Trump filed bankruptcy not only for the Trump Taj Mahal, but for Trump Marina and Trump Plaza casinos, with debt of about $1.8 million. After this, Trump rebranded as Trump Entertainment Resorts, Inc., which eventually declared bankruptcy as well, following which Trump stepped down as chairman.

The Important Mentoring Influence of Roy Cohn[1]

Young Trump, within two years of graduating from the University of Pennsylvania and still living in Queens, was on the hunt for attractive women. He joined a private disco, "Le Club," in Manhattan, which he described as a "hot" social club. There he met and developed a close relationship with Roy Cohn, who was infamous as Senator Joseph McCarthy's right-hand man and lawyer during his notorious investigations for the House Un-American Activities Committee. Trump and Cohn instantly hit it off. As Cohn was later to reflect, both Trump and he were men of action, who preferred their deeds to speak for them, rather than speaking in portentous tones like the political class.

While it was his father, Fred Trump, who identified Donald as his successor, bringing him as "crown Prince" into the family real estate rental business in middle-class Brooklyn and Queens, it was Cohn who encouraged Donald Trump to transcend the cautionary boundaries his father had set and cross the river and enter the lists with the major Manhattan real estate entrepreneurs. Cohn introduced the ambitious young man to the social and political elite of Manhattan.

Cohn was an important mentor for Trump, teaching him always to fight back, never to settle. Cohn linked Trump to mob-owned construction companies. Trump described Cohn as someone who could be "vicious" for him and would "brutalize" his opponents. Cohn became, in Trump's words, "like a second father to him."

So, when the federal government sued Fred Trump and his son Donald in 1972 for racial discrimination in their rental apartments, at Cohn's urging they countersued for $100 million. The government had found after a careful investigation that black rental applicants were denied, with their cards marked "C" (for colored), whereas a white couple applying immediately afterward would be accepted. The judge threw out the countersuit, identifying the grounds for the countersuit as spurious, and there was an adverse settlement. Trump was to state after this settlement, "I'd rather fight than fold, because as soon as you fold once, you get the reputation," clearly echoing his new lawyer, Roy Cohn, who was considered one of the most powerful and famous lawyers in America. Although the case was a complete loss for the Trumps, Donald spun it as a terrific win, exemplifying one of Cohn's lessons, to never admit defeat.

When Trump was applying for a casino operator's license, he managed to persuade the New Jersey attorney general to limit the scope of the investigation, thus obscuring his mob connections and several major federal investigations. This pattern of limiting investigations of his past, and his awareness of the vulnerability of his less than savory history, continues to the present day.

Roy Cohn, representing Trump interests, played a major role in assisting Abraham Beame in a tight race for mayor of New York in a primary run against Mario Biaggi. Through selective leaks detrimental to Biaggi in the *New York Times*, Beame fended off a major challenger for the nomination and went on to win the election.

During a time of crisis for Mayor Beame, Trump saw a major opportunity for using the bankrupt Penn Central railroad as a site for the long-promised convention center. Trump's progress was impeded by Ned Eichler, VP of Palmieri & Co., the firm that was to disburse Penn Central's real estate holdings. Trump pursued Eichler to his sparse office. Eichler found in Trump "a blond young man fairly bursting with ambition." When a meeting was arranged, Beame told Eichler, who was representing Palmieri, "Whatever my friends Fred and Donald Trump want in this town, they get."

Trump had the vision to see the possibilities for refurbishing the Commodore Hotel. He was encouraged by Cohn in pursuing this vision. His father strictly opposed this risky development. By creatively portraying the refurbishing of this hotel next door to Grand Central Station as an act of public service, fighting the deterioration of midtown, Trump managed to persuade the city to aid in financing.

Without detailing all the deals of Trump's real estate career, as in the "big deal" just reviewed, Trump used charm and creative imagination to portray and get financing for large projects with very little personal money at risk. He describes a very flat organization with no cumbersome bureaucracy, so that if one of his employees had a good idea he could come into Trump's office, they would review it, and if Trump approved, that was it.

This style is engraved in Trump's experiential memory, and Trump uncritically seems to assume that the same leadership style he used so effectively as a real estate entrepreneur will work without modification in any way in running the country. One cannot help but be reminded of Robert McNamara, who served as secretary of defense during the Vietnam War under presidents Kennedy and Johnson. All of the brilliant statistics McNamara had used so effectively in his post as president of the Ford Motor Company were of little help in coping with the impact on the American psyche of service personnel returning home in body bags, which were the metric he used for his statistics.

Roy Cohn was a major influence on Trump's life. And since Cohn's death in 1989 due to complications from AIDS, Trump has frequently remarked how much he misses him, often asking: "Where is my Roy Cohn?," a sentiment he has given voice to even as president, following Attorney General Jeff Sessions's decision to recuse himself.[2] The styles of Trump and Cohn were very complementary. And their friendship was equally important to both men, with Cohn serving as emcee for Trump's birthday party at the nightclub Studio 54, while Trump hosted a birthday party for Cohn in Trump Tower. In fact, it was Cohn who had stressed to Trump the importance of keeping his name in the papers.

The Entertainer

Donald Trump has long sought recognition for his wealth and success by trying to gain celebrity status. As he once stated, "If you don't tell people about your success, they probably won't know about it."[3] This need for recognition is an aspect of his narcissism; he has an exaggerated sense of self-importance that is manifested as extreme self-centeredness, egocentricity, and self-absorption, which is compensating for underlying insecurity.

Early Celebrity Status

Since 1981, Donald Trump has appeared in over 130 TV series, fifty TV specials, sixty documentaries, and twenty movies. He has been continuously interviewed on news programs, and in newspapers and magazines. In addition, since 1987 Donald Trump has published fourteen books, as well as a board game and a video game.

During the eighties, Donald Trump first began appearing as himself in TV shows and movies, including two appearances on *The Jeffersons*. He also began appearing in a number of documentaries, TV miniseries, and such specials as *WrestleMania*. Throughout the eighties, Trump was often a punchline in popular culture, as a frequent target of the satirical *Spy* magazine and serving as the inspiration for the villain Biff Tannen in the 1989 movie *Back to the Future Part II*.

Donald Trump came out with his first book, *The Art of the Deal*, in 1987. The book, which is coauthored with Tony Schwartz, is part memoir and part business advice. It was number one on the *New York Times* bestseller list for thirteen weeks, remaining there for a total of forty-eight weeks. In a *Washington Post* article published in May 2017, Schwartz described his experience working with Trump during the writing of *The Art of the Deal*. He stated that "early on, I recognized that Trump's sense of self-worth is forever at risk. When he feels aggrieved, he reacts impulsively and defensively, constructing a self-justifying story that doesn't depend on facts and always directs the blame to others."[4]

Trump has cited this book as being one of his proudest accomplishments, stating that it is his second favorite book after the Bible. During an interview with CNN during the 2016 presidential campaign, Trump said: "I wrote a book called *The Art of the Deal*, the No. 1 selling business book of all time, at least I think, but I'm pretty sure it is. And certainly, a big monster, the No. 1 bestseller."[5]

A component of Trump's narcissism is that he unrealistically overestimates his abilities and achievements, as seen not only in his great pride for *The Art of the Deal*, but in his expectations for his board game. In 1989, the Donald Trump board game, Trump: The Game, was released. Following the release of his game, Trump stated, "I didn't want a game based solely on chance. I wanted a game based on talent. And I wanted to teach people if they have business instincts. It's great if they can learn that from a game instead of having to go out and lose your shirt." Although it sold poorly after its initial release, selling only 800,000 copies out of an anticipated two million, the game was released in 2004 following the success of Trump's show *The Apprentice*. The board game, which is modeled after Monopoly, is based on Trump's career and *The Art of the Deal*. Trump initially assumed he would make millions from his board game, representing the overestimation he had of his abilities and popularity at that time.[6]

Just as Trump's narcissism causes an overestimation of success, he views setbacks as conveying a sense of special unworthiness. Trump must control the image that is projected of him to the world, as witnessed during the nineties. By the nineties, Trump, who was gracing the tabloids with his divorces and bankruptcies, focused heavily on his TV persona. He appeared on a number of sitcoms in an attempt to control his own image to the public, including *The Fresh Prince of Bel-Air* in 1994, *The Nanny* in 1996, and *Sex and the City* in 1999. According to Christopher Lasch in his 1979 social commentary *The Culture of Narcissism*, underneath the surface arrogance and grandiosity of the narcissist is profound self-doubt and inner uncertainty, looking to others for confirmation of his worth: "The other person tends to be used to make the narcissist feel good, and well-being depends upon receiving a continuously adequate quantity of positive regard."[7]

In the 1990s, Trump also began associating himself with *Playboy*, giving interviews there in 1990 and 1997. (In 2000, Trump even had a cameo role in a pornographic *Playboy* documentary.) In his 1990 *Playboy* interview, when asked, "With so much poverty on the city streets, isn't it embarrassing for you to flaunt your wealth?" Trump replied, "There has always been a display of wealth and always will be, until the depression comes, which it always does. And let me tell you, a display is a good thing. It shows people that you can be successful. It can show you a way of life. *Dynasty* did it on TV. It's very important that people aspire to be successful. The only way you can do it is if you look at somebody who is."[8] Donald Trump looks not only for a confirmation of his wealth, but admiration. He desires an admiring response from his audience, constantly displaying himself, his wealth, and his success to evoke attention from others.

He cannot be satisfied, craving more attention and recognition from new audiences, as witnessed through his increased TV and movie appearances throughout the 1990s into the early 2000s, as well as his books and his video game. Donald Trump's video game, *Donald Trump's Real Estate Tycoon,* was first released in 2002. In this single-player game the player had to try and defeat Donald Trump by becoming a business magnate.

Miss Universe

This desire for admiration can also be witnessed in Trump's co-ownership of the Miss Universe Organization, which included the Miss USA and Miss Teen

USA pageants from 1996 to 2015. As discussed by former Miss Arizona Tasha Dixon, who had been a contestant in the Miss USA pageant, employees of the pageant encouraged the contestants to lavish Trump with attention when he came into the dressing areas. Trump has come under a great deal of fire over his conduct while co-owner of the Miss Universe Organization. Allegations have been made that Trump would walk into the contestants' dressing areas while they were partially undressed or completely naked, including during the Miss Teen USA pageant where girls as young as fifteen were undressed. Mariah Billado, who was Miss Teen Vermont in 1997, recalls her experience with Trump during the Miss Teen USA pageant, stating, "I remember putting on my dress really quick because I was like, 'Oh my God, there's a man in here.'" Three other teenage contestants from the same year confirmed the story. Similar allegations have been made by former contestants of the Miss USA pageant. Dixon recalled Trump entering the dressing areas during the 2001 pageant, stating:

> He just came strolling right in. There was no second to put a robe on or any sort of clothing or anything. Some girls were topless. Other girls were naked. Our first introduction to him was when we were at the dress rehearsal and half-naked changing into our bikinis.

This was coupled with encouragement by the employees to shower him with attention, as Dixon goes on to state:

> To have the owner come waltzing in, when we're naked, or half-naked, in a very physically vulnerable position and then to have the pressure of the people that worked for him telling us to go fawn all over him, go walk up to him, talk to him, get his attention . . .

While Trump's political campaign failed to respond to these allegations in 2016, Trump himself admitted to and even bragged about this conduct on the Howard Stern show in 2005.

> Trump: Well, I'll tell you the funniest is that I'll go backstage before a show.
>
> Stern: Yes.

Trump: And everyone is getting dressed and ready, and everything else and then there are no men anywhere, and I'm allowed to go in because I'm the owner of the pageant and therefore I'm inspecting it. You know, I'm inspecting it.

Robin Quivers [female co-host]: Right.

Trump: You know I'm inspecting it, I wanna make sure that everything is . . .

Stern: You're like a doctor, you need to be there.

Trump: Yeah, the dress . . . "Is everyone okay? Is everybody okay?" And you see these incredible looking women. And so I sort of get away with things like that, but . . .

Trump viewed his co-ownership of the Miss Universe Organization as reinforcing his business and his brand, often having the Miss Universe pageant hosted in cities where he had business interests. Finalists normally came from countries where the competition had strong television ratings. One former Miss Universe contestant from 2012, Adwoa Yamoah, who competed as Miss Canada, stated that after contestants first met Trump:

He made comments about every girl: "I've been to that country." "We're building a Trump Tower there." It was clear the countries that he liked did well. He'd whisper to Paula [Shugart, president of the Miss Universe Organization] about the girls, and she'd write it down. He basically told us he picked nine of the top fifteen.

Similar sentiments have been made by other former contestants, including two contestants from 2013, Kerrie Baylis and Shi Lim. Baylis, who was Miss Jamaica, stated that when the finalists were announced, "the list looked like the countries that Donald Trump did business with, or wanted to do business with." Lim, who was Miss Singapore, also stated that "the finalists were picked by Trump. He was really in charge. We called it the Trump card."

The Apprentice

Donald Trump has often sought to control his image in the media, and following business downturns he has always attempted to use his celebrity status to alter his image to the world. Donald Trump rather successfully did this through his TV show *The Apprentice*. His reality TV game show first aired in January 2004, with Trump starring until 2015. On *The Apprentice*, contestants compete for a one-year $250,000 contract to run one of Donald Trump's companies. It was on *The Apprentice* that Donald Trump coined one of his signature phrases, "You're fired!" As was discussed in "The TV That Created Donald Trump" by Emily Nussbaum in the *New Yorker*:

> It's become a wearying, ugly observation, a media truism at once superficial and deep: if *The Apprentice* didn't get Trump elected, it is surely what made him electable. Over fourteen seasons, the television producer Mark Burnett helped turn the Donald Trump of the late nineties—the disgraced huckster who had trashed Atlantic City; a tabloid pariah to whom no bank would lend—into a titan of industry, nationally admired for being, in his own words, "the highest-quality brand."[9]

Trump himself recognized how popular *The Apprentice* made him, stating in an interview for *Playboy* in 2004:

> Certainly a businessperson on television has never had anything close to this success. It's like being a rock star. Six people do nothing but sort my mail. People come in and want my secretary Robin's autograph. If a limo pulls up in front of Trump Tower, hundreds of people gather around, even if it's not mine. I ask, "Can this be a normal life?" Maybe it's the power that comes from having the hottest show on television, but people like me much better than they did before *The Apprentice*. And if you think about it, all I did on the show was fire people, which proves how bad my reputation must have been before this.[10]

And in fact, one of the main purposes of the show was to help rebrand Donald Trump's image. In an interview for the *New Yorker*, author Patrick

Radden Keefe discusses how *The Apprentice*'s producer Mark Burnett "resurrected Trump as an icon of American success":

> *The Apprentice* portrayed Trump not as a skeezy hustler who huddles with local mobsters but as a plutocrat with impeccable business instincts and unparalleled wealth—a titan who always seemed to be climbing out of helicopters or into limousines. "Most of us knew he was a fake," [video editor Jonathon] Braun told me. "He had just gone through I don't know how many bankruptcies. But we made him out to be the most important person in the world. It was like making the court jester the king." Bill Pruitt, another producer, recalled, "We walked through the offices and saw chipped furniture. We saw a crumbling empire at every turn. Our job was to make it seem otherwise."[11]

While the show provided viewers with a false image of Trump's business success, it did more than just that: it provided an almost mythical figure to the audience. A successful and immensely wealthy businessman who could make others successful and rich like him. And the shows were debuted at times when Americans needed a success story, they needed to believe in something. *The Apprentice* itself debuted in 2004, nearly a year after the invasion of Iraq and at the same time it had been announced to Congress that no evidence was found of Saddam Hussein harboring weapons of mass destruction. Then the show's spin-off, *The Celebrity Apprentice,* debuted in 2008 following the United States entering one of the worst economic downturns that had been seen since the Great Depression. The show didn't just provide the American people with the amusement of a reality TV series, it gave them someone to admire, an admiration Trump had always wanted from the American public. An admiration he would seek once again from the American public by running for president of the United States.

4

The Relationships of a Narcissist

Wives

Trump has chosen his wives based upon attributes that help to bolster his own image, primarily being their attractiveness and age. The physical attributes of his wives make them an ideal match for him. A number of comments from Trump in the past concerning his wives include, "You know, it really doesn't matter what the media write as long as you've got a young, and beautiful, piece of ass," and "I think the only difference between me and the other candidates is that I'm more honest and my women are more beautiful." When discussing his first wife Ivana in his book *Trump: Surviving at the Top*, he wrote:

> I knew from the start that Ivana was different from just about all of the other women I'd been spending time with. Good looks had been my top—and sometimes, to be honest, my only—priority in my man-about-town days. Ivana was gorgeous, but she was also ambitious and intelligent. When I introduced her to friends and associates, I said, "Believe me. This one's different." Everyone knew what I meant, and I think everyone sensed that I found the

combination of beauty and brains almost unbelievable. I suppose I
was a little naive, and perhaps, like a lot of men, I had been taught
by Hollywood that one woman couldn't have both.[1]

He uses his "other half" and her physical and psychological attributes to create a fuller sense of himself, they become a self-object. According to the psychoanalyst Heinz Kohut, the primary function of an individual in a narcissist's personal surround is to shore up his or her self-esteem, to provide reassurance for the fragile self, serving as a self-object that completes the famished self of the narcissist. Trump's current wife, a former model from Slovenia whom he married in 2005, has been described as his perfect mate by a number of close friends, including Lisa Bytner, who had worked in public relations for Trump Model Management, saying, "She doesn't make waves. She speaks only when spoken to. She's just very sweet." Another close friend, decorator William Eubanks, stated of Melania, "She enjoys her role of stepping back and letting him take center stage."[2] Trump's wife is meant to serve as a boost to his own self-esteem and to make him appear more successful.

In his book *The Art of the Comeback*, Trump wrote:

> Often, I will tell friends whose wives are constantly nagging them about this or that that they're better off leaving and cutting their losses. I'm not a great believer in always trying to work things out, because it just doesn't happen that way. For a man to be successful he needs support at home, just like my father had from my mother, not someone who is always griping and bitching. When a man has to endure a woman who is not supportive and complains constantly about his not being home enough or not being attentive enough, he will not be very successful unless he is able to cut the cord.[3]

It is not at all surprising that Trump, who views his wives as self-objects, is on his third marriage.

Trump's past two divorces and his extramarital affair were based upon those partners no longer meeting the criteria of the perfect individual he had in mind to complement himself. Trump's underlying vulnerability and sense of worthlessness is triggered when his spouse no longer mirrors the image he has of himself. Rather than accommodating to the inevitable vicissitudes of marriage, he divorces and seeks a partner who is able to mirror him in the way his famished ego needs. Without the structure a relationship like this provides, he feels incomplete. When speaking of his first wife, Ivana, in an interview with Oprah Winfrey in April 1988, Trump stated, "There's not a lot of disagreement because, ultimately, Ivana does exactly as I tell her to do."[4] Trump's marriage to Ivana ended in a divorce that was finalized in 1992. Ivana no longer mirrored him in a manner that his famished ego desired, largely because she began focusing more heavily on work. In *The Art of the Comeback*, Trump wrote:

> My big mistake with Ivana was taking her out of the role of wife and allowing her to run one of my casinos in Atlantic City, then the Plaza Hotel. The problem was, work was all she wanted to talk about. When I got home at night, rather than talking about the softer subjects of life, she wanted to tell me how well the Plaza was doing, or what a great day the casino had. I really appreciated all her efforts, but it was just too much . . . I will never again give a wife responsibility within my business. Ivana worked very hard, and I appreciated the effort, but I soon began to realize that I was married to a businessperson rather than a wife.

Trump continued to blame their martial issues on Ivana's choosing to work, stating:

> There was a great softness to Ivana, and she still has that softness, but during this period of time, she became an executive, not a wife. . . . You know, I don't want to sound too much like a chauvinist, but when I come home and dinner's not ready, I'll go through the roof, okay?[5]

His marriage to Ivana ended over his reportedly having an affair with the twenty-five-year-old beauty pageant contestant Marla Maples. Marla, who was fifteen years younger than Ivana, would become Trump's second wife in 1993. Marla and Donald would divorce six years later. *New York Post* columnist Cindy Adams, a longtime friend of Trump's, stated of the divorce that "he basically didn't want to get married. It was lust, not really love. She loved him very much. But Donald is somebody who's in love mostly with himself." When discussing his divorce from Marla in *The Art of the Comeback*, Trump wrote:

Marla was always wanting me to spend more time with her. "Why can't you be home at five o'clock like other husbands?" she would ask. Sometimes, when I was in the wrong mood, I would give a very materialistic answer. "Look, I like working. You don't mind traveling around in beautiful helicopters and airplanes, and you don't mind living at the top of Trump Tower, or at Mar-a-Lago, or traveling to the best hotels, or shopping in the best stores and never having to worry about money, do you? If you want me to be home at five o'clock, maybe these other things wouldn't happen, and you'd be complaining about that too. Why would you want to take something that I enjoy and change it?" I always viewed her whys as being very selfish. But the fact is, in a marriage both sides have to be happy.[6]

Trump has no ability to empathize with his wives as individuals who have needs and feelings of their own. He is unable to see his wives beyond the manner in which they fulfill his own narcissistic needs, forming only a shallow attachment to them. In Trump's Mother's Day tweet for his wife Melania, the picture Trump shared was of the two of them walking together, with Trump a foot in front of Melania, placing him in a more prominent position in the photo than her. This Mother's Day tweet was not to honor her for being a mother, but to show her as being the mother of his child. This has been a major component of their relationship from the beginning. When the couple first started dating in 1999, Melania participated in an on-air interview with Donald Trump and Howard Stern, as they discussed her body parts, including her chest and whether or not she may have stolen money from him.

Melania Trump: A Mini Political Personality Profile

Melania Trump was born Melanija Knavs in Slovenia (at that time part of Yugoslavia) on April 26, 1970. Her father, Viktor Knavs, managed dealerships for a state-owned vehicle manufacturer. He was a part of the League of Communists of Slovenia, which advocated for a policy of state atheism. Her mother worked as a patternmaker at a children's clothing manufacturer, where Melania first began doing fashion shows along with the children of other factory workers. At the age of sixteen she began doing commercial modeling, signing a modeling contract in Italy at the age of eighteen. By 1996, she moved to New York City to continue her modeling career, where she met Donald Trump two years later at a party. As discussed previously, Melania's relationship with Trump gained attention on *The Howard Stern Show*. In one interview from 1999, Trump spoke by phone with Stern while in bed with Melania, in which she describes herself as being almost nude, at which point Stern's co-host Robin Quivers states:

> "That's Donald's girl, you gotta get your own girl."[7] Over the course of the interview, Trump and Stern joke that Trump shouldn't marry Melania because of her accent, with Trump describing his ex-wife Ivana's accent as: "Yes, it was amazing. It was so cute, and then one day I woke up that it was terrible. I couldn't stand it anymore." Stern goes on to ask Trump to have sexual relations with Melania while on the phone, as well as discuss Trump's consideration for running as a presidential candidate for the Reform Party. Stern states: "That is why you're a great candidate, because you're refreshingly honest. Clinton is doing the same stuff [i.e., his affair with Monica Lewinsky], he's just not talking about it."[8] In fact, Melania was a focal point during Trump's first attempt at running for president with the Reform Party in 1999 (which is discussed in Chapter 9). When asked what type of First Lady she would be, Melania replied: "I would be very traditional, like Betty Ford or Jackie Kennedy."[9] In early 2000, Melania attended a number of political events with Trump. Melania and Trump were married in 2004 and had their son Barron in 2006.

Melania has been noted for playing a small role in Trump's presidential campaign, however, in November 2015, Melania stated about her husband running for president: "I encouraged him because I know what he will do and what he can do for America. He loves the American people and he wants to help them."[10] In her role as First Lady, she announced her public awareness campaign, Be Best, in May 2018, which focuses on combating cyberbullying and drug use in America's youth. Her campaign, however, came under heavy criticism following its announcement over the campaign's booklet, which was nearly identical to a booklet released by the Federal Trade Commission under the Obama administration. Melania has also been questioned regarding Trump's harsh stance on immigration, as she is the first First Lady to be a naturalized citizen. In regard to border separation of families, Melania has stated she "hates to see children separated from their families and hopes both sides of the aisle [Republicans and Democrats in Congress] can finally come together to achieve successful immigration reform."[11] However, Melania came under criticism once again during her June 2018 visit to McAllen, Texas, one of the major areas under focus for family separation, in which she wore a jacket that said, "I really don't care. Do U?" At first, Melania fired back at the media saying it was just a jacket and there was no hidden meaning. Trump himself tweeted: "'I REALLY DON'T CARE, DO U?' written on the back of Melania's jacket, refers to the Fake News Media. Melania has learned how dishonest they are, and she truly no longer cares!"[12] A few months later Melania changed her original stance on the jacket to match Trump's claim, saying during an interview on ABC News that she wore the jacket "for the people and for the left-wing media who are criticizing me. And I want to show them that I don't care." Often Melania appears to serve as a media distraction from her husband's controversies, as witnessed by her July 24, 2019 tweets concerning Christmas plans for the White House, tweets which coincided with former special counsel Robert Mueller's congressional hearings.

Children

Just as Trump's wives have served as self-objects to complete his famished self, so have his children. In his book *Crippled America*, Trump wrote:

> I don't mind criticism. People call me thin-skinned, but I have thick skin. I have a wonderful and beautiful wife. I've got billions of dollars. My children are highly intelligent and accomplished executives who work with me.[13]

Trump's children not only fulfill his narcissistic needs by idealizing him, but by bolstering his image. His three eldest children (Donald Jr., Eric, and Ivanka) all went to top schools and now have successful careers, as well as marriages and children. Donald Jr., Ivanka, and Tiffany all graduated with their bachelors from Donald Trump's alma mater the University of Pennsylvania, with both Donald Jr. and Ivanka graduating from the Wharton Business School. Trump has regularly implied he, too, is an MBA graduate of

Wharton, but he is an undergraduate economics graduate of the University of Pennsylvania. Eric Trump graduated with his bachelors from Georgetown University, where Tiffany began law school in the Fall of 2017. As for his two daughters, Ivanka and Tiffany, their physical appearance is also of the upmost importance to Trump. Both daughters have even worked as models. Trump has often commented about Ivanka's beauty, once saying, "I've said if Ivanka weren't my daughter, perhaps I'd be dating her." As for Tiffany, who is noted for being an "internet celebrity," Trump has written, "She was always a great student and a very popular person no matter where she went."

Trump looks at his children as a reflection of himself, equating their success to his success. In an interview with Anderson Cooper on CNN in the summer of 2016, Trump commented:

> I've always been a very good father. They come to me, friends of mine, very successful people, and their children have problems with drugs and problems with alcohol and problems with a lot of things, and they say: "Could you speak to my son? Could you speak to my daughter?" And I'm always very honored to do that.[14]

However, his claims of being a wonderful father are contradictory to comments made in the past that he never spent a great deal of time with his own children, saying in 2005 on Howard Stern's radio show, "'Cause I like kids. I mean, I won't do anything to take care of them. I'll supply funds and she'll take care of the kids. It's not like I'm gonna be walking the kids down Central Park." Trump appears to have the same lack of involvement with his youngest son Barron, born in 2006, who is primarily taken care of by Melania. Despite the lack of involvement in his children's lives, specifically his eldest children, he appears to be much closer to them as adults. Donald Jr., Eric, and Ivanka, as well as Ivanka's husband Jared Kushner, all played vital roles in Trump's campaign and are now a part of his inner circle.

Donald Trump Jr.: A Mini Political Personality Profile

Donald Trump Jr. is the first child of Donald Trump's marriage to Ivana Trump. Donald Jr. did not have the closest relationship to his father growing up. In an interview with *The Atlantic* in 2016, Donald Jr. remarked that his dad wasn't the kind to take his kids out to toss a ball, saying, "He made time for us, but it was always on his terms." Donald Trump Jr., Eric, and Ivanka actually spent most of their time with Ivana's parents. In an interview with *New York Magazine*, Donald Trump Jr. commented, "My father is a very hardworking guy, and that's his focus in life, so I got a lot of the paternal attention that a boy wants and needs from my grandfather."[15]

By the age of twelve, Donald Trump and Ivana started going through a very public and scandalous divorce, resulting in the couple sending their children off to boarding school, with Donald Trump Jr. and Eric going to The Hill School in Pennsylvania and Ivanka to Choate in Connecticut. In the same interview with *New York Magazine*, Donald Trump Jr. stated:

> Listen, it's tough to be a twelve-year-old. You're not quite a man, but you think you are. You think you know everything. Being driven into school every day and you see the front page and it's divorce! THE BEST SEX I EVER HAD! And you don't even know what that means. At that age, kids are naturally cruel. Your private life becomes very public, and I didn't have anything to do with it: My parents did.[16]

Donald Jr. blamed his father for the divorce, leading to a difficult relationship between them. This difficult relationship apparently continued into Donald Jr.'s early adulthood. In an unconfirmed Facebook post, Scott Melker, who attended the University of Pennsylvania with Donald Jr., described the horrible relationship he witnessed between father and son:

> I was hanging out in a freshman dorm with some friends, next door to Donald Jr.'s room. I walked out of the room to find Donald Trump at his son's door, there to pick him up for a baseball game. There were quite a few students standing around watching, trying to catch a glimpse of the famed real estate magnate. Don Jr. opened the door, wearing a Yankee jersey. Without saying a word, his father slapped him across the face, knocking him to the floor in front of all of his classmates. He simply said "put on a suit and meet me outside," and closed the door.
>
> Donald Jr. was a drunk in college. Every memory I have of him is of him stumbling around campus falling over or passing out in public, with his arm in a sling from injuring himself while

drinking. He absolutely despised his father, and hated the attention that his last name afforded him. His nickname was "Diaper Don," because of his tendency to fall asleep drunk in other people's beds and urinate. I always felt terrible for him.[17]

Donald Jr. appears to have become closer to his father once he began working for him in 2001, after spending a year in Colorado, where, against his father's wishes, he spent his time fishing, hunting, and camping. It is unclear what caused Donald Jr. finally to join the family business or what actually mended the relationship between him and his father. But after 2001, the two appeared to be much closer, with Donald Trump grooming his eldest son in the business. As discussed in Robert Slater's *No Such Thing as Over-Exposure: Inside the Life and Celebrity of Donald Trump*:

> Of course, when the boss makes a point of staying close to the office, subordinates get the hint that they must be on hand as well. Sometimes, Trump gets that point across subtly, sometimes not. When his son, Donald Trump Jr., planned a two-week trip to Africa in the summer of 2004, his father told him that he did not like his going away for that long, "because you can come back and your business is no longer there." Trump's fear was that his son would be out of touch for too long. "You've got to find some other things that you like to do," he urged his son. Golf was the father's own passion, if only because "you play for three hours and you come back to the office."[18]

In 2003, Donald Jr. was introduced to his future wife, Vanessa Haydon, by his father at a fashion show. Donald Jr. and Vanessa married two years later in Donald Trump's vacation home, Mar-a-Lago, Florida. They now have five children. Donald Jr. started on his father's show *The Apprentice* for roughly ten seasons, serving as a boardroom adviser.

Throughout the election, Donald Trump Jr. continually defended his father, especially over his controversial statements, with Donald Jr. making a number of controversial statements himself. In early September 2016, while defending his father on a radio show, Donald Jr. stated:

> The media has been her [Hillary Clinton's] number one surrogate in this. Without the media, this wouldn't even be a contest, but the

media has built her up. They've let her slide on every discrepancy, on every lie, on every DNC game trying to get Bernie Sanders out of this thing. If Republicans were doing that, they'd be warming up the gas chamber right now. Every day everyone's throwing everything they can possibly throw at him.[19]

Later that month, Donald Trump Jr. explained how he viewed the refugee crisis by stating in a tweet, "If I had a bowl of Skittles and I told you just three would kill you, would you take a handful? That's our Syrian refugee problem."[20] Although he did not join the White House like his sister, Donald Jr., who took over his father's business, has continued to be a major aspect of his father's inner circle. Serving as a sycophant for his father, Donald Jr. has continued to defend his father's controversies to the media, making numerous controversial statements of his own. This has included the propagation of conspiracy theories through Twitter, including accusations that migrant children separated from their families at the borders are actors. Donald Jr. has also supported the anti-Semitic conspiracy theory that American-Hungarian Jewish businessman, George Soros, was a Nazi collaborator during the Holocaust. Donald Trump Jr. has also made media headlines due to the Mueller investigation. Donald Jr., along with Trump campaign chairman Paul Manafort and Jared Kushner, were investigated over their June 9, 2016 meeting with Russian lawyer Natalia Veselnitskaya at Trump Tower. However, Donald Jr., was ultimately not prosecuted for campaign finance violations because it could not be proven that he willfully broke the law.

Eric Trump: A Mini Political Personality Profile

Eric Trump is the third child of Donald Trump's marriage to Ivana Trump. In an interview on *48 Hours*, when he was only nineteen years old, Eric describes his memories of his father growing up, as well as his parents' divorce:

> I remember traveling a lot with him. I also remember spending a lot of time in the office, building Lego cities while he was negotiating deals when I was five or six. People often stared and pointed. Growing up, that's something that gets to you.[21]

Eric went on to say that, much like Ivanka, he has grown up wanting to work for his father's organization, with Donald Trump remarking:

> He's got a wonderful capability. And then at some point he'll be tested, and tested very strongly. And then he's going to see whether or not he likes it. But I suspect that Eric will do well, and he's going to like it.[22]

After the interviewer made a joke regarding what would happen if Trump Tower eventually became the Eric Trump Tower, Donald Trump replied, "He'd be dismissed from the company immediately." To which Eric added, "Surely disowned. I know my place." Eric Trump went on to say about his father:

> He has an amazing work ethic. I really look up to him. I think it's amazing that you can find a job that you love and enjoy so much that you'd rather be doing it than taking vacations.[23]

Eric Trump, much like his two elder siblings, spent time during the campaign defending his father. However, Eric, like Donald Jr., also brought controversy to the campaign, due to claims of tax evasion and accusations that he stole money from his charity. Following the inauguration in February, Eric faced more criticism due to a nearly $100,000 Secret Service bill for a business trip to Uruguay. It is unclear how much of a role Eric plays within his father's inner circle, but he is most likely a sycophant just like Donald Jr.

Ivanka Trump: A Mini Political Personality Profile

Ivanka Trump is the second child of Donald Trump's marriage to Ivana Trump. While Donald Jr. had a difficult relationship with their father growing up, Ivanka often comments about how she grew up playing with blocks on the floor of her father's office, wanting to follow in his footsteps into the world of real estate. Ivanka is often seen as the second most famous Trump, serving, like her brother Donald Jr., as a boardroom adviser on *The Apprentice*. Over the years Ivanka has attempted to create her own brand as a hard-working and successful businesswoman. Ivanka Trump has her own lifestyle website, "Ivanka Trump HQ," the stated objective of which is to help in "inspiring and empowering women to create the lives they want to live." The website has a number of sections, including "style," "work," "home," "play," "travel," and "wise words," where numerous articles are posted giving women advice on getting a job, dressing professionally, exercising, buying gifts, planning a wedding, and cooking. Ivanka's first book, *The Trump Card: Playing to Win in Work and Life*, came out in 2009. Not unlike her father's books, Ivanka discusses her experiences in the business world and offers business advice for her readership.[24] Her 2017 book, *Women Who Work: Rewriting the Rules for Success*, is filled with inspirational quotes from figures like Oprah Winfrey, Toni Morrison, Maya Angelou, as well as Ellen Johnson Sirleaf, the president of Liberia.[25] However, despite the famous and inspirational figures she draws upon, the use of the quotes, as well as her own advice and conclusions, makes relatively little sense. She has drawn much criticism in a number of literary reviews, including one in the *New Yorker* titled "Ivanka Trump Wrote a Painfully Oblivious Book for Basically No One" by Jia Tolentino:

> The other quoted experts—and there are hundreds—are all over the map. There's Stephen Covey, the business consultant and teacher who wrote *7 Habits of Highly Effective People*. There's Socrates. There's Toni Morrison, who is quoted as saying, "Bit by bit, she had claimed herself. Freeing yourself was one thing, claiming ownership of that freed self was another." (Ivanka does not note that those lines are from the novel *Beloved* and refer to freedom from actual slavery; in this context, they are used as the chapter divider before a section on time management, in which she asks women, "Are you a slave to your time or the master of it?")[26]

In a similar review for NPR, Annalisa Quinn wrote:

> Many of the inspiring quotations Trump stakes a claim to here seem to have been culled from apocryphal inspiration memes. For instance, on the subject of asking for a raise, she quotes another black woman writing on racism, Maya Angelou: "Ask for what you want and be prepared to get it."[27]

But the real, very different line is from Angelou's memoir *The Heart of a Woman*, and it is a piece of advice about living in a racist world. "Ask for what you want," Angelou's mother tells her, "and be prepared to pay for what you get."

In addition to her books and lifestyle website, Ivanka has her own fashion line that has been carried in a number of major U.S. department store chains. However, over the years, her fashion line has come under sharp criticism, including from a number of animal rights groups for her line using rabbit fur. In 2016, the U.S. Consumer Product Safety Commission recalled scarves from her line due to burn risk, stating that they did not meet with federal flammability standards. In February 2017, her line was dropped by Nordstrom due to "poor performance." Her line came under fire once again during Donald Trump's "Made in America" campaign due to the fact that almost all of her clothes are produced outside of the United States, in countries such as China, Vietnam, Bangladesh, and Indonesia.

Ivanka Trump has long been viewed as the voice of moderation at her father's side, not only during his current presidency and election campaign, but even as one of his boardroom advisers on *The Apprentice*. Throughout the campaign, much like her brothers Donald Jr. and Eric, Ivanka worked to defend her father to the media. However, as opposed to making controversial statements herself, like Donald Jr., Ivanka attempted to provide a more warm and personal view of her father. When Donald Trump was criticized for sexism, Ivanka would speak out publicly stating that she herself wouldn't have made it this far in her career if her father "didn't believe in opportunities for women." Rather than taking the "witch hunt" and "Nazi Germany" rhetoric of her father and eldest brother, she has simply called this news "sensationalized" and that her father is just "very blunt." Throughout the election the media often commented that Ivanka served as "his de facto first lady in waiting," as she appeared more regularly than Melania and was the one to introduce Trump when he announced he was going to run for president. In an interview in August 2016 with Sean Hannity, Trump named Ivanka as the person he counts on the most and that she was the member of his inner circle that he had consulted over his debates that were moderated by Megyn Kelly.

Ivanka is Trump's only child to take an active role in the White House, along with her husband Jared Kushner, becoming an adviser to her father. Upon taking this role, Ivanka stated, "I'm still at the early stages of learning how everything works, but I know enough now to be a much more proactive voice inside the White House."²⁸ Both Ivanka and her husband have come under heavy criticism for their roles in the White House, with one criticism for Ivanka being that she took her father's place at the G20 Summit. While Jared has been criticized for his role in handling the administration's foreign policy in the Middle East. Despite the view that Ivanka would serve as a moderate force within the White House, as she publicly differs with her father on a number of issues, she has done little to advance any of her own opinions. For instance, climate change and paid family leave are two issues Ivanka has been rather vocal about, yet very little to nothing has been done to advance her agenda. In fact, quite the opposite, with Trump proposing major cuts to the Environmental Protection Agency (EPA) and withdrawing from the Paris climate agreement. Ivanka made arguments against the United States withdrawing and had met with a number of business leaders to urge them to make a case to her father for staying in the agreement. And despite Ivanka's comments in the past airing support for the LGBTQ community, Trump tweeted on July 26, 2017, his decision to ban transgender individuals from serving in the U.S. military.

Both Ivanka and her husband have been used to defend Trump against accusations of anti-Semitism. Jared, who is a self-identified observant Jew, used his paper the *New York Observer*, to defend his father-in-law during the 2016 campaign, writing:

> Donald Trump is not anti-Semitic and he's not a racist. Despite the best efforts of his political opponents and a large swath of the media to hold Donald Trump accountable for the utterances of even the most fringe of his supporters—a standard to which no other candidate is ever held—the worst that his detractors can fairly say about him is that he has been careless in retweeting imagery that can be interpreted as offensive.

While both Ivanka and her husband have been used to soften Trump's public appearance, Ivanka specifically, she does not appear to hold much sway over him. Despite claims that he trusts her opinion and often seeks her counsel for advice, Trump's actions speak to the contrary, as exemplified by the Paris climate agreement. Going forward it does not appear that, at least for now, Ivanka will have much sway over her father's opinions or actions, despite any claims she makes to the media.

Friends

In addition to viewing his family, including his wives and children, as self-objects, Trump views his friends as self-objects as well. Relationships in general tend to be difficult to sustain. And in fact, it has often been questioned how many close friendships Trump has maintained over the years. It is always "what have you done for me lately?" While he has often kept the company of business and even political elites, Trump appears to prefer the self-validation he receives from his followers, rather than from any meaningful friendships. One of his longest maintained friendships is that with the billionaire real estate investor, Tom Barrack. Barrack, who became close to Trump during a number of business dealings in the 1980s, has helped Trump through some of his financial troubles. He has continued to prove himself as a useful friend over the years, helping both Trump and members of Trump's family maintain their debt. In 2017, Barrack was also on the committee for Trump's inauguration.

However, friends of narcissists can be bewildered at how easily what they thought was a solid relationship and deep friendship can suddenly disappear. Consider Jeff Sessions, the first in the Senate to endorse Trump, and who was rewarded by being appointed attorney general. But then he had the effrontery to recuse himself from the Mueller investigation because of his role in the campaign. So Trump went on the attack mercilessly, and characterized Sessions as weak, with the clear goal of forcing him to resign, so that he could appoint a new attorney general who could fire the special counsel. This is another example of loyalty as a one-way street for Trump.

5

King Donald

In 1999, Donald's father, Fred Trump, the King of his real estate empire in Brooklyn and Queens, died. Crown Prince Donald, who had absorbed his father's management lessons, inherited the kingdom and became King Donald. Donald, the King of New York, and eventually King of Real Estate. In an interview with Trump conducted by *BELLA* magazine prior to his announcing his candidacy for president titled "The King of New York: Donald Trump," the author Daniel G. Hall wrote: "There is a larger-than-life perception about Trump, and with good reason—the brand Trump built is synonymous with worldwide luxury and prestige."[1]

The Italian Baroque master Caravaggio is particularly noted for his rendering of the myth of Narcissus, from the poet Ovid. Consumed by his own beauty, Narcissus is depicted transfixed by his own image reflected in a pond. He cannot tear his eyes away from the beautiful image and dies. This was my concept which animated the cover illustration *Narcissus Dreaming of His Glorious Future* for my 2015 book with Cambridge University Press, *Narcissism and Politics: Dreams of Glory*, marvelously rendered by Montana DeBor, a graduate student in fine art at George Washington University. The crown and the Nobel Prize gold medal on the image of Narcissus are intended to illustrate the dreams of glory which consume the narcissist.

Trump has been consumed by dreams of glory since his youth. For most narcissists, the dreams are not fulfilled, the ambitions not achieved. But, what happens when the dreams of glory are achieved? There is an explosion of narcissism.

It is said that Trump really did not expect to win the 2016 election and entered the presidential lists almost as a lark. That may account for the apparent lack of preparation to assume the role. Indeed, the inner circle in different ways thought they would win by losing, i.e., be identified as being ready for a major job.

Yet, at another level, he was raised from boyhood on as Crown Prince to succeed his father, the real estate King of Brooklyn and Queens, eventually himself becoming the King of New York and the King of Real Estate. When Donald's older brother Fred Jr., an alcoholic who did not approve of the way his father conducted business, chose a career in aviation, Donald's father designated Donald as successor. Donald's ambition was not only to follow in his father's path but to go on to the next level.

However, this man who was once the King of New York and eventually the King of Real Estate, has in his presidential role transitioned into King Donald of the United States. In fact, the June 2018 cover of *Time* contained a rendering of Trump looking at himself in the mirror and seeing himself as a king, with the title "King Me."[2] Politicians in the Democratic Party have may similar accusations against Trump viewing himself as a king. For instance, following Trump's claim that not only was the Mueller investigation unconstitutional but that he had an "absolute right" to pardon himself, Democratic politicians responding by stating: "You are not a king." Representative Ted Deutch stated: "Let us remind you of something, we don't live in a monarchy." While Senator Chuck Schumer stated: "We don't have a king. We are a nation of laws, not men. That's what the Founding Fathers created America all about. They didn't like the monarchies. But if a president can pardon himself, it's virtually a monarchy—at least as far as the president is concerned."[3] And in many ways Trump has continuously channeled the 18th century royalty that America's Founding Fathers fought against.

Emperor Trump

And perhaps in his wildest dreams of glory, Trump's ultimate goal is not to be just the King of the United States, but eventually Emperor Trump. Take for instance his obsession with building a wall on the United States' southern border with Mexico. This fixation can be likened to his shining skyscrapers, which bear the TRUMP brand. In fact Trump has even been referred to as the "King of Branding" in the media. It can also be likened to Trump's admiration of the Great Wall of China, which Melania visited on Trump's 2017 trip to China. He may be seeking to emulate the achievement of Emperor Qin. Qin, the first emperor of a united China, was the first to conceive of and build the great wall of China. This is a glory to which Trump apparently aspires, wanting to not merely be president but also to be an emperor, hoping to brand the "great wall of Trump" as he branded the international spread of Trump Towers when he was the King of New York and King of Real Estate. In fact, in 2015 on Fox Business Network's *Mornings with Maria*, the then presidential candidate stated: ". . . you look at the Great Wall of China that was built 2,500 years ago. It's 13,000 miles . . . As you know, I know how to build. I know how to get it done. We'll have a great wall. We'll call it the Great Wall of Trump."[4] However, Trump later said he was being facetious about calling it "the Great Wall of Trump," being careful to never refer to the wall in such a manner again.

Rules of the Kingdom

To understand Trump's leadership style as President of the United States, it is important to examine him as a business leader, essentially examining the rules of the kingdom set forth by King Donald. One of the best ways to examine his business leadership style is through the rules Trump has created for himself (and for others) over the years. This is the series of leadership rules that can be found in a number of his books. There is reason to believe that Trump has uncritically extrapolated these rules to the world of politics and the challenges of being president.

In Trump's *The Art of the Deal* he gives his readers tips and advice that he uses to guide his own life and his business. When discussing publicity, he writes, "Good publicity is preferable to bad, but from a bottom-line perspective, bad publicity is sometimes better than no publicity at all. Controversy, in short, sells."[5] He also advocates his belief in "fighting back," a common theme in a number of his books, which was exemplified by Roy Cohn:

> [W]hen people treat me badly or unfairly or try to take advantage of me, my general attitude, all my life, has been to fight back very hard. The risk is you'll make a bad situation worse, and I certainly don't recommend this approach to everyone. But my experience

is that if you're fighting for something you believe in—even if it means alienating some people along the way—things usually work out for the best in the end.⁶

Trump's *The Art of the Comeback* starts with "Trump's Top Ten Comeback Tips," which are as follows:

1. PLAY GOLF
It helped me relax and concentrate. It took my mind off my problems; I only thought about putting the ball in the hole. And, the irony is, I made lots of money on the golf course—making contacts and deals and coming up with ideas.

2. STAY FOCUSED
I am convinced that if I had maintained the same work ethic I had during the 1970s and most of the 1980s, there would have been no recession for me. I wasn't focused and really thought that life and success just came hand in hand. I thought I was better than the rest. When I began to relax and take it a little—or perhaps a lot—easier, things being to fall apart.

3. BE PARANOID
I have noticed over the years that people who are guarded or, to put it coldly, slightly paranoid, end up being the most successful. Let some paranoia reign! You've got to realize that you have something other people want. Don't let them take it away.

4. BE PASSIONATE
This is a key ingredient to success and to coming back. If you don't have passion about who you are, about what you are trying to be, about where you are going, you might as well close this book right now and give up. Go get a job and relax, because you have no chance of making it. Passion is the essence of life and certainly the essence of success.

5. GO AGAINST THE TIDE
When I decided to keep 40 Wall Street as an office building, everyone in Lower Manhattan was converting their buildings to

residential space—and with good reason. The apartment market is hot as a pistol. I decided to head in the exact opposite direction, and now I am signing up tenants at rents far higher than anything I expected.

6. GO WITH YOUR GUT

Some of the greatest investors I have ever known invest by instinct, rather than research, study, or hard work. If you look back over history, this is the way the greatest fortunes have been built. People had ideas that they truly believed in.

7. WORK WITH PEOPLE YOU LIKE

If you go to the office and don't find the energy in the people you are with, it is highly unlikely that you will be energized toward success.

8. BE LUCKY

I hate to put this in the book because it can't be acquired. People who inherit fortunes are lucky; I call them members of the lucky sperm club. But you can help coax luck into your life by working hard and being at the right place at the right time.

9. GET EVEN

During the bad times, I learned who was loyal and who wasn't. I believe in an eye for an eye. A couple of people who betrayed me need my help now, and I am screwing them against the wall! I am doing a number . . . and I'm having so much fun.

10. ALWAYS HAVE A PRENUPTIAL AGREEMENT

Anyone in a complicated business should be institutionalized if he or she gets married without one. I know firsthand that you can't come back if you're spending all your time fighting for your financial life with a spouse.[7]

In Trump's book *Think Big*, each chapter ended with a list of key points for his readers. One will note a paranoid tone to the following selection of those key points:

- Hire the best people, and do not trust them.
- Get even with people who do you wrong.
- Always get a prenuptial agreement.
- Get all the facts, then go with your gut.
- Always think positively and expect the best.
- Protect your back by thinking negatively.
- Do not have illusions; the world is a brutal place full of vicious people.
- Everyone wants to kill the fastest gun.
- Lions kill for food, humans kill for sport.
- Get some respect, and do not give a damn if people like you.
- When somebody screws you, screw them back in spades.
- When someone attacks you publicly, always strike back.
- If you want to stop a bully, hit them right between the eyes. They will think twice about doing it again.
- Go for the jugular so that people watching will not want to mess with you.
- If someone knows they made a mistake and they apologize, forgive them and move on, but never trust them again.
- Give yourself a big definition.
- Draw positive conclusions about yourself.
- Always think of yourself as someone who is important.
- Speak out like a big thinker.[8]

Trump also wrote in *Think Big*:

When someone crosses you, my advice is "Get even!" That is not typical advice, but it is real-life advice. If you do not get even, you are just a schmuck! When people wrong you, go after those people, because it is a good feeling and because other people will see you doing it. I love getting even. I get screwed all the time. I go after people, and you know what? People do not play around with me as much as they do with others. They know that if they do, they are in for a big fight. Always get even. Go after people that go after you. Don't let people push you around. Always fight back and always get even. It's a jungle out there, filled with bullies of all kinds who will try to push you around. If you're afraid to fight back people will think of you as a loser, a "schmuck!" They will know they can get away with insulting you, disrespecting you, and taking advantage of you. Don't let it happen! Always fight back and get even.[9]

It is easy to see how Trump is continuing to be guided by his rules, even as president of the United States. Thus far, Trump has treated the presidency as if he were still a business tycoon and as if he were still the King of Real Estate. He seems to lack an understanding of governing and how to develop consensus and work with Congress. The dominant themes of "not trusting anyone" and "be paranoid" specifically impede his ability to work effectively with Congress. His difficulty with empathy and taking a disagreement as an insult further exacerbates this difficulty.

There is nothing resembling thoughtful logical analysis in Trump's decision-making process. There is a discomfort with shades of gray. If it is a good idea, i.e., if Trump thought of it, it is to be defended. And for someone to challenge an idea produces anger, as it is taken as a personal criticism. And this is particularly stressful for the White House staff and the inner circle, who are so wary of insulting Trump and inciting his anger, that it produces a reflexive sycophancy. The brilliance of the narcissistic leader means by their very nature their ideas are perfect and not to be challenged. And the anger in the face of challenge betrays the underlying insecurity. First and foremost, what does this do for Donald J. Trump? Secondly, what does this do for his base? And finally, what is best for America? This all makes for impulsive, rigid decision-making.

Overall, his leadership style is very different from other presidents. Acting as a king, or perhaps as an emperor, not considering things carefully but acting on impulse, often tweeting in the early morning to announce his imperial decision. Consider the decision to withdraw U.S. forces from Syria. President Trump announced this major policy with an early morning tweet. General Joseph Votel, the four-star commander of the U.S. Central Command (CentCom) responsible for Middle East strategy and operations, stated on CNN International, "I was not consulted" on the Syria withdrawal.[10] He announced his retirement shortly thereafter. This was followed by the announcement by the secretary of defense, General James Mattis, that he was resigning as defense secretary following a clash with the president over the policy of withdrawing troops from Syria. He stated in his letter of resignation that the president deserved someone in charge of the Pentagon "better aligned with his views."[11] Democrats in congress had touted him as their best hope for reining in the president-elect who had unorthodox views on matters of war and peace. With the resignation of Votel and Mattis, there was no longer a leader of enough stature to provide a stabilizing presence; the other so-called adults in the room had already left: John Kelly and H. R. McMaster, generals who provided a stabilizing force. His decision-making style is regal, similar to that he employed in leading the Trump Organization.

In his books describing his management style at the Trump Organization, Trump proudly described an open-door style, that anyone from the janitor to senior executives, anyone with a good idea, was invited in to discuss his idea with King Donald. And if it struck a positive chord, it would be put into effect without staffing it out. It would seem that this is the same style he has implemented in the presidency. It is a style that imparts an impulsive quality to Trump's decision-making. Another major aspect of his leadership style is lying.

Liar-in-Chief

One of the most remarkable features of the Trump presidency is the frequency of untruths being spoken from the presidential podium. Hitler coined the term "big lies" in his 1925 book *Mein Kampf* about the use of a lie so "colossal" that no one would believe that someone "could have the impudence to distort the truth so infamously." His minister of propaganda, Joseph Goebbels, stated that "if you can't lie, you'll never get anywhere."

Preceding Trump's manipulation of public opinion through big lies or fake truths was Richard Nixon. The distinguished historian/biographer Fawn Brodie of UCLA singled out the role of lying in the formation of Nixon's character. She indicates that almost all of Nixon's victories were "won as a result of lying attack on the unexpected and fortuitous death of others." It is one thing to propagate "the big lie." It is quite another to habitually propagate little lies with no apparent reason, and that the core of Nixon's character was not built on lies but ambition by comparison to Trump's. Barry Goldwater famously called Nixon "the most dishonest individual I have ever met in my life." He asserted that Nixon "lied to his wife, his family, his friends, long time colleagues in the U.S. Congress, lifetime members of his own political party, the American people and the world." Trump, himself, has a long history of lying. For instance, according to Jonathan Greenberg of *Forbes*, Trump lied to get onto the Forbes 400 richest people list in 1982. Greenberg stated: "He was worth under $5 million that year when I put him in at $100 million. He should have never been on that list and neither should his father.... He totally snowed me."[12]

According to the *Washington Post* Fact Checker column, in his first year as president, Trump made 2,140 false claims. In the next six months, he has lied at the rate of 4,229 per annum—nearly double. It was at the rallies, the signature event of Trump's presidency, that Trump was particularly liable to give voice to false and misleading claims. At one rally in August 2019, Trump made thirty-five false claims. Trump's predisposition to lie, especially at his rallies, can best be explained by Trump himself in *The Art of the Deal*: "People may not always think big themselves, but they can still get very excited by those who do. That's why a little hyperbole never hurts. People want to believe that something is the biggest and the greatest and the most spectacular."[13] Since the Fact Checker column began its work, Trump repeated nearly 150 untruths at least three times.

When presidential spokeswoman Sarah Huckabee Sanders repeated an untruth that had already been debunked, she cited the president as her source: "I'm here to speak on behalf of the president. He's made his comments clear." The White House assault on the truth is not an accident, it is intentional.

6

Political Personality

Political Personality Description

APPEARANCE

The goal of a narcissist like Trump is achieving unlimited power, wealth, fame, and beauty. Donald Trump's appearance is an important aspect of his self-worth; in his constant search for admiration and attention he focuses more heavily on appearance rather than substance. When asked what he believed made him so popular, Trump replied, "Honestly, it's my looks. I'm very handsome."[1] When it was remarked Trump did not act in the manner that a president would, he replied that he looks the part, saying, "Do I look like a president? How handsome am I, right? How handsome?"[2] In fact, Trump has long thought that appearance was important for a presidential candidate. In a 1981 segment of *Rona Barrett Looks at Today's Super Rich*, after being asked if he would ever consider running for president, Trump remarked how television has ruined politics to the point that not even Abraham Lincoln could be elected, saying, "He was not a handsome man and he did not smile at all."[3]

However, underneath Trump's vanity is a deep sea of insecurity. It has been reported in an interview in the *New York Times* with Trump's doctor that he uses a prostate-related drug, Propecia, to prevent male-pattern baldness.[4] For years Trump has been sensitive to comments made about his hair, tweeting in April 2013, "As everybody knows, but the haters and losers refuse to acknowledge, I do not wear a 'wig.' My hair may not be perfect but it's mine."[5] Trump made a similar statement in his 2004 book *Trump: How to Get Rich*, stating, "I do not wear a rug. My hair is 100 percent mine. No animals have been harmed in the creation of my hairstyle."[6]

Trump has also reacted very negatively to comments made during the election regarding the size of his hands. In one broadcast, while holding up his hands for viewers to see, Trump stated, "Look at those hands, are they small hands? And, he referred to my hands—'if they're small, something else must be small.' I guarantee you there's no problem. I guarantee."[7] Trump has often taken remarks about the size of his hands to be disparaging remarks about the size of his genitalia, previously stating, "My fingers are long and beautiful, as, it has been well documented, are various other parts of my body."[8]

JUDGMENT

It is as if every thought that passes through Trump's tumultuous mind must be expressed. The early morning twitter storms, which led the journalist David Brooks to characterize him as bipolar and manic, are perhaps the most vivid illustration of this. As a narcissist, his thoughts are particularly important, very valuable, and not easily opposed or given up. And it as if by merely having the transient thought, it will become actualized. There is a kind of royal imperative to the thought, and without consulting anyone, "it shall be done." Consider announcing the transgender policy thought without first consulting with the military, which had been working on this complex issue for years. He has the big ideas and lets his subordinates sweat the details. And the rapidity with which his ideas change! It does seem that there are no core ideas, apart from the centrality of Donald J. Trump.

In his early morning tweet storms, Trump gives voice to a policy idea, and then, in an inversion of the traditional manner of staffing out policy positions, tasks his analytic units with developing an intellectual framework for the policy.

A striking example of this was the announcement on Trump's twitter account that the United States would be withdrawing its troops from Syria, as mentioned in the previous chapter. First General Joseph Votel, CentCom commander, who was quite bitter about being bypassed, submitted a letter of resignation, and took a farewell tour. Shortly thereafter, on December 20,

2018, General James Mattis, the secretary of defense, who also had been bypassed, sent President Trump a letter of resignation in which he stated:

> One core belief I have always held is that our strength as a nation is inextricably linked to the strength of our unique and comprehensive system of alliances and partnerships. While the U.S. remains the indispensable nation in the free world, we cannot protect our interests or serve that role effectively without maintaining strong alliances and showing respect to those allies.[9]

Characterized as a "stinging rebuke" by Joseph Fuchs on CNN, the letter not only emphasizes the value of our network of alliances, stressing the importance of NATO after the 9/11 terrorist attacks on the World Trade Center and the Pentagon, but also the importance of consulting with our allies.

Making it clear that it was not acceptable to him in his role as secretary of defense to be bypassed in major military decisions, Mattis wrote in his letter of resignation:

> Because you have the right to a Secretary of Defense whose views are better aligned with yours on these and other subjects, I believe it is right for me to step down from my position.[10]

KNOWLEDGE

When asked in an interview during the election if he reads, Donald Trump responded, "I never have. I'm always busy doing a lot. Now I'm more busy (sic), I guess, than ever before." During this interview, the reporter noted that Donald Trump's office was bare of any books, with not even a computer on his desk. The only reading material to be found was a stack of magazines with Trump's face on the cover. Trump has an overwhelming lack of curiosity. When questioned about his lack of knowledge over critical policy issues, Trump argues that the details are either unimportant or that it is only the media out to "get him." In discussing an interview Trump had with Hugh Hewitt in his book *Crippled America*, Trump wrote:

> During the show, he started asking me a series of questions about an Iranian general and various terrorist leaders. "I'm looking for

the next commander in chief to know who Hassan Nasrallah is, and Zawahiri, and al-Julani, and al-Baghdadi. Do you know the players without a scorecard yet?" What a ridiculous question! I don't think knowing the names of each terrorist leader more than a year before the election is a test of whether someone is qualified. We're not playing Trivial Pursuit. Every question Hugh asked me was like that—although I noticed he didn't ask too many questions about our economic policy or about reforming the tax system—things I've spent my life mastering. Instead, he asked these "gotcha" questions that proved nothing except that he was able to read some names and pronounce them correctly. Does anybody believe George W. Bush and Barack Obama could name the leaders of all terrorist organizations? (Not that they are the standard!)[11]

However, even a few months into his presidency Trump was still vastly unaware of even the major details of a number of terrorist organizations. In an address given by the president in the Rose Garden in late July 2017, Trump stated that Lebanon was "on the front lines" fighting Hezbollah (whose leader is Hassan Nasrallah), seemingly unaware that Hezbollah is currently a party within the Lebanese parliament.

In Trump's *Think Big*, he discusses what he considers to be his "Formula of Knowledge":

> The Formula of Knowledge is the best way to learn because learning from someone else's mistakes is faster and easier than making them yourself. For example, you don't have to go through an early 1990s real estate crash like I did to know what to do in that situation. Because of the way things go in life, lots of times life forces you to learn from your own mistakes, but it is much better if you can learn from others' mistakes rather than your own.[12]

Trump advises his audience to learn from the mistakes of others, while seemingly admitting that he doesn't do so himself; rather he learns from his own mistakes, including the real estate crash of the 1990s. This is an attitude he has carried with him into his presidency. Trump has already acknowledged that he has not read any presidential biographies (a stark contrast with his predecessors, including Barack Obama, George W. Bush, Bill Clinton, and

George H. W. Bush), nor does he plan to read any soon. As discussed by Julian Zelizer, a professor of history and public affairs at Princeton University, "They [the four aforementioned former presidents] were all people who had read about the past, they were invested in thinking of themselves in the trajectory of other presidents. That's not who [Trump] is . . . He's not someone who reads deeply, he's not someone who even identifies, necessarily, with the long trajectory of presidents." He has an overwhelming lack of curiosity, not only about the history of American presidents, but of American history in general. In the past Trump has made numerous inaccurate comments on American history, including stating that abolitionist Frederick Douglass was still alive, as well as praising two bitter American rivals Andrew Jackson and Henry Clay.

In addition to his lack of intellectual curiosity, Trump has a relatively low vocabulary and poor grammar. Although he is not the first president to be called out for this issue, as former President George W. Bush was throughout his presidency, according to studies, Trump's grammar and vocabulary are well below that of any recent president. While during speeches on average a president or presidential candidate will speak at a 6th to 8th grade level, Trump's grammar and vocabulary is below that of a 6th grader; indeed, some studies have likened his vocabulary to that of a 3rd grade level. According to Maxine Eskenazi, a scientist in the Carnegie Mellon University's Language Technologies Institute, "we would expect that we could see the word 'win' fairly frequently in third grade documents while the word 'successful' would be more frequent in, say, seventh grade documents."[13] Among his most tweeted words are "great," "win," and "loser." There has also been much speculation concerning Trump's inability to retain information, including information during his intelligence briefings, with one *Washington Post* article stating, "President Trump consumes classified intelligence like he does most everything else in life: ravenously and impatiently, eager to ingest glinting nuggets but often indifferent to subtleties."[14] Top intelligence officials, including former CIA director Mike Pompeo, have discussed the intelligence community's efforts to deliver information to President Trump in a manner he can best understand, which is largely through visuals like maps, charts, pictures, and videos.

It is very difficult to convey new information to President Trump, as he seeks to establish the superiority of his knowledge to anyone trying to bring him new information. Trump regularly boasts about his intellect and the superiority of his knowledge on a wide range of subjects. When he was asked a question about the major shortfall in senior state department positions and to identify which experts he consults with in developing foreign policy, he responded: "I'm speaking with myself, number one, because I have a very good brain and I've said a lot of things."[15] Then when he was asked on *Morning Joe* who he consulted with on foreign policy consistently, he responded: "I know what I'm doing, and I listen to a lot of people. But my primary consultant is myself. And I have a good instinct for this stuff." In the same interview when he was questioned if his foreign policy was neo-isolationist, he responded, "I wouldn't say that at all."[16]

Scope of His Claimed Knowledge

He has laid claim to a wide variety of expertise, including:

DRONES AND DRONE TECHNOLOGY
"I know more about drones than anybody. I know about every form of safety that you can have."
"Having a drone fly overhead—and I think nobody knows much more about technology, this type of technology certainly, than I do."

TV RATINGS
"I know more about people who get (TV) ratings than anyone."

ISIS
"I know more about ISIS than the generals do."

SOCIAL MEDIA
"I understand social media. I understand the power of Twitter. I understand the power of Facebook, maybe better than almost anybody, based on my results, right?"

COURTS
"I know more about courts than any human being on Earth."

LAWSUITS

"(W)ho knows more about lawsuits than I do? I'm the king."

THE VISA SYSTEM

"Nobody knows the system better than me. I know the H1B. I know the H2B . . . Nobody else on this dais knows how to change it like I do, believe me."

TRADE

"Nobody knows more about trade than me."

THE U.S. GOVERNMENT SYSTEM

"Nobody knows the system better than I do."

RENEWABLE ENERGY

"I know more about renewables than any human being on Earth."

TAXES

"I think nobody knows more about taxes than I do, maybe in the history of the world."

DEBT

"I'm the king of debt. I'm great with debt. Nobody knows debt better than me."

MONEY

"I understand money better than anybody."

INFRASTRUCTURE

"Look, as a builder, nobody in the history of this country has known so much about infrastructure as Donald Trump."

SENATOR CORY BOOKER

"I know more about Cory than he knows about himself."

DEMOCRATS
"I think I know more about the other side than almost anybody."

CONSTRUCTION
"Nobody knows more about construction than I do."

THE ECONOMY
"I think I know about it better than [the Federal Reserve.]"

TECHNOLOGY
"Technology—nobody knows more about technology than me."

This boasting about the scope of his knowledge has been present throughout his career. In 1999, for example, speaking of Campaign Finance, he boasted, "I think nobody knows more about campaign finance than I do, because I'm the biggest contributor."

It is this kind of arrogance that interferes with his accepting expert briefings in general, but especially from his military and intelligence experts. He made an uncoordinated comment, for example, about having defeated ISIS, when there were reliable reports of 10,000 to 20,000 ISIS cadres scattered throughout Iraq and other countries, keeping a low profile but ready to be activated, which contributed to the frustration that led to the resignations of generals Votel and Mattis over the uncoordinated Syria withdrawal announcement.

The regal reference is particularly interesting in terms of his decision-making. If, in his own mind's eye, he knows everything about lawsuits (and everything else), this helps explain his difficulty in relying on experts. Again, and again, he has boasted that he's "like really smart" and "a very stable genius" as questions have been raised concerning his mental fitness to be president, with reference to the Twenty-Fifth Amendment.

With reference to the claimed expertise in technology, there have been numerous reports that Trump is unable to retain even a small portion of the information presented to him. It is important to note that the characteristics of the narcissist can cause serious problems in information processing and problem solving. Rather than viewing problems as, "What are the threats to our nation?" and "What can be done to meet these threats?," the narcissist views information as "How can I use this situation to either preserve or improve my personal situation?"

While Trump speaks fondly of his NYMI experience, saying he received more rigorous military training than he would have in the army, when the school fell on hard times and requested $7 million from its wealthiest alumnus, Trump turned them down, saying it was a "failing enterprise."

Emotional Reactions

Trump is extremely emotional, volatile, and unpredictable. He is often overwhelmed by powerful emotions, leading to emotional outbursts, including his now infamous Twitter storms. Trump's Twitter storms are a form of narcissistic rage. As I detailed in *Narcissism and Politics: Dreams of Glory,* narcissistic rage is a result of the narcissist triad:

> The narcissist triad consists of (1) narcissistic entitlement, which inevitably leads to (2) disappointment and disillusionment, which in turn produces (3) retaliatory rage due to the rejection of the "entitlement." This rage is strongly associated with the frustration of narcissistic entitlement and insatiable narcissistic needs.

As a narcissist's grandiose façade and unlimited dreams of glory mask a sea of insecurity and doubt, any attempt to dash their self-created reality will result in strong reactions. Take for instance Trump's Twitter storm against Macy's on July 1, 2015, after they dropped his fashion line, the Donald J. Trump Collection. The Donald J. Trump Collection, a line of clothes, watches, and ties that had debuted in Macy's in 2004, was dropped only two weeks after Trump made a number of controversial statements about Mexico. In a statement issued by Macy's, the company stated:

> We are disappointed and distressed by recent remarks about immigrants from Mexico. We do not believe the disparaging characterizations portray an accurate picture of the many Mexicans, Mexican Americans and Latinos who have made so many valuable contributions to the success of our nation. In light of statements made by Donald Trump, which are inconsistent with Macy's

values, we have decided to discontinue our business relationship with Mr. Trump and will phase-out the Trump menswear collection, which has been sold at Macy's since 2004.[17]

A number of Trump's Twitter storms have also been directed at individuals who have threatened Trump's sense of entitlement, including (but not limited to) senators Marco Rubio, John McCain, Elizabeth Warren, and Richard Blumenthal, as well as Hillary Clinton, Barack Obama, Jeff Sessions, James Comey, Megyn Kelly, Alicia Machado, and Mika Brzezinski. These Twitter storms represent his underlying insecurities and self-doubt.

The Russia investigation, in particular, has sparked a number of Trump Twitter storms. On the morning of July 22, 2017, Trump tweeted nearly a dozen times concerning the ongoing investigation, citing stories from the *Washington Post* and the *New York Times* as being "Fake News," as well as attacking Hillary Clinton, tweeting ". . . What about all of the Clinton ties to Russia, including Podesta Company, Uranium deal, Russian Reset, big dollar speeches etc." and "My son Donald openly gave his e-mails to the media & authorities whereas Crooked Hillary Clinton deleted (& acid washed) her 33,000 e-mails!" The Senate voting down the repeal of Obamacare caused a similar emotional outburst from Trump. On the morning of July 25, 2017, Trump tweeted, "This will be a very interesting day for HealthCare. The Dems are obstructionists but the Republicans can have a great victory for the people!" He would make similar tweets on the morning of July 27, 2017, but by that evening he would begin a tirade of tweets against the Senate vote for two days, including a tweet on the 29th that said ". . . 8 Dems totally control the U.S. Senate. Many great Republican bills will never pass, like Kate's Law and complete Healthcare. Get smart!"

Trump's emotional outbursts have often been rewarded. Trump's hard-line supporters revel in his twitter storms, due to the shock value of Trump's lack of regard for social and political norms. Trump's continuous insults against those who oppose him have become a vital component of his appeal to his hard-line supporters, and more often than not he acts in a manner to appease his hard-liners. The tweets he posts during one of his Twitter storms or those attacking people often receive the most likes. Tweets against the Clintons usually gain over 100,000 likes, including a tweet against Chelsea Clinton on July 10, 2017, where he wrote, "If Chelsea Clinton were asked to hold the seat for her mother, as her mother gave our country away, the Fake News would say CHELSEA FOR PRES!" Tweet attacks against Comey have also received over 100,000 likes. One tweet on June 9, 2017, where he wrote, "Despite so many false statements and lies, total and complete vindication ... and WOW, Comey is a leaker!" A tweet that received over 125,000 likes, while more positive tweets garner less likes, for instance his "Made in America" week tweets often had less than 60,000 likes.

"Swiss Cheese Conscience"

Trump has a "Swiss cheese conscience." A Swiss cheese conscience is when an individual has strict moral prohibitions, but can satisfy his own needs without moral prohibition, pouring through the holes of the cheese, justifying one's own actions while condemning others. While spouting a conservative ideology focused on "strong family values," Trump has already had two very public divorces. Trump's narcissistic entitlement allows for him to feel justified in decrying individuals or actions he himself commits, as if he were living in *a rarefied stratum* possessing a superior nature that lifts him above the moral expectations and laws that apply to mere mortals. As exemplified by Trump's comments during the election regarding infidelity in the Clintons' marriage, attacking Hillary over Bill's affair and even suggesting that Hillary may have had an affair herself. Trump made light of Bill Clinton's affair in the 1990s, while Trump himself has a failed marriage due to infidelity. His first marriage to Ivana ended because of his affair with Marla Maples, a divorce that was finalized in 1992. In a *Vanity Fair* article from September 1990, when discussing his affair with Marla, Trump was quoted as saying, "When a man leaves a woman, especially when it was perceived that he has left for a piece of ass—a good one!—there are 50 percent of the population who will love the woman who was left."

It is this lack of moral obligations for himself that has allowed Trump to make numerous offensive, racist, and/or sexist comments throughout the years. This includes Trump's recorded comments with Billy Bush from 2005, when he stated, "You know, I'm automatically attracted to beautiful—I just start kissing them. It's like a magnet. Just kiss. I don't even wait. And when you're a star, they let you do it. You can do anything. . . . Grab them by the pussy. You can do anything."[18] He also commented on President Obama's conduct of the role of commander in chief. Trump has continued to make comments without any moral obligation throughout his election and into his presidency. Comments that include attacks against specific races, ethnicities, and countries, such as:

> When Mexico sends its people, they're not sending the best. They're not sending you, they're sending people that have lots of problems and they're bringing those problems with us. They're bringing drugs. They're bring crime. They're rapists . . . And some, I assume, are good people.

And also:

> I will build a great wall—and nobody builds walls better than me, believe me—and I'll build them very inexpensively. I will build a great, great wall on our southern border, and I will make Mexico pay for that wall. Mark my words.

Trump's comments such as these will be discussed in a later chapter.

PART II

The Political Psychology of Trump's Followership

7

The Charismatic Leader-Follower Relationship

One of the remarkable features of the Trump psycho-political phenomenon is the durability of the base. One would think that the most extreme of his impulsive behaviors and extremist language would severely injure his popularity, yet polls continue to reflect 38–43% support, often as high as 48%.

The relationship between Trump and his hard-line followers represents a charismatic leader-follower relationship, whereby aspects of the leader's psychology unlock, like a key, aspects of his followers' psychology. A strong hypothesis concerning the psychology of followers of charismatic leaders is that articulated by Abse and Ullman, who studied the Jonestown massacre—"in times of crisis, individuals regress to a state of delegated omnipotence and demand a leader who will rescue them, take care of them."

Trump has a mirror-hungry leader personality, which feeds off of the adoration of his followers in the charismatic leader-follower relationship he has with his base. This personality pattern results from the "injured self," whose grandiose façade feeds off of confirming and admiring responses.

There are two pathways to the "wounded self": the individual who has been deprived of mirroring adoration from rejecting parents, and a more subtle variant, the individual who has been raised to be special, contingent upon his success. Douglas MacArthur, as described in the introduction, is an example. His mother made it clear in her remarkable poem that her success was contingent upon MacArthur's success, and indeed she moved to a residence near West Point to ensure MacArthur sufficiently concentrated on his studies. But this is a heavy burden.

It is the second pathway, the expectation of success and the insecurity that it generates, that was the pathway of Donald Trump. But it was his father who was raising Donald to succeed him as real estate giant, in effect nominating him to be Crown Prince, while his mother seemed more absorbed in herself.

The individual feels compelled to display himself in order to evoke the attention of others. However, no matter how much positive attention they receive they are never satisfied, consistently seeking new audiences from whom they can receive the continuing attention and recognition they crave. This constant need for new and more attention led the successful businessman Trump to continually seek prominent celebrity status since the early 1980s, appearing in TV series and specials as well as movies well into the 1990s, eventually culminating in his hit TV reality game show *The Apprentice* in the 2000s. However, the attention he received from this show could not satisfy him, causing him to seek a new audience of attention by running for president of the United States, where he received not only greater attention from U.S. citizens, but received a larger international audience as well.

Central to the "mirror-hungry" leaders' ability to elicit the admiration they require is their ability to convey a sense of grandeur, omnipotence, and strength. Leaders such as Trump, who convey this sense of grandiose omnipotence, are attractive to individuals seeking idealized sources of strength; they convey a sense of conviction and certainty to those who are consumed by doubt and uncertainty. This was evident in Trump's support from rural areas and the working class, where Trump's motto "Make American Great Again" (MAGA) had a strong resonance. Despite his lack of any concrete policy, his tweets concerning "JOBS, JOBS, JOBS" had resonated with many of his followers, especially those who are struggling and feel abandoned by the last administration.

"Mirror-hungry" charismatic leaders are often drawn to large crowds, where the roar of admiration becomes music to their ears. It was evident during the election how much Trump thrived off of his large rallies with people shouting his name. This is why even after the election ended, he has continued to hold giant rallies across the country because he needs to continue to thrive off the admiration of his followers as another form of compensation for his insecurity and self-doubt. It is also important to note that these rallies have been vital for his supporters as well. There is a quality of mutual intoxication for both sides, whereby Trump reassures his followers who in turn reassure him of his self-worth. Even before current rallies, his followers will line up hours early, waiting to fill even sports stadiums that can seat 10,000, continuing to chant "Lock her up!" During the rallies, Trump continues to use his externalizing rhetoric attacking any opponents or focusing on the immigrant crisis, despite calls from fellow Republicans to focus on issues like the economy. But it is this rhetoric that draws in his followers, who chant, "Build the wall! Build the wall!" One can compare it to a hypnotist mesmerizing his audience. But the power of the hypnotist ultimately depends upon the eagerness of their subjects to yield their authority, to cede control of their autonomy, to surrender their will to the hypnotist's authority.

Garrett Fagan has described the "lure of the arena" in referring to the Roman games in the colosseum, "when Romans turned out in the tens of thousands to watch the violence of brutal gladiatorial games."[1] This seems an apt metaphor for the Trump rallies both during the campaign and as president, when his remarks seemingly designed to encourage violence. He applauded Rep. Greg Gianforte's 2017 attack on a reporter when he said, "Any guy who can do a body slam, he is my type."[2] Despite screening of attendants, occasional protesters will infiltrate the rallies, and Trump, appealing to the majority, will call for attacking the minority protesters, calling for "slapping the face" of the protester, indicating: "I'd like to punch him in the face." Of another protester he said, "Get him out. Try not to hurt him. If you do, I'll try to defend you in court. Don't worry about it."

During the election campaign, Trump was able to tap into the already existing rhetoric of the alt-right in the United States. His comments against foreigners, Latinos, Muslims, and a number of other groups fit into the existing rhetoric of a number of alt-right parties.

It was comments such as these that led to widespread support among the alt-right, including from the Ku Klux Klan. Trump has received support from a number of high-ranking KKK members, including former Grand Wizard David Duke and current spokeswoman for the Knights Party, Rachel Pendergraft. On November 2, 2016, Pendergraft tweeted "KKK's official newspaper supports Donald Trump for president." Trump continues to be supported by the

KKK on their radio program, *White Resistance News*, where the two hosts (including Pendergraft) also bash anyone who opposes Trump. After the press conference following Charlottesville, after he became publicly pro-neo–Nazi and white supremacist, he was publicly thanked by David Duke. After the fatal riot between white supremacists and those protesting their actions, Trump did not disavow the white supremacist extremism but stated, "There are fine people on both sides," a relativistic comment which won him widespread opprobrium. Trump has also received support from alt-right leader and white supremacist Richard Spencer. Following Trump's State of the Union address on January 30, 2018, where he focused largely on his immigration views, stating that "Americans are dreamers too," Spencer tweeted:

> Trump said that he wants to maintain the "nuclear family" by ending chain migration. Basically, he's implying the superiority of the Protestant "wife and kids" over the South American and African extended family. Interesting rhetoric.[3]

It is important to note that there are complex socio-cultural, political, and historical factors that must be taken into consideration in addition to the features of the charismatic leader-follower relationship. One of the remarkable aspects of the Trump phenomenon is the stability and psychological power of his followership.

The hypnotic pull of the charismatic leader is compelling for the ideal-hungry follower. The wounded follower feels incomplete by himself and seeks to attach himself to an ideal other. Thus, there is a powerful, almost chemical attraction between the mirror-hungry charismatic leader and the ideal-hungry charismatic follower. And if Trump thrives on the adoring mirroring response of his followers, he provides for them a sense of completeness. Incomplete unto themselves, they have an enduring need to attach themselves to an idealized other.

We wish to emphasize that we assuredly are by no means implying that all those who voted for Donald Trump were narcissistically wounded individuals. But in trying to understand the resilience of Trump's followership and the core of his base, we are suggesting that Trump's political personality is particularly appealing to wounded individuals seeking an externalizing leadership and that Trump is particularly talented in appealing to individuals who are seeking a heroic rescuer.

But temporarily overwhelmed individuals will also respond to a heroic rescuer. Consider how the temporarily overwhelmed British people during the blitz responded to the remarkable charismatic leadership of Winston Churchill. Yet after the war was over, when the British people no longer needed a rescuer and returned to their customary self-sufficiency, Churchill was cast aside. When Trump assured voters in West Virginia, Pennsylvania, and Ohio that coal mining would be returning, he was sending a rescuing message to a socio-economic bloc that was situationally overwhelmed and needed a powerful rescuer.

The base will continue to be the core of Trump's support as long as the externalizing rhetoric and solutions Trump supplies continue to provide solace to his wounded followers. While two-thirds of Americans polled by CNN opposed Trump's family separation policy, 58% of self-identified Republicans supported it. Importantly, the percentage of the electorate identified as Republicans in Gallop polls is shrinking, from 32.7% before the election to 28.6% recently.[4] But the purity of the Trump base will continue to provide a solid—and reassuring—floor of support for the president. And when the roar of the crowd is interfered with by protesters, emphasizing freedom of the press, Trump's rhetoric will encourage the most recent use of violence by his supporters to quiet the protest and convey to him unambiguously the strength of the admiration of his followers.

These rallies can be taken as iconic miniature samples of the charismatic attraction between Trump and his followers. There are two types of charismatic relationships between a leader and his followers. The reparative charismatic leader, as exemplified by Mohandas Gandhi and Martin Luther King, heal the splits in their society as they are healing the splits in their own psychology. The destructive reparative leader, as exemplified by Adolf Hitler, pulls his followers together as he exports hatred to an external enemy. When Trump stimulates the attendees at his rallies to chant in guttural tones "Lock her up!," this is the hateful rhetoric of the followers of destructive charismatic leaders. It reassures the leader of the powerful support of their followers. And as their chants fill the auditorium, it reassures them that they are followers of a godlike leader who will lead them out of their wounded state, are united in their followership, and will uncritically follow the leader's call for violence against the protesters.

8

The Tea Party

History of the Tea Party

In February 2009, CNBC reporter Rick Santelli delivered a rant against policies of the Obama administration on the floor of the Chicago Mercantile Exchange, which struck receptive chords. Santelli threatened to hold a Chicago Tea Party rally later that year in which "some derivative securities" would be dumped in Lake Michigan by capitalists. Santelli's 2009 speech is widely credited with sparking the Tea Party movement. The *New York Post* reported, "The movement may not go anywhere—but it sure gives overtaxed, tapped-out folks a place to let off steam." Santelli, observing the remarkable manner that his rant went viral on YouTube, called his fiery speech "a match in a dried tinder box."[1]

Then on February 27, 2009, the Tea Party grabbed national attention with nationwide protests and rallies whereby protesters dumped tea or tea substitutes into local bodies of water. Evoking the symbolism of the Boston Tea Party of 1773, whereby dozens of colonists dumped forty-five tons of tea from three East India Company ships into the Boston Harbor, these modern-day protests wanted to urge Congress to repeal the *stimulus package*. The symbolism of the Boston Tea Party is still vital to numerous Tea Party groups, as seen on one Tea Party website, TeaParty.Org:

Many claim to be the founders of this movement; however, it was the brave souls of the men and women in 1773, known today as the Boston Tea Party, who dared to defy the greatest military might on earth. We are the beneficiaries of their courage. The Tea Party includes those who possess a strong belief in the Judeo-Christian values embedded in our great founding documents. We believe the responsibility of our beloved nation is etched upon the hearts of true Patriots from every race, religion, national origin, and walk of life sharing a common belief in the values which made and keep our beloved nation great. This belief led to the creation of the modern-day Tea Party.[2]

While those affiliated with the Tea Party movement refer to it as a "grassroots" movement that emerged in the 2000s, the history of the Tea Party goes back much further than 2009. In fact, the Tea Party has been described not as a grassroots movement, but rather as "corporate astroturfing" whereby it is an organization that "appears to be grassroots, but is either funded, created, or conceived by a corporation or industry trade association, political interest group or public relations firm."[3] The first website for the Tea Party was created in 2002 by the Citizens for a Sound Economy (CSE). The CSE, a conservative political group, was founded by Charles and David Koch in 1984. It is discussed by Jeff Nesbit in his book *Poison Tea: How Big Oil and Big Tobacco Invented the Tea Party and Captured the GOP*:

CSE was, in effect, a wholly owned subsidiary of Koch Industries, the second-largest privately owned company in the United States, with interests in manufacturing, trade, and investments. CSE hoped, and planned, to expand its reach to other funders such as oil, pharmaceutical, and tobacco companies. But at the time, CSE largely survived on the philanthropy and political aims of the Koch brothers, Charles and David, who owned the mammoth private corporation based in Wichita, Kansas, named after this family.[4]

While the CSE, the predecessor to the Tea Party, was founded by the Koch brothers, a study funded by the National Cancer Institute of the National Institute of Health found that they were also heavily backed and received over $5.3 million between 1991 and 2001 from tobacco companies like

Philip Morris. In 1990, the head of national field operations for R.J. Reynolds Tobacco Company, Tim Hyde, described why groups like CSE were vital to the tobacco industry:

> . . . coalition building should proceed along two tracks: a) a grassroots organizational and largely local track; b) and a national, intellectual track within the DC-New York corridor. Ultimately, we are talking about a "movement," a national effort to change the way people think about government's (and big business) role in our lives. Any such effort requires an intellectual foundation—a set of theoretical and ideological arguments on its behalf.[5]

Not only did the tobacco industry support CSE, but also its successor organizations the Americans for Prosperity and FreedomWorks, in an effort to continue trying to oppose smoke-free laws and more importantly tobacco taxes. These two organizations, in particular, were instrumental in providing training and materials for the first main Tea Party activities in February 2009. The AFP and FreedomWorks continued to help local Tea Parties which helped to support "the tobacco companies' political agenda by mobilizing local Tea Party opposition to tobacco taxes and smoke-free laws."[6]

Who is a Tea Partyer?

From 2010 to 2012, numerous polls were conducted to help figure out who the average Tea Partyer was and what the Tea Party believed. As described in one article by CBS in 2012, "They're white. They're older. And they're angry." But what exactly does this mean? And what truth is there to this statement? According to that poll conducted by CBS News, 18% of Americans identified as Tea Party supporters. Of those 18% they found that: 89% were white; 75% were forty-five years old or older; 59% were men; roughly 75% identified as conservative; and 60% identified as always or usually voting Republican. Other notable demographics identified in this poll included a Tea Partyer being more likely to be educated and more likely to attend religious services, with over 61% being Protestant. Another key characteristic was that they described themselves as "angry" over the current political situation, specifically having a high disapproval rate of then current president Barack Obama.

However, a majority of those who described themselves as a Tea Party supporter, 78%, had never attended a rally or even visited a Tea Party website.[7]

In fact, numerous polls have found that most individuals who identified themselves as Tea Party supporters have never attended one of their rallies. A similar poll conducted by Gallup found that many people who considered themselves supporters of the Tea Party had never been to a rally or a local meeting. In addition according to the Gallup poll, there was relatively no difference in age, employment status, and educational background of Tea Party supporters in comparison to the overall U.S. adult population. Where the demographics for Tea Party supporters may differ from overall U.S. adult demographics is in who attends the rallies, as well as the organizers of the group.[8] Chris Good of *The Atlantic* found that in speaking with organizers and leaders of local Tea Party groups that many of them were "older, middle-aged and upper-middle-aged, and many of them (certainly a disproportionate amount, compared to the national population) have been small business owners."[9] This observation was reiterated in a phone interview he had with Bob Porto, a Tea Party organizer from Arkansas, who stated, "I would say that the majority of them are middle class, and I would say that the majority of them are either established in their career as an employee at a company or that they have had or are a business owner."[10]

A number of these polls have also reported that Tea Party supporters state they care more about economic issues than social issues. While initial Tea Party protests focused on urging Congress to repeal the stimulus package, other issues have gained popularity among Tea Partyers, including a number of social issues. According to constitutional law professor, Elizabeth Price Foley, in her book *The Tea Party: Three Principles*:

> Although there are certainly a wide range of issues important to the Tea Party groups scattered across the country, there appear to be three core principles shared by all of them, which are unique and essential to American identity: (1) limited government—protecting and defending the idea that the federal government possess only those powers enumerated in the Constitution; (2) unapologetic U.S. sovereignty—protecting and defending America's borders and independent position in the world; and (3) constitutional originalism—interpreting the Constitution in a manner consistent with the meaning ascribed by those who wrote and ratified the

text. These three core principles are reflected in a variety of current issues of importance to the Tea Party, including health-care reform, fiscal responsibility, immigration, internationalism, and the war on terror.[11]

While the Tea Party claims their major focus is on economic issues, social issues have been equally as important to many Tea Party members, which includes abortion and LGBTQ issues.[12] One of the reasons that social issues might play a larger role in the Tea Party than what has been implied by the party is the high rate of evangelical Tea Partyers. Evangelical Tea Partyers have also been referred to as "teavangelicals," a phrase coined by David Brody in his book *The Teavangelicals: The Inside Story of How the Evangelicals and the Tea Party Are Taking Back America*. According to Mike Huckabee, who wrote the forward to the book: "With the word *Teavangelicals*, David had coined a term that . . . also explains the unique blend of a biblical worldview with the Tea Party emphasis on conservatism and the Constitution . . . His insights help explain the passion and the principles that have given a voice to millions of Americans . . . The Teavangelicals are not so much traditional Republicans as they are traditional Americans."[13]

Trump and the Tea Party

In a 2011 poll by NBC News and the *Wall Street Journal*, Donald Trump was the favored potential Republican candidate for 2012 by Tea Party supporters at 20%, more than any of his potential Republican rivals. Mike Huckabee was favored by 17% of Republican supporters, while Mitt Romney was at 21%.[14] The day after the release of this poll, Donald Trump stated on the *Today* show, in reference to the Tea Party, "I'm very proud of some of the ideas they put forth. They want to stop this ridiculous, absolutely killer spending that's going on. What's going on in this country—the way we're spending money like drunken sailors—we are absolutely, I'm telling you, we're going to destroy our own freedom."[15] In discussing his popularity in the poll, Trump went on to state, "I think that I connect with people because I happen to be smart, I happen to have a lot of common sense, I happen to know what I'm doing, I built a great company." And when asked if he considered himself a Tea Partyer, Trump answered, "I think so."[16]

Trump's popularity at this time came as a bit of a surprise to some. In a *Washington Post* article following the poll, political strategists identified three main categories that accounted for his popularity: 1) name identification; 2) confrontation sells; and 3) business credentials. Peter Hart, a Democratic pollster, stated, "The voters know Trump; they do not know many of the others. For the Tea Party followers—gone is Palin, so Trump is their current flavor du jour."[17] According to one party strategist, "People want to be like him." While Carl Forti, of the Black Rock Group, stated, "People want economic hope. They want a job . . . Trump's a businessman, so in theory, he knows what he's doing."[18] And perhaps one of the key factors in his popularity, under the category of "confrontation sells," was Trump's criticism of then president Barack Obama. During this time, Trump gave voice to the birther conspiracy theories. Actually starting in March 2011, just prior to the release of this poll, Trump went on a tirade of making birther claims for roughly six weeks:

> "Why doesn't he show his birth certificate? There's something on that birth certificate that he doesn't like."
> —March 23, 2011, on *The View*[19]

> "He's spent millions of dollars trying to get away from this issue. Millions of dollars in legal fees trying to get away from this issue. And I'll tell you what, I brought it up, just routinely, and all of a sudden a lot facts are emerging and I'm starting to wonder myself whether or not he was born in this country."
> —March 28, 2011, on Fox News[20]

> "He doesn't have a birth certificate, or if he does, there's something on that certificate that is very bad for him. Now, somebody told me—and I have no idea if this is bad for him or not, but perhaps it would be—that where it says 'religion,' it might have 'Muslim.' And if you're a Muslim, you don't change your religion, by the way."
> —March 30, 2011, on
> *The Laura Ingraham Show*[21]

Trump continued to ramp up these claims, especially in the days following the release of the poll:

> "I have people that have been studying this [Obama's birth certificate] and they cannot believe what they're finding . . . I would like to have him show his birth certificate, and can I be honest with you, I hope he can. Because if he can't, if he can't, if he wasn't born in this country, which is a real possibility . . . then he has pulled one of the great cons in the history of politics and beyond."
>
> —April 7, 2011, on the *Today* show[22]

> "His grandmother in Kenya said, 'Oh, no, he was born in Kenya and I was there and I witnessed the birth.' She's on tape. I think that tape's going to be produced fairly soon. Somebody is coming out with a book in two weeks, it will be very interesting."
>
> —April 7, 2011, on *Morning Joe*[23]

In addition, a few days following the release of the NBC News/*Wall Street Journal* poll, Trump spoke at a Tea Party event in Florida, an event that was part of a series of "Tax Day" protests by Tea Partyers throughout the country. At the speech some Tea Partyers were wearing shirts that said "Draftthedonald.com."[24] The shirts, of which there were roughly a thousand, and the website it promoted, were created by Jerry Hochfelsen. Hochfelsen stated, "We need a businessman. Twenty-five years ago I thought [former Chrysler chairman] Lee Iacocca should have run for president. Today it's Trump." During his speech at the event Trump said:

> The opportunity to address this group of really hard-working, incredible people is my great honor. Believe me . . . I've said on numerous occasions, that countries like China, India, South Korea, Mexico, the OPEC nations, and many others view our leaders as weak and ineffective. And we have repeatedly, unfortunately been taken advantage of to the tune of hundreds of billions of dollars a year. We have to take our country back . . . We can't afford education. We can't afford to build the roads. And yet we're in Iraq, Afghanistan, now Libya. How about Libya, isn't that a beauty? We don't want to change the regime. We want nothing to do with the regime, but we want them out. I can just imagine our soldiers and pilots—they're probably saying, "What does he (Obama) mean? He said he's not going to be involved in the regime change. And

then in another speech he says, we want him out. What does it mean?" In the meantime, it's a total disaster. Because nobody knows what the hell they're doing. And Gaddafi is winning . . . You can't have China taking our jobs, taking our money, making our products. And the amazing thing, then they do all of this and then they loan us money and we pay them interest. And what do they do? They manipulate our currency. Now I know how to stop it . . . *Businessweek* magazine said in a vote of its readers, that Donald Trump was the world's most competitive businessperson. With Bill Gates being number two and Warren Buffett being number three. Steve Forbes stated that I was one of the greatest entrepreneurs in the history of free trade.[25]

Overall, the first wave of the Tea Party, specifically their beliefs, were rather predictive of Donald Trump's presidential campaign and his presidency. For instance, Tea Partyers were more likely to see illegal immigration as a problem, in comparison to other Americans, including Republicans. Trump's campaign, as well as his presidency, has heavily focused on illegal immigration, as witnessed by his rhetoric of "America First" and "Build the Wall." Tea Partyers were also more likely to doubt the impact of global warming, another issue for Trump, who for years has debated whether or not climate change and global warming is a hoax. In addition, over half of the Tea Party members believed that America's best years were behind us, a belief that Trump has apparently shared as witnessed by his choice in slogans: "Make America Great Again." Almost 90% of Tea Partyers also believed Obama had expanded the role of government too much. Since 2014, Trump himself has criticized Obama for his use of the executive power, arguing that Obama over expanded his power (although Trump now as president has signed more executive orders than any president since Johnson). Another politician that both a majority of Tea Partyers and Trump himself viewed unfavorably was John McCain. As discussed in the chapter "The Quintessential Narcissist," Trump has had a long history of attacking John McCain, even now after McCain's passing from brain cancer in 2018. Trump's overall view of America also closely resembled that portrayed by the Tea Party, as discussed by Bryan Gervais and Irwin Morris, who stated:

> Trump's campaign was predicated on a gloomy portrait of life in this country. In his inaugural address, he famously spoke of

"American carnage." This same theme was also present among Tea Party legislators. They were more likely than other House Republicans to describe an America in decline, one in which Americans had experienced losses at the hands of a failing, and even abusive federal government led by President Barack Obama, and one in which even the American way of life was under threat, including from Muslims and undocumented immigrants.[26]

Despite support from the Tea Party in 2011, reports from during the 2016 Republican primary race and presidential campaign argued that many Tea Party members at that time actually supported Texas senator Ted Cruz over Donald Trump. In a *Washington Post* article by Elizabeth A. Yates, she states that Tea Partyers did not support Trump because he was not considered to be a conservative and that "many are offended by his demeanor, language, and ego." Yates goes on to discuss that it was not until after Trump was voted in as the Republican nominee that he received more support from the Tea Party, in an effort to counter the Democrats who "represented creeping socialism that threatened American democracy."[27] Others, like Lisa Mascaro of the *Los Angeles Times*, argued that the rivalry between the campaigns of Donald Trump and "tea party darling Sen. Ted Cruz" was threatening to break the Tea Party. One way in which Trump gained popularity with Tea Partyers over other candidates like Cruz was his willingness to go to extremes. Take for instance his stance on immigration. Trump's rhetoric was also very popular with conservative news sources, like *Fox News* and *Breitbart News*.[28] However, by November 2016, article headlines by news outlets like Fox News would read, "How the Tea Helped Trump Win the Election."[29] So did the Tea Party support Donald Trump and did they help him to win the presidential election? One of the best ways to examine the real relationship between Donald Trump and the Tea Party is to examine his relationship with Steve Bannon.

Steve Bannon and Donald Trump

Steve Bannon first met Trump through David Bossie, a Republican political activist, in 2011. Bannon was introduced to Trump in order to provide him with advice on a potential presidential bid. However, Bannon didn't believe that at that time Trump had much chance of winning, doubting that Trump would even run. Although Trump ended up not running at the time, Bannon began advising him nonetheless, helping strengthen his nationalist views, including the formulation of anti-immigration policies. It was at this time that Trump became a more avid reader of *Breitbart News*, with Bannon printing out articles for Trump and having them delivered to him by his staff in a manila folder. According to Joshua Green, author of *Devil's Bargain: Steve Bannon, Donald Trump, and the Storming of the Presidency*:

> It was no accident that Trump's formal declaration of his candidacy, on June 16, 2015, took the form of a bitter paean to American nationalism that quickly veered into an attack on Mexican immigrants as "criminals" and "rapists." Nor was it a coincidence that one of his first trips as a bona fide presidential candidate was a circus-like visit to the U.S.-Mexican border crossing in Laredo, Texas. Bannon, who established [a] *Breitbart* Texas bureau in 2013 to focus on immigration, had worked for weeks with sympathetic border agents to help arrange the trip. And while Trump's remarks were pilloried by the press and by many of his fellow Republicans—("extraordinarily ugly," Jeb Bush called them; House Speaker Paul Ryan said he was "sickened" by them)—that wasn't what registered most with the candidate himself. By the time he left Texas, Trump had rocketed to first place in polls of Republican primary voters.[30]

Bannon officially joined Trump's presidential campaign at a crucial time in August 2016 when most people believed Trump was heading for a landslide loss. By this point Trump had already gone through two campaign managers, Corey Lewandowski and Paul Manafort. While the media and those in Washington viewed Bannon's appointment as being the nail in the coffin of Trump's campaign, Bannon fit in perfectly with Trump's "outsider campaign."

Following Trump's inauguration, Bannon was made White House chief strategist. Over the past few months, Bannon's role within the White House often appeared to be a role of counteracting other members of Trump's inner circle. Consider, for example, his brief service on the National Security Council, a role White House officials claimed Bannon took in order to counteract Michael Flynn. However, Bannon's role became increasingly controversial within the White House. Bannon was reportedly a source of tension, coming into conflict with other White House officials, including

Ivanka Trump and Jared Kushner. Bannon was officially dismissed from his position on August 18, 2017.

Steve Bannon: A Mini Political Personality Profile

Steve Bannon was born in 1953 into a working-class, Irish Catholic, Democratic family in Norfolk, Virginia. His father was an AT&T telephone lineman and his mother a homemaker. Growing up Bannon wanted to have a military career, however, after attending Benedictine College Preparatory, a private Roman Catholic military high school in Richmond, Virginia, Bannon needed a break from military discipline. So he enrolled at Virginia Tech, where he studied urban planning. After graduating, Bannon joined the U.S. Navy Reserve; however, his experience as a junior naval officer was nothing like he imagined it would be, describing the men he worked with as looking "like they had been given a choice between jail and the Navy." Bannon later received his MA from Georgetown University in national security studies and an MBA from Harvard University. Throughout the 1980s, 1990s, and 2000s, Bannon had a number of different careers, including as an investment banker at Goldman Sachs, acting director of the Earth science research project Biosphere 2, as well as an executive producer in Hollywood.[31] Then, in 2007, Bannon was a founding member of *Breitbart*, which has come under severe criticism for its publications, with Philip Elliott and Zeke J. Miller of *Time* stating that it has "pushed racist, sexist, xenophobic and anti–Semitic material into the vein of the alternative right."

Trump and the Tea Party Today

While very few reports have examined the relationship between the Tea Party and Trump during his presidency, the argument can be made that he still has a large number of supporters among Tea Partyers. In fact, a number of Tea Partyers who did not support Trump as a presidential candidate now support him as president. In a video by NBC News, titled the "Evolution of Anger," Tea Partyers like Jenny Beth Martin and those from the Tea Party Patriots discuss how they have come to support the president as a "voice of the outsider."[32] On March 4, 2017, over sixty pro–Trump rallies occurred throughout the country. These "Spirit of America" rallies, as they were called, were organized by current and former Tea Party members.[33] However, a number of Trump's policies, have called into question his support among Tea Partyers, including major increases in government spending.[34] One Tea Party activist, Jennifer Stefano, discusses in an op-ed in the *New York Times* some of the accomplishments made by activists during the Obama presidency, but goes on to write: "No one can take those accomplishments away from us, but today, I and many of my fellow accidental activists feel that President Trump and Congress are taking action on spending that is undoing our hard work. President Trump's Tax Cuts and Jobs Act was a victory for Americans . . . Yet when it came to spending, some of the same politicians who championed tax cuts and claimed to be for limiting government caved to Washington's political culture."[35]

9

A Divided Republican Party

Trump and the Republican Party

During the 2016 presidential candidate campaigns, Jeb Bush stated, "Mr. Trump doesn't have a proven conservative record. He was a Democrat longer in the last decade than he was a Republican."[1] This wasn't the first time Trump has been accused of not being a true Republican and it surely wasn't the last. Even now during his presidency, it has been debated whether Donald Trump is actually Republican. Looking back, Trump's support for the Republican Party has wavered. In fact, his political opinions appear to have wavered so much that since 1987, his party affiliation has changed five times. In 1987, Trump registered as a Republican. Then in 1999, he changed his party to the Independence Party of New York. From 2001 to 2009 he was registered as a Democrat, until he came back to the Republican Party. In a 2004 interview on CNN, Trump stated:

> In many cases, I probably identify more as Democrat. It just seems that the economy does better under the Democrats than the Republicans. Now, it shouldn't be that way. But if you go

back, I mean it just seems that the economy does better under the Democrats . . . But certainly we had some very good economies under Democrats, as well as Republicans. But we've had some pretty bad disasters under the Republicans.[2]

However, in 2011, he switched to having no party affiliation. Then in 2012, he once again registered as a Republican.

In addition to his party affiliation, it is important to analyze his political donations. While two-thirds of the roughly $1.4 million he has donated to national-level parties, candidates, and other committees since 1989 have gone to Republicans, it is important to note that 40% of those donations were made after 2010.[3] In 2014 alone Trump donated to thirty-four Republican politicians. In fact, from 2010 to 2015, 97% of his political donations went to Republicans. However, prior to 2010, more than half of his political donations went to Democrats.[4]

Even when he first began considering running for political office, Trump didn't believe he would run as a Republican. In an interview with *Playboy* in 1990, he stated, "Well, if I ever ran for office, I'd do better as a Democrat than as a Republican. And that's not because I'd be more liberal, because I'm conservative. But the working guy would elect me. He likes me." In fact, the first time Trump launched a presidential campaign it wasn't with the Republican Party. In 2000, Trump aspired to be the presidential candidate for the Reform Party, which was created by Texas billionaire and 1992 presidential candidate Ross Perot in 1995. According to the Reform Party's website, the party is "a moderate, centrist and populist party that sits in the center of the political spectrum. It has moderate fiscal and economic platforms mixed with strong calls for ethics and electoral reform based on populist beliefs."[5] In his 2000 campaign, Trump focused on issues such as fair trade, eliminating the national debt, and creating universal healthcare. He outlined these issues in his book (coauthored by Dave Shiflett), *The America We Deserve*, which was published in 2000. He wrote:

> My star, however, seemed to be rising. In early October I announced the formation of a committee to explore a run for the presidency. At that time I announced that my first choice for vice president would be Oprah Winfrey. Again the political elites chortled—Oprah Winfrey! They just don't understand how many Americans respect and admire Oprah for her intelligence and caring. She has provided

inspiration for millions of women to improve their lives, go back to school, learn to read, and take responsibility for themselves. If I can't get Oprah, I'd like someone like her.[6]

Other individuals Trump discussed as being interested in recruiting for his potential administration was General Electric chairman and CEO Jack Welch, Muhammad Ali, Teamsters chief James P. Hoffa, New Jersey senator Bob Torricelli, and Florida governor Jeb Bush.

Trump's bid to be a presidential candidate in 2000 drew interesting responses, including a *Washington Post* article by Al Kamen from January of that year, saying, "President Donald Trump? Most Beltway insiders—and many others—dismiss the notion as absurd, figuring only a national nervous breakdown, or worse, could put the real estate developer and noted egomaniac in the White House."[7] However, Trump eventually withdrew from the race on February 14, 2000, stating that the Reform Party was not "conducive to victory" and that he would not be able to win the election as the party's candidate.[8]

Republican Party During the Election

Trump first announced that he would be officially running to be the Republican nominee for the 2016 presidential election on June 16, 2015, during a rally at Trump Tower in New York City. During his announcement speech, he covered a variety of topics including Islamic terrorism, healthcare, foreign relations, and illegal immigration. Trump's speech, which introduced his slogan "Make American Great Again," was a launching point for a lot of his rhetoric, as seen in the following statements:

> I will be the greatest jobs president that God ever created. I tell you that. I'll bring back our jobs from China, from Mexico, from Japan, from so many places. I'll bring back our jobs, and I'll bring back our money.
>
> I would build a great wall. And nobody builds walls better than me, believe me. And I'll build them very inexpensively. I will build a great great wall on our southern border and I'll have Mexico pay for that wall.

When do we beat Mexico at the border? They're laughing at us, at our stupidity. And now they are beating us economically. They are not our friend, believe me. But they're killing us economically. . . . When Mexico sends its people, they're not sending their best. They're not sending you. They're not sending you. They're sending people that have lots of problems and they're bringing those problems with us. They're bringing drugs, they're bringing crime, they're rapists, and some, I assume, are good people.[9]

While initial polls, prior to him officially joining the race in 2015, showed Trump as being heavily disliked by Republican voters, his announcement speech was a major boost. Trump went from being accused of paying a company to hire actors to attend his announcement rally to leading in the polls among his fellow GOP primary contenders following this speech.

Since Donald Trump made that initial announcement, Republicans have had mixed opinions about the then candidate and now president. In fact, some of his campaign promises conflicted with the ideology of the Republican Party. For instance, his New Deal–style proposal to create jobs by building infrastructure, which conflicts with the Republican Party's small-government beliefs. In an interview with *New York Times* following the election, Trump stated, "That's not a very Republican thing—I didn't even know that, frankly."[10]

Numerous Republicans did not support Trump, at least not until he became the Republican nominee or even until he became president. Republican strategist and top aide for Mitt Romney's 2012 campaign Katie Packer even started a super PAC in January 2016 called Our Principles PAC. The goal of said PAC was to oppose Donald Trump's bid to be the Republican nominee. In March 2016, the PAC sent out mailers attacking Trump in Iowa ahead of the Iowa caucuses. The PAC also released a video of women reciting some of Trump's most sexist statements.

Donald Trump and Other Republican Politicians

Just as Trump's support from Republican Party members has been shaky since he first announced that he was running for president, so has his support from other Republican politicians. Trump's relationship with fellow Republicans can be viewed in three main categories: those who have shown him continual support since first announcing his presidency; those who didn't initially support him but flipped their opinion either after he became the nominee or after he became president; and those Republicans who have never supported him.

Continual Support

A number of Republican politicians, including Newt Gingrich and Mike Huckabee, have heavily supported Donald Trump from the very beginning. One of the first establishment Republicans to endorse Trump during his campaign was Gingrich. He had been considered a strong contender for Trump's vice presidential running mate. Huckabee has even defended Trump before the Republican Party, comparing Trump to Winston Churchill. In a tweet from 2017, after viewing *Darkest Hour*, a film about Churchill at war, Huckabee tweeted, "Churchill was hated by his own party, opposition party, and press. Feared by King as reckless, and despised for his bluntness. But unlike Neville Chamberlain, he didn't retreat. We had a Chamberlain for 8 yrs; in @realDonaldTrump we have a Churchill."[11]

Huckabee has continued not only to be a major supporter of Trump, but his defender and champion. At the end of 2018, as Trump continued to come under criticism for his high turnover rate in the White House, Huckabee stated that while the staff turnover rate was "a little higher than normal" it was because of Trump's "vigor of somebody who's about thirty-two years old."[12] Huckabee went on to state on the Fox Business Network's *Mornings with Maria*, "This is a tough president to work for, and not because he's a difficult person individually, but he is very demanding and very few people can keep up with him." Huckabee has consistently defended Trump and his administration, specifically his own daughter, Sarah Huckabee Sanders, who serves as Trump's press secretary. In August 2018, Huckabee tweeted, "I know I'm objective about @PressSec as @NYTimes new hateful, racist hire Sarah Jeong is about white people, but I still think @PressSec is the WINDSHIELD and little Jim Acosta is the BUG."[13] This was an attack on CNN reporter Jim Acosta who had heavily questioned Sanders during a press conference on whether she considered the media to be "the enemy of the people." Sarah Sanders began as Trump's senior adviser for his 2016 presidential campaign, where she worked on the communications staff, specifically communications for coalitions. Following Trump's election, Sanders was appointed to the position of deputy White House press secretary. She served in this position until Sean Spicer resigned on July 21, 2017, at which point she assumed the role of White House press secretary.

As White House press secretary, Sanders has come under a great deal of controversy. With the release of the Mueller Report on April 18, 2019, Sanders came under fire for delivering a false statement regarding President Trump's decision to fire FBI director James B. Comey, whereby she repeatedly said in 2017 that she had communicated with "countless" FBI officials who were happy with Trump's decision. She has since said that was a "slip of the tongue" and not based on any facts. On *Good Morning America* a day after a release of the report, Sanders explained the statement was made in the heat of the moment and was not "a scripted talking point." She went on to say, "I'm sorry that I wasn't a robot like the Democrat Party that went out for two and a half years and repeated time and time again that there was definitely Russian collusion between the president and his campaign."[14]

Flipped

There are numerous Republican politicians who didn't at first support Trump, but eventually became supporters, whether after he became the Republican nominee or president. This includes former vice president Dick Cheney, who in February 2016 said that Trump sounded like a "liberal Democrat" and voiced his disagreement over comments made by Trump regarding 9/11. However, by May of that year, Cheney went on to state that he would back Trump as the nominee.[15] Former governor of Louisiana, Bobby Jindal, a fellow Republican nominee during the 2015 race, during his own campaign called Trump a "narcissist" and an "egomaniacal madman." After dropping out of the race in November 2015, Jindal supported Marco Rubio to be the Republican nominee, until Rubio also dropped out in March 2016. In May 2016, Jindal, in a column in the *Wall Street Journal*, stated that he would be voting for Trump "warts and all."[16]

One of the most notable politicians who eventually became a major Trump supporter is Lindsey Graham. In 2016, Graham called Trump "a kook" who was "unfit for office," however, by 2017 he would attack others for making similar claims. Graham himself noted his initial dislike of Trump during the

February 2019 Conservative Political Action Conference (CPAC), stating, "So President Trump and I did not start off well. I remember being there the night he got elected and he said, 'Hey, Lindsey, I don't have your phone number,' and I said, 'There's a reason for that.'"[17] Once one of Trump's biggest GOP opponents, Graham is now one of his biggest supporters, going on at the conference to state, "I couldn't be more proud of the fact that he talks to me and asks my opinion. And we've got a lot in common now: I like him and he likes him."[18] As discussed by Mark Leibovich in his *New York Times* feature on Lindsey Graham:

> It can be jarring to watch Graham enact, in real time, the broader shift the Republican Party has undergone under Trump. The conversions tend to fall into a few basic categories. There are the elected Republicans who once had little use for Trump but would prefer to keep their heads down and hope that their Trump-loving constituents forget the terrible things they said about the future president during the 2016 campaign. There are the most powerful Republicans, like Mitch McConnell, the Senate majority leader, and until early 2019 Paul Ryan, the former speaker of the House, who might have had little use for the president in private but couldn't risk alienating him. And there are once-dubious Republicans who have not only come around to supporting Trump but who have also caked their about-faces in ostentatious heaps of flattery for "my president."
>
> And then there is Graham, who would seem to occupy his own distinct category of Trump-era contortionist.... Graham's rush to Trump's side is particularly baffling because not long ago he was best known for his bipartisan deal-making on issues like climate change and immigration. He subscribed, at least theoretically, to the country-over-party credo of his departed Senate co-conspirator John McCain. McCain's diagnosis of brain cancer and eventual death coincided approximately with Graham's emergence as Trump's most prominent Senate defender and whisperer.[19]

While it may be difficult to determine why various politicians flipped, and whether or not they are truly his supporters, many most likely flipped for political reasons. Whether to stay on Trump's good side and reap the rewards of his presidential power or to appease their own political bases, which were in many cases largely made up of Trump supporters.

Opposed to Trump

It is important to note that there are several Republican politicians who were not and have continued not to be supporters of Donald Trump. This includes U.S. senator, former governor, and presidential candidate, Mitt Romney. In May 2016, Romney told the *Wall Street Journal*:

> I wanted my grandkids to see that I simply couldn't ignore what Mr. Trump was saying and doing, which revealed a character and temperament unfit for the leader of the free world. I know that some people are offended that someone who lost and is the former nominee continues to speak, but that's how I can sleep at night.[20]

While Romney has continued to be a critic of Donald Trump, he also wrote in an op-ed in the *Salt Lake Tribune* in June 2018, "I will support the president's policies when I believe they are in the best interest of Utah and the nation." He goes on to discuss the Trump policies he has agreed with, including the keeping "corporate tax code globally competitive," reducing "unnecessary regulations," and restoring "multiple use on Utah public land." Romney goes on to write:

> I have and will continue to speak out when the president says or does something which is divisive, racist, sexist, anti-immigrant, dishonest or destructive to democratic institutions . . . I believe that when you are known as a member of a "team," and the captain says or does something you feel is morally wrong, if you stay silent you tacitly assent to the captain's posture.[21]

Then in a *Washington Post* op-ed from January 1, 2019, Romney wrote:

> It is well known that Donald Trump was not my first choice . . . After he became the nominee, I hoped his campaign would refrain from resentment and name-calling. It did not. When he won the

election, I hoped he would rise to the occasion . . . But, on balance, his conduct over the past two years, particularly his actions last month, is evidence that the president has not risen to the mantle of the office.

Romney went on:

> To a great degree, a presidency shapes the public character of the nation. A president should unite us and inspire us to follow "our better angels." A president should demonstrate the essential qualities of honesty and integrity, and elevate the national discourse with comity and mutual respect . . . With the nation so divided, resentful and angry, presidential leadership in qualities of character is indispensable. And it is in this province where the incumbent's shortfall has been most glaring.[22]

Then, following the release on the Mueller Report, Romney wrote, "It is good news that there was insufficient evidence to charge the President of the United States with having conspired with a foreign adversary or with having obstructed justice. . . . Even so, I am sickened at the extent and pervasiveness of dishonesty and misdirection by individuals in the highest office of the land, including the President."[23] This received backlash from Trump supporter Mike Huckabee, who tweeted, "Know what makes me sick, Mitt? Not how disingenuous you were to take @realDonaldTrump $$ and then 4 yrs later jealously trash him & then love him again when you begged to be Sec of State, but makes me sick that you got GOP nomination and could have been @POTUS."[24]

John Warner, the former longtime Republican Virginia senator and former secretary of the navy, endorsed Hillary Clinton over Donald Trump in the election. Warner's criticism of Trump focused largely on his unfitness to be commander in chief, stating that he was "distressed" over Trump's comments on the might of the U.S. military. Warner stated:

> We have today the strongest military in the world. No one can compare with us. Does it need to be modified and changed and added to and modernized? You bet it has. But it is not in shambles. It is not the admirals and the generals and the seniors and rubble

in the hallways of the Pentagon . . . They're still as vibrant as the day I left there during the war in Vietnam.[25]

Warner also criticized Trump's treatment of the family of Gold Star recipient U.S. Army Captain Humayun Khan, stating, "No one should have the audacity to stand up and degrade the purple heart, degrade military families, or talk about the military being in a state of disaster. That's wrong."[26] Warner also criticized Trump for his lack of experience in national security matters, saying, "You do not pull up a quick text like 'National Security for Dummies.' You have to build on a foundation of experience for how you will go forward in the leadership of this country." Warner's views on Trump have not changed, saying in 2018:

> It's a very serious time for the country. I did not support Trump. I'm deeply troubled by the central issues. So much of my life has been devoted to the intelligence work and national security—and I'm just not comfortable with the way he's handling these national security issues . . . He has no inner compass at all. He's put a tremendous divide in this country.[27]

Warner even supported a number of Democratic candidates during the 2018 midterm elections, stating, "It goes beyond politics now. I'm a Republican, I'll finish a Republican as I cruise through my 91st year. But you've got to put the nation's interests and the state's interests ahead of politics."[28]

Non-Followers

Republicans who are not supporters of Trump have been commonly referred to as "Never Trump" Republicans or even "anti-Trump" conservatives by the media, as well as the "Stop Trump movement" and "Dump Trump." The Never Trump movement began as an effort to prevent Trump from becoming the Republican nominee for the 2016 election.[29] As discussed earlier in this chapter, Mitt Romney's former top aide Katie Packer started the Our Principles PAC to oppose Trump's bid to be the Republican nominee. In an interview from March 2016 with NPR's Ari Shapiro, Packer stated, "I didn't really expect Donald Trump to pick up steam. He was somebody that I thought everybody would recognize as kind of a phony and a fraud. And when that didn't happen, I felt like somebody had to do it. And I got together with some other people that agreed that this guy would be a problem for our party, that we would lose badly in the general election and that he would be terrible for our country."[30] Our Principles was not the only conservative PAC to counter Trump's bid for the Republican nomination. The Club for Growth's PAC, the Club for Growth Action, spent millions on anti–Trump ads in 2015 and 2016 in states like Iowa and Florida that stated that he supported liberal policies. In September 2015, Trump threatened to sue the organization when his lawyer Alan Garten sent a letter to the organization's president David McIntosh, stating, "Your Attack Ad blatantly misrepresents to the public that Mr. Trump 'supports higher taxes', nothing could be further from the truth."[31]

Following his nomination and eventual presidential victory, just as Republican politicians flipped in their opinion of Trump, so did numerous "Never Trump" Republicans. Specifically, the "Never Trump" Republicans who did not support him because they believed he would never become president and was a disastrous choice for the Republican Party. However, the movement has continued. According to a study published in *Research and Politics* by Lauren R. Johnson, Deon McCray, and Jordan M. Ragusa, those most likely to be a part of the Never Trump movement were female Republicans and Latter-day Saints (Mormons).[32] And while the initial goal of the movement was to oppose Trump becoming the Republican nominee and then preventing him from winning in 2016, the new goal of the movement is to have another Republican nominee for the 2020 election. A number of Republican politicians have already expressed interest in running, including: U.S. senator from Tennessee Bob Corker; governor of Maryland Larry Hogan; and governor of Ohio John Kasich. And former Massachusetts governor Bill Weld established an exploratory committee on February 15, 2019, and submitted for FEC Statement of Candidacy filing on April 15, 2019.

Followers

Donald Trump's followers, especially those in the Republican Party, need to be examined from different perspectives. While his supporters may have been drawn to him for more than one reason, it is important to note that there are certain aspects of Trump, particularly in his rhetoric and the issues he has chosen to champion, that has drawn in supporters.

Rhetorical Appeal

"MAKE AMERICA GREAT AGAIN"

Trump's official slogan, "Make America Great Again," was officially launched during his announcement speech in 2015. However, it was not the first time that Trump used the phrase nor was it the first time the phrase was used by an American politician. During his 1980 presidential campaign, Ronald Reagan used the phrase "Let's make America great again" in reference to the economic issues the United States was facing at that time. Although not an official slogan, the phrase was also used by Bill Clinton during the 1992 presidential campaign and in a 2008 radio ad for Hillary Clinton's 2008 Democratic primary campaign.[33] Trump later said he was unaware of Reagan's use of the phrase. It was first used in reference to Trump in 2011 by Roger Stone, who had worked on Reagan's 1980 campaign and as a political adviser to Trump. Stone tweeted, "Make America Great Again—TRUMP HUCKABEE 2012 #nomormons."

Trump's "Make America Great Again" slogan has strongly resonated with his followers. The concept of making America great again appeals to individuals who want to return society to an idealized golden age of the past, perhaps a golden age that never actually existed. Whether or not this golden age did indeed exist, Trump's supporters believe that he will "make America great again." But what is perhaps most appealing about this rhetoric is how it has been left open to interpretation by his followers, for them to envision when they believe America was "great" and how they believe America can be "great again." In an interview, Trump explained he believed America was great at the beginning of the 20th century and following World War II, highlighting them as periods of military and industrial expansion. He stated: "If you look back, it really was, there was a period of time when we were developing at the turn of the century which was a pretty wild time for this country and pretty wild in terms of building that machine, that machine was really based on entrepreneurship."[34] However, this is not a strong aspect of the rhetoric he uses for his slogan; the vagueness in which he uses it at his rallies or in speeches allows for his supporters to interpret the message for themselves. For some Americans, it is about American jobs. As described by one Trump supporter, Ryan Moore, in a *USA Today* opinion piece:

I'm very proud to wear my MAGA hat. All of the official MAGA hats are made in the USA. The hat is a symbol of wanting to put America first and wanting products to be made in America and wanting them to be made by Americans . . . How absurd would it be to put the interests of other nations ahead of our own? The phrase "Make America Great Again" and the MAGA hat have absolutely nothing to do with race or gender. The "Again" does not mean anyone wants to go back to a time before all races and both sexes had full equality. It is simply the fact that there are some things in America's past that are better than they are now and of course there are other things that are better in present day America.[35]

Moore also describes feeling targeted for wearing a MAGA hat, writing: "White men are the most hated and discriminated against group of people in the United States now. If you don't believe that, you simply aren't paying attention or looking at it objectively."[36] For other supporters it has to do with identifying the United States with Christian values and beliefs. In an opinion piece from Fox News, Trump supporter Kristan Hawkins writes: "The hats are meant to harken Americans back to better days—not the dark days of slavery and segregation, but days when lawmakers actually got along and compromised; when Democrats were actually allowed to be pro-life; when Americans didn't check their neighbors' political affiliation on Facebook before deciding if they could be friends."[37] In fact, there is no clear concise view on even what year or decade America was "great." In a poll conducted by the *New York Times*, Trump supporters gave a wide range of answers for the time they believed America was "great," including 1955, 1960, 1970, 1985, and the most popular answer being in 2000. A similar study found that a majority of Republicans believe "life was better for people like them" fifty years ago, especially Trump supporters who believed that life was better in the 1960s.[38]

"BUILD THE WALL"

While not his main slogan, "Build the Wall" has been a major component of Trump's rhetoric. And it is not surprising that it has appealed to so many of his supporters. In a study from 2016 on Trump supporters' views of immigration, the study found that 66% of them viewed immigration as a "very big" problem, as opposed to 17% of Clinton supporters. This percentage was almost identical to the percentage of Trump supporters, 65%, who viewed terrorism as a "very big" problem as opposed to 36% of Clinton supporters. The study also found that 79% of his voters supported building the wall, with only 18% opposing and 88% of Clinton supporters opposing it. However, his supporters appeared to have mixed views of undocumented immigrants, with 35% believing they take jobs away from U.S. citizens; roughly 33% believing they are not as hard-working and are less honest than U.S. citizens; 50% believing they "are more likely than American citizens to commit serious crimes"; and 59% of those who support Trump strongly associating undocumented immigrants with criminal behavior.[39] And while "Build the Wall" appeals to economic fears of some Americans, as discussed in Chapter 9, and the anti-immigration and racist views of other Americans, as discussed in Chapter 10, there is another aspect to the appeal of Trump's rhetoric of "Build the Wall."

In addition to the views on immigration and economic fears that make Trump's mantra of "Build the Wall" so appealing is also the allure of Trump's abrasive personality and rhetoric style, the belief that he is against being politically correct. In the study, "The Immigrant as Bogeyman: Examining Donald Trump and the Right's Anti-Immigrant, Anti-PC Rhetoric," by Laura Finley and Luigi Esposito, they:

> ... argue that Trump's anti-immigrant rhetoric can be understood as (1) a response against current norms associated with political correctness, which include a heightened sensitivity to racially offensive language, xenophobia, and social injustice, and (2) a rejection of the tendency to subordinate patriotism, U.S. sovereignty, and national interests to a neoliberal political economy that emphasizes "globalism" and prioritizes "free trade" over the interests of working Americans.[40]

Trump is not the only politician to target political correctness in the United States. It has been a focal point for numerous conservatives, like Dr. Ben Carson, Trump supporter and secretary of Housing and Urban Development, who has referred to political correctness as being a weapon for suppressing free speech and a tool to suppress Americans and enslave them. It is also a focal point for numerous conservative news outlets, like *Breitbart*. In a report,

"Hidden Tribes: A Study of America's Polarized Landscape," by Stephen Hawkins, Daniel Yudkin, Míriam Juan-Torres, and Tim Dixon, they found that most Americans have an aversion to PC culture, with roughly 80% of the population believing that "political correctness is a problem in our country."[41] The study also found that age and race were not proper indicators for whether or not an individual supports political correctness, rather that income and education were better indicators. They found that individuals who make less than $50,000 were more likely to dislike political correctness and that those who never attended college were more likely to think that political correctness is becoming a problem. However, the authors stated that the most significant indicator of beliefs on political correctness was what the authors referred to as "political tribe." The study found that 97% of "devoted conservatives" believe political correctness is a problem, as well as 61% of "traditional liberals." The group to most likely support political correctness was "progressive activists," with only 30% seeing it as a problem.[42]

"DRAIN THE SWAMP"

Another major component of Trump's rhetoric has been his message that he will "drain the swamp." During a rally in Wisconsin in October 2016, Trump stated, "It is time to drain the swamp in Washington, D.C. This is why I'm proposing a package of ethics reforms to make our government honest once again." However, the idea to "drain the swamp," a phrase also used by Ronald Reagan in 1983, dates back to the early 1900s and early socialist American politicians like Winfield R. Gaylord and Victor L. Berger, who vowed to "drain" the "capitalist swamp."[43]

But it was the way in which Trump used this rhetoric of "drain the swamp" that individuals like John Pudner, director of conservative good-government group Take Back Our Republic, say helped Trump win the election. Pudner himself stated that it was this promise that "is a central topic to why President Trump won this election."[44] In fact, Trump's five-point plan for draining the swamp that he unveiled in October 2016 (most likely to draw attention away from the 2005 *Access Hollywood* tape that had just been released) received praise from a number of government-reform advocates, including nonpartisan groups that do not endorse candidates. On October 17, 2016, Trump stated, "If we let the Clinton Cartel run this government, history will record that 2017 was the year America lost its independence. We will not let that happen.

It is time to drain the swamp in Washington, D.C." At that point he revealed his five-point plan:

> First: I am going to reinstitute a five-year ban on all executive branch officials lobbying the government for five years after they leave government service. I am going to ask Congress to pass this ban into law so that it cannot be lifted by executive order.
>
> Second: I am going to ask Congress to institute its own five-year ban on lobbying by former members of Congress and their staffs.
>
> Third: I am going to expand the definition of lobbyist so we close all the loopholes that former government officials use by labeling themselves consultants and advisers when we all know they are lobbyists.
>
> Fourth: I am going to issue a lifetime ban against senior executive branch officials lobbying on behalf of a foreign government.
>
> And Fifth: I am going to ask Congress to pass a campaign finance reform that prevents registered foreign lobbyists from raising money in American elections.[45]

Aaron Scherb, director of legislative affairs for the nonpartisan advocacy group Common Cause, said of this five-point plan, "These are certainly steps in the right direction, and Common Cause certainly agrees with them and would like to see them enacted."[46]

This definitely appealed to a specific faction of his followers. In Eric Bolling's *The Swamp: Washington's Murky Pool of Corruption and Cronyism and How Trump Can Drain It*, he states:

> However, one of the most important themes President Donald Trump tapped into in his history-making election campaign of 2016, and continued to sound once in office, was the inhabitants of the D.C. Swamp don't necessarily think in the same nationalist terms that the average American does. It's not as simple, however, as saying that the D.C. crowd is too left-wing for right-wing

citizens. It's not just a matter of the federal government overseas. Nor an issue of "transnational" corporations caring more about the bottom line than about inhabitants of any one land.

After all, we want the United States to be friendly with other governments if the alternative is war. We want U.S. companies to export goods to other nations. But while the average American still lives his or her life in a single state and may not even own a passport, the elite have become so accustomed to working with, traveling with, communicating with, and, more worryingly, governing with their elite counterparts in other nations, it becomes unclear whether they remain, at heart, Americans first.[47]

There are other politicians who at the start of Trump's presidency supported him because they believed that he could potentially "drain the swamp," including Congressman Ken Buck, who wrote in his book *Drain the Swamp: How Washington Corruption is Worse than You Think* (with Bill Blankschaen):

> President Trump is a brash, frank, and outspoken man. If he insists on transparency from Congress; if he shines a light on how Congress actually does its business; he can send a lot of the swamp creatures skittering away, and he can encourage the American people to pursue the sort of lasting congressional reform that I've outlined in this book. In his first days in office President Trump instituted a hiring freeze on civilian federal workers. He noted that many federal workers are overpaid (and have better benefits) compared to workers who do similar work in the private sector. He hinted that he intended to right this injustice to the taxpayers. He made clear his intention to slash unnecessary federal regulation. And he said that he planned to cut the federal budget by more than ten trillion dollars over the next ten years. These are all steps in the right direction. It's my job—and the job of every conservative in this country—to make sure he follows through.[48]

While Trump has continued to tout that as president he has drained "the swamp," a number of reports have shown a conflicting viewpoint, including the high number of former lobbyists he currently has working in the administration.

"NOT A POLITICIAN"

Another component of Trump's appeal is to anti-politician voters. The fact that Donald Trump was not a politician, or at least hadn't been up until this point, was very appealing to many of his followers and a fact that he often exploited in his rallies. For example, during a rally in Manchester, New Hampshire, in July 2015, Trump told the audience that because he was a businessman and not a politician, he was the only one who could solve the nation's problems. Trump had realized early on that this could be a major selling point for him. As discussed in his book from 2000, *The America We Deserve*:

> Last May a Washington-based Democratic pollster, Rob Schroth, conducted a nationwide survey of one thousand voters. Schroth's thesis was that figures from disciplines outside of politics were better known and more trusted than the current crop of politicians seeking the U.S. presidency. Schroth tested athletes, businessmen, newscasters, and entertainers; he tested the popularity of public figures like Clint Eastwood, Michael Jordan, Barbra Streisand, Bill Gates, Katie Couric, Ted Turner, Robert Redford, Barbara Walters, John Elway, and Donald Trump.
>
> It was no surprise to me that 97 percent of the American people knew who I was. It was also no surprise that I was particularly popular with some segments of the American population. Working people, African Americans, Latinos, and people making under $25,000 a year all had a favorable opinion. Rich people did not like me. Rich people who don't know me *never* like me. Rich people who know me like me.[49]

And in fact it was a major selling point. In a series of interviews with Trump supporters from every state titled "Trump Nation," conducted by the *USA Today Network* in 2016, a number of his supporters cited that a reason they were voting for him was that he was a businessman and not a politician. Don Knight, a sixty-year-old business man from Alabama, stated, "I'm a businessman, I have been for forty-two years, and I like the idea that he is a businessman, he's not a politician. I think with him being a businessman and building the empire that he's built, that I think he could do the same thing for the United States."⁵⁰ Meredith Mason, from South Carolina, stated:

> He's not a politician in the strictest sense of the word. He doesn't owe anybody anything after the election. So I think he'll have at least a chance to accomplish something, to straighten out the business end of what's happened with government. I don't like the fact that he is very verbally disrespectful sometimes, but I think he's very honest, and it's not something we see. Usually politicians will tell this group what they want to hear and then they'll go tell the next group what they want to hear. It's refreshing to have somebody who actually has an opinion and is not afraid to voice it.⁵¹

Don Bates Jr., a forty-six-year-old from Indiana, stated:

> Well, number one, I'm a proud Republican, and so I'm going to support the Republican ticket. I like Donald Trump's business background. I think he brings a fresh perspective to politics that I think a lot of people are hungry for. I think people are tired of career politicians, and I think that's why Trump is resonating. I think there are a lot of skeletons in the closet. The email scandal really concerns me, but, if it's not that scandal, it's a lot of scandals and they never did tell the truth about Benghazi, and so I think there's a trust factor there that's seriously lacking. The threat of radical Islamic terrorism is a major threat, and this current administration does not appear to be taking that threat seriously, and so I think we have a national security issue and our next president has to be willing to face that and realize that it's a serious problem here in the United States. I think a lot of people are energized. When you look on the Republican side, Donald Trump got more votes than any Republican ever in the history of Republican primaries, and so I think there's going to be a ton of energy. I think there will be on both sides, but I sense a lot of excitement in this race.⁵²

Trump has kept to similar rhetoric, even now as president. In a rally in Tampa in July 2018, he told his followers, "I'm not like other politicians. You see what happened. I've kept my promises."

Issue Appeal

EVANGELICALS

Evangelicals, specifically white evangelicals, have been a cornerstone of Trump's base. In a poll from early 2019, it was found that 69% of white evangelicals "approve of how Donald Trump is handling his job as president of the United States," however, this number is lower than a previously reported 78% approval rate. In John Fea's *Believe Me: The Evangelical Road to Donald Trump*, he states:

> Too many conservative evangelicals view the past through the lens of nostalgia. Scholar Svetlana Boym describes nostalgia as a "sentiment of loss and displacement" that "inevitably reappears as a defense mechanism in a time of accelerated rhythms of life and historical upheavals." In this sense, nostalgia is closely related to fear. In times of great social and cultural change, the nostalgic person will turn to a real or an imagined past as an island of safety amid the raging storms of progress. . . . Sometimes evangelicals will seek refuge from change in a Christian past that never existed in the first place . . . Nostalgia is thus a powerful political tool. A politician who claims to have the power to take people back to a time when America was great stands a good chance of winning the votes of fearful men and women.[53]

As stated by one of Trump's most prominent evangelical supporters, Robert Jeffress of the First Baptist Church in Dallas:

> I realize it is [politically] incorrect to say this, but it is nevertheless true. America was not founded as a Muslim nation. America was not founded as a Hindu nation. America was not founded as a nation that is neutral toward Christianity. America was founded as a Christian nation, and today we are going to discover that truth from history.

Trump's popularity with evangelicals, especially evangelical Republicans, is best understood by looking at how he has appealed to the pro-life issue.

While Trump once described himself as "very pro-choice," he has taken a stronger pro-life stance as president. As described by his evangelical, pro-life vice president, Mike Pence: "In one short year, President Donald Trump has made a difference for life."[54] Trump reiterated his pro-life rhetoric during the 2019 State of the Union address, in which he stated: "Let us work together to build a culture that cherishes innocent life. And let us reaffirm a fundamental truth: All children—born and unborn—are made in the holy image of God."[55] It was the first time Trump has made such a comment in a presidential address to Congress, and while the message was not necessarily intended for Congress, it was intended as an appeal to his base, especially before the 2020 election. In April 2019, Trump also chose to show during a White House movie night the pro-life film, *Gosnell: The Trial of America's Biggest Serial Killer*. During his past White House movie nights, Trump has chosen to show *Finding Dory* and *The Post*.

It is also important in understanding Trump's follower relationship with evangelicals, to examine Donald Trump's vice president Mike Pence. As stated by Richard Land, president of the Southern Evangelical Seminary and one of Trump's faith advisers, "Mike Pence is the 24-karat-gold model of what we want in an evangelical politician. I don't know anyone who's more consistent in bringing his evangelical-Christian worldview to public policy."[56]

Michael Richard "Mike" Pence: A Mini Political Personality Profile

Mike Pence was born in 1959 in Columbus, Indiana, to an Irish Catholic Democratic family. Mike's father, Edward Pence, owned a number of gas stations and was a Korean War veteran. Edward was awarded a Bronze Star in 1953, a commendation for which Mike is extremely proud of his father, displaying it, as well as his father's commendation letter and reception photo, in his office. Mike received his BA in History from Hanover College in 1981 and his JD from Indiana University in 1986. Pence first tried running for Congress in 1988 in Indiana, but lost to the Democratic incumbent Phil Sharp. During Pence's second attempt against Sharp in 1990, he ran a TV ad with an actor dressed in stereotypical Middle Eastern attire. The actor, who spoke in a fake Middle Eastern accent, thanked Sharp for not helping the United States wean itself off of imported oil. Pence came under heavy criticism for the ad and lost the election once again. However, Pence was able to rejuvenate his political career in 2000, finally making it to the House of Representatives. After a number of years in Congress, Pence began to rise in prominence in the Republican Party, becoming chairman of the Republican Study Committee from 2005 to 2007. Pence ran for governor of Indiana in 2012, assuming office in 2013.

At the start of the 2016 Republican presidential primaries, Pence initially endorsed Ted Cruz. Pence was later considered for vice president by Trump, along with a number of other individuals, including Chris Christie and Newt Gingrich, with Trump officially announcing Pence as his running mate in July 2016. At the start Pence was highly supportive of Trump, even of the remarks and policies that Trump came under fire for, including immigration bans and the border wall. However, as the election progressed it appeared to become more and more difficult for Pence to defend Trump. For instance, when Trump's 2005 conversation with Billy Bush surfaced, Pence publicly stated, "I do not condone his remarks and cannot defend them." However, Pence continued to stand by Trump's side. It was at this time that the media began speculating whether Pence would drop off the ticket, an accusation Pence stated was false. Pence's relationship with Trump continues to be a rocky one. While Pence may not agree with all of Trump's opinions or actions, he is choosing to stay by Trump's side in order to advance his own position.

Gun Rights

Trump has also strongly appealed to Americans who are pro–gun rights and advocates for the Second Amendment. In his book *Crippled America*, in the chapter "The Right to Bear Arms," Trump states, "I own guns. Fortunately, I have never had to use them, but, believe me, I feel a lot safer knowing that they are there. I also have a concealed-carry permit that allows me to carry a concealed weapon." Trump goes on to state, "I took the time and the effort to get that permit because the constitutional right to defend yourself doesn't stop at the end of your driveway. That doesn't apply just to me either. It applies to all our driveways or front doors. That's why I'm very much in favor of making all concealed-carry permits valid in every state."[57] Then in an interview Donald Trump and Donald Trump Jr. had with Anthony Licata in *Field & Stream* in January 2016:

Anthony Licata: Are you a gun owner, a hunter? The two of you?

Donald Trump: I do have a gun, and I have a concealed-carry permit, actually, which is a very hard thing to get in New York. And, of course, the problem is once you get to the borderline of New Jersey or anyplace else, you can't do it, which is ridiculous, because I'm a very big Second Amendment person. But I do have a gun, and my sons are major hunters, and I'm a member of the NRA [National Rifle Association].[58]

Appealing to gun owners and gun rights advocates was a major issue he focused on during his campaign. During a presidential campaign rally in Nevada, Trump told his supporters: "We love the Second Amendment, folks. Nobody loves it more than us, so just remember that." The "we" Trump is referring to in this statement are his sons Donald Jr. and Eric. Trump has used not only himself as a symbol of gun rights in the United States, but his sons as pro–gun rights symbols as well. Donald Trump Jr. in particular has had a strong relationship with the pro–gun rights community, including a relationship with the gun silencer manufacturer SilencerCo. In September 2016, he even appeared in a YouTube video for SilencerCo., where he discusses teaching "little kids" how to use guns:

> It's about safety. It's about hearing protection. It's a health issue, frankly, uh, for me. Uh, you know? Getting little, you know, little kids into the game? You know, it greatly reduces recoil. I mean, it's a, it's a great—it's just a great instrument. There's nothing, you know, there's nothing bad about it at all. It makes—it makes total sense, it's where we should be going.[59]

During his interview with SilencerCo CEO Joshua Waldron, Donald Jr. also discusses the importance of the Second Amendment, stating: "This wasn't an afterthought. It's a basic right of an American, and we have to defend that."[60] Waldron and his wife are both Trump supporters who donated both to his campaign and to the Trump Victory Fund.

In April 2017, Trump became the first sitting president since Ronald Reagan to address the NRA, where he stated at the gun lobby's annual meeting, "The eight-year assault on your Second Amendment freedoms has come to a crashing end." Trump went on to state, "You have a true friend and champion in the White House." Trump again addressed the NRA's annual meeting in 2018, where he made the following statements:

> These are real patriots, they really are, and they don't get the kind of adulation. But really, they do and we know that.

> Your Second Amendment rights are under siege, but they will never, ever be under siege as long as I'm your president.[61]

Trump has continued his rhetoric to gun rights advocates that if he was not president, and especially that if he is not reelected in 2020, that their rights would be taken away. He has used this rhetoric not only with the NRA, but at the Conservative Political Action Conference as well, stating in 2018: "I will protect you, because it all has to come through my office, and we hopefully are going to be here for six more years, so you're in good shape."[62] Then at the NRA convention on April 26, 2019, Trump told the audience:

> Our sacred charge is to preserve the freedoms that our ancestors gave their very lives to secure. Because no matter how many centuries go by, how much the world changes, the central drama of human history remains the same. On one side are those who seek power, control and domination. And on the other side are patriots.... We will make America stronger, safer and greater than ever, ever, ever before.

Trump had also told the audience that he plans to have the United States back out of the United Nations Arms Trade Treaty. The treaty, which had been signed by Obama but never ratified by Congress, is meant to regulate international conventional weapons sales in an effort to prevent weapons from being sold to human rights abusers. Trump's relationship with the NRA prior to 2016 came into question during the Mueller investigation.[63] Donald Jr. has also maintained his relationship with the gun rights community, attending a turkey hunt prior to joining his father at the NRA convention on April 26. Donald Jr. also made headlines that same weekend, when it was reported that he almost didn't buy his new $4.5 million Hamptons vacation home with his new girlfriend, former Fox News host Kimberly Guilfoyle, because it didn't have a gun room.

A New Republican Party

Donald Trump represents to many today what the Republican Party should be, believing that the old Republican Party is a thing of the past. As stated by Ann Coulter in her book *In Trump We Trust*:

> The only deep insight Republicans have had for the past three decades is: *Be Reagan!* This wouldn't be a bad plan, inasmuch as Reagan was a wildly successful president (followed by a typically incompetent Bush), except: (1) Reagan was president in the 1980s, and (2) today's Republicans don't seem to remember Reagan. They are the political version of the cargo cult, a primitive tribe that worshiped modern technology without understanding how it worked, holding coconuts up to their ears as if they were air traffic controllers. Republicans believe they can capture Reagan's greatness by repeating his answers to the problems of three decades ago.[64]

Trump has been successful in understanding what some established Republicans have yet to do, in that for many today, the ideology of the party that grew out of the 1970s no longer holds as much appeal. This is evident among Republican politicians Trump has also endorsed and supported. Take, for instance, Corey Stewart, who unsuccessfully ran for senator from Virginia in the 2018 midterm elections. Stewart, who is known for being pro–Confederate symbols and anti-immigration, once exclaimed: "This is the new Republican Party." And that those resisting change in the Republican Party are "dinosaurs. They need to wake up and understand that President Trump has fundamentally remade the Republican Party." Trump had tweeted his support for Stewart in June 2018: "Congratulations to Corey Stewart for his great victory for senator from Virginia. Now he runs against a total stiff, Tim Kaine, who is weak on crime and borders, and wants to raise your taxes through the roof. Don't underestimate Corey, a major chance of winning!"[65] While Trump has maintained some of the traditional values of the Republican Party, he has shifted away from other longstanding beliefs, including supporting free trade and increasing national debt. And it's not just beliefs that Trump has altered, it is the overall attitude of the Republican Party.

10

The Working Class and Rural Areas

Since the beginning of his campaign Trump has focused on building his base among the working class and rural areas. But how has Trump received a great deal of support from those areas? While both groups (with some of the working class also living in rural areas) are drawn to Trump for similar reasons as discussed in the previous "A Divided Republican Party" chapter, there are aspects that are more unique to these two groups. In both cases, Trump was successful in appealing to groups that have felt overlooked in U.S. politics, sometimes for decades.

Working Class

In many ways for years Trump has identified himself with the working class, even to be referred to by some of his supporters as the "blue-collar president." In *The Art of the Deal*, Trump describes his upbringing:

> We had a very traditional family. My father was the power and the breadwinner, and my mother was the perfect housewife. That didn't mean she sat around playing bridge and talking on the phone. There were five children in all and besides taking care

of us, she cooked and cleaned and darned socks and did charity work at the local hospital. We lived in a large house, but we never thought of ourselves as rich kids. We were brought up to know the value of a dollar and to appreciate the importance of hard work. Our family was always very close, and to this day they are my closest friends. My parents had no pretensions. My father still works out of a small, modest back office on Avenue Z in the Sheepshead Bay section of Brooklyn, in a building he put up in 1948. It's simply never occurred to him to move.[1]

Newt Gingrich cites this very passage in his book *Understanding Trump*, saying that it is "an upbringing that's similar to many working-class Americans." Gingrich goes on to state:

In Washington, if you can name the capitals of forty-two countries, you are thought of as a sophisticated person. (If you know the appropriate wine to drink in each of these countries, you are a superstar.) Whether that information is useful is of secondary concern . . . Trump is exactly the opposite. He makes certain he knows what he needs to know to be successful at the time he needs to know it. This is an entrepreneurial approach to knowledge rather than an academic one. In fact, in stark contrast to the Washington intelligentsia, this is how most Americans learn—when they are motivated out of a need to accomplish something. The type of blue-collar, practical Americans who make up Trump's base of support understand this, which is why Trump's apparent lack of knowledge about the finer details of public and foreign policy did not derail his campaign.[2]

Trump has long identified himself as being a self-made billionaire, often stating, "I built what I built myself." And in fact, many people believe this, and not just his supporters. In one study published in *Political Behavior* it was found that not only were most people uninformed about Trump's background, but that they are misinformed. Three different surveys conducted from 2016 to 2018 found that roughly half of all Americans, supporters and non-supporters, were unaware that Trump was born into a wealthy family. In fact, becoming aware of Trump's background has shown to have a significant effect on perception of him and his presidency. In a 2018 survey conducted by Jared McDonald, David Karol, and Lilliana Mason, half of the participants were asked: "To what extent were you aware that Donald Trump grew up the son of wealthy real estate businessman Fred Trump, started his business with loans from his father, and received loans worth millions of dollars from his father in order to keep his businesses afloat?"[3] Responses indicated that Democrats who were provided with this question viewed him as being even less empathetic, but that for Republicans this question reduced their perception of Trump as being empathetic by 10%. This question also reduced both Democrats' and Republicans' perception of Trump's business competence.

Not only has Trump painted himself as once having been part of the working class, but he uses language and rhetoric that is meant to appeal to his followers in the working class. And it was not just about appealing to the working class, specifically the white working class, but any individual in a lower-paying job. As discussed by Harvard professor Michèle Lamont, who has researched the relationship between Trump's rhetoric and the working class, "We could immediately see how he was appealing to workers by talking about blaming globalization, saying he was going to give [them] jobs . . . His populist argument was oriented toward appealing to all workers, but at the same time, he was [engaged in] veiled racism by talking about 'the inner city' and things like that."[4] Lamont also explained, however, that it wasn't just an appeal to white workers, but African Americans and Latinos as well. Lamont went on to state:

> For the working class to find themselves with no job is both an economic tragedy and a cultural tragedy, since their self-concept is very much about being hard-working. So by telling them, "It's globalization, and it's the people who pushed globalization, such as Hillary Clinton, who are responsible for your downfall" . . . We have to remember, many workers, they want to think of themselves—and they are—as extremely hard-working, and they want jobs . . . He's trying to give them their dignity back by saying, "I know that you're hard-working people, and you're capable of doing this."[5]

This is rhetoric he has continued well into his presidency in order to maintain his followership among the working class. On September 4, 2018, the White House released a fact sheet entitled "President Donald J. Trump is Delivering Results for American Workers," which quotes Trump as saying, "Every day, we are lifting our forgotten Americans off the sidelines, out of the margins, and back into the workforce." The document reads:

> GETTING BACK TO WORK: President Donald J. Trump's agenda is driving an economic resurgence that is creating more and more employment opportunities for American workers.
>
> WORKING FOR ALL AMERICANS: President Trump's pro-growth economic policies are generating tremendous benefits for American workers and raising optimism to new heights.
>
> BUILDING UP OUR WORKFORCE: President Trump is ensuring that students and workers have access to education and training that will equip them to compete and win in the global economy.[6]

Trump provides his followers in the working class with an external source at which to direct their anger and blame their economic issues, thus removing their personal responsibility. What this represents is splitting. Splitting is one of the defense mechanisms of individuals with a damaged self-concept. Individuals who rely on splitting and externalization look outward for the source of their difficulties. They need an external source or enemy to blame. This is a dominant mechanism of the destructive charismatic, like Trump, who projects the devalued part of himself onto the interpersonal environment and then attacks and scapegoats the enemy without. Unable to face his own inadequacies, the individual with this personality style needs a target to blame and attack for his own inner weakness and inadequacies. And in his rhetoric for the working class the external sources or enemy he has focused on includes: globalization; immigration; and environmentalism.

Globalization

Trump first announced that "America First" would be "the major and overriding theme" of his presidency during his 2016 campaign. Trump proclaimed that he would be "the best jobs president that God ever created" and that meant to target globalization.[7] This also meant enforcing trade policies that include tariffs, duties, and other forms of protecting domestic industries. A major component of this America First policy was the promise to bring back manufacturing jobs, revive the struggling Rust Belt sector, and punish companies who move their factories out of the United States. Following the election in 2016, Trump visited the Carrier Corporation plant in Indianapolis, where he stated: "These companies aren't going to be leaving anymore."[8] This was in reference to a deal he had brokered that prevented Carrier from closing its Indianapolis plant, which employed over one thousand people, and opening a plant in Mexico. While Trump received a warm welcome, not only from employees of Carrier, but from the broader manufacturing community, Carrier would eventually still lay off 632 employees in favor of cheaper labor in Mexico. In addition to stating that he would prevent companies from moving their factories, Trump claimed he would end outsourcing of manufacturing jobs to countries like China, Japan, and Mexico, which included his decision to pull the United States out of the Trans-Pacific Partnership and to renegotiate the North American Free Trade Agreement (NAFTA).

Immigration

Trump's America First rhetoric has targeted not only globalization as an enemy of the working class, but immigration as well. As part of his America First rhetoric Trump focused on the belief that immigrants, specifically illegal immigrants, are taking jobs away from Americans. In 2015, Trump stated about illegal immigration: "They're taking our jobs, they're taking our manufacturing jobs, they're taking our money, they're killing us."[9] Within the working class, Trump has specifically focused this rhetoric on those who work manufacturing jobs, or those especially who have lost their manufacturing jobs. Manufacturing jobs in the United States have seen a major decline since the 1980s. Between 2000 and 2010 was a particularly rough decade for those working in the manufacturing sector. In addition to his anti-globalization rhetoric, in which Trump blames companies for moving factories overseas and giving jobs to "foreigners," Trump also blames "foreigners" in our own country for taking away American jobs. Trump's rhetoric of not only America First, but "Build the Wall," focuses on the belief that not only does illegal immigration increase crime in the United States, but it takes away jobs from American citizens. He has maintained a similar rhetoric for his working class about the impact immigration supposedly has on them, stating in 2019: "Working-class Americans are left to pay the price for mass illegal immigration: reduced jobs, lower wages, overburdened schools, hospitals that are so crowded you can't get in, increased crime, and a depleted social safety net."[10]

Environmentalism

In 2009 Trump reportedly signed a letter to President Obama urging action be taken to reach a global climate deal.[11] But by 2010, Trump argued that Al Gore should have his Nobel Prize taken away: "Gore wants us to clean up our factories and plants in order to protect us from global warming, when China and other countries couldn't care less. It would make us totally noncompetitive in the manufacturing world, and China, Japan, and India are laughing at America's stupidity." This marks not only a change in Trump's beliefs regarding the environment, but a change in how he focused his rhetoric about the environment toward working-class Americans, focusing on manufacturing. This can be witnessed in one of Trump's tweets from 2012: "The concept of global warming was created by and for the Chinese in order to make U.S. manufacturing non-competitive." While in 2016, Trump claimed that the years of comments calling global warming a hoax by the Chinese was a joke, he continued his rhetoric about the environment. In 2016, Trump was then endorsed by the West Virginia Coal Association following promises he made to "bring back coal mining jobs," by repealing environmental regulations drawn up under Obama. During this time, Trump supporters held signs that read "Trump Digs Coal." At a rally in 2017 in Kentucky, Trump made a similar pledge to coal miners: "We are going to put our coal miners back to work. They have not been treated well, but they're going to be treated well now . . . As we speak, we are preparing new executive actions to save our coal industry and to save our wonderful coal miners from continuing to be put out of work. The miners are coming back." Trump has continued this rhetoric as president, making conflicting statements regarding his beliefs on global warming and about China. As president, Trump pulled the United States out of the Paris Agreement on climate change, which he viewed as a waste of taxpayer money, and put a climate-change skeptic in charge of the Environmental Protection Agency (EPA).

It is important to note that anti-environmental rhetoric is not entirely new in U.S. politics. While established Republicans, such as the late senator John

McCain, advocated for environmental policies, Republicans like Trump have been quite taken by global warming hoax theories. As stated by Republican strategist Whit Ayres, who worked on Marco Rubio's presidential campaign: "Most Republicans still do not regard climate change as a hoax. But the entire climate change debate has now been caught up in the broader polarization of American politics. In some ways it's become yet another of the long list of litmus test issues that determine whether or not you're a good Republican."[12] However, environmentalism and climate change have been discussed behind the political scenes for years by players in the fossil fuel industry, like Charles and David Koch. In 2008, the Americans for Prosperity, a foundation funded by the Koch brothers that was an organization split off from Citizens for a Sound Economy, the group that started the Tea Party, drafted the initiative No Climate Tax. The initiative included a pledge for congressional members to sign that stated: "I will oppose any legislation relating to climate change that includes a net increase in government revenue."[13] By 2010, the pledge had been signed by over 150 congressional members and candidates. The next few years saw an increase in debates concerning environmental issues, like climate change, between select Republicans and Democrats, especially following various environmental regulations passed by the Obama administration. By 2016, Trump had clearly latched on to this movement that had been gaining steam among politicians in Washington, D.C., and targeted it to the working class. He targeted the environmental regulations passed by Obama to those who worked manufacturing jobs or to coal miners, who continuously saw their jobs slipping away.

It was through this rhetoric of him being against globalization, immigration, and even environmentalism that he persuaded various groups within the working class to follow him. A major component of the charismatic leader-follower relationship is the skillful use of rhetoric, whereby a leader is able to persuade his needy audience: "Follow me and I will take care of you. Together we can make a new beginning and create a new society. The fault is not within us but out there, and the only barrier to the happiness, peace, and prosperity we deserve is the outside enemy out to destroy us." Many of his supporters continue to support this rhetoric, even as the unemployment rate among the working-class continues to increase.[14]

And despite any of Trump's policies, even those that hurt the working class, his support among the working class is largely unwavering. Scott Paul, head of the Alliance for American Manufacturing, said: "There's a lot of forgiveness.

There's kind of a list of reasons why he hasn't done this or hasn't done that."[15] In a Harris Poll conducted by surveying over one thousand working-class Americans, the results showed that 55% of workers surveyed say they are in a better economic situation now than they were under the Obama administration. In addition, 85% say their lives are heading in the right direction, 69% say their local communities are on the right track, and 51% say that the United States is heading in the right direction under Trump.[16] This specific poll was discussed in an article published in September 2018 by the conservative news source, *Breitbart*, where John Binder states: "The optimism of America's blue collar workers comes as Trump has sought to revitalize economic patriotism in the U.S. economy through immigration enforcement and tariffs to protect American industry and jobs."[17]

Rural Areas

The 2016 election was viewed as greatly increasing the rural-urban voter divide, with researchers referring to Trump's high level of support in rural areas as being a form of "rural resentment." According to Katherine Cramer, a political science professor at the University of Wisconsin, "There's this sense that people in those communities are not getting their fair share compared to people in the cities. They feel like their communities are dying, and they perceive that all that stuff—the young people, the money, the livelihood—is going somewhere, and it's going to the cities."[18]

An observation that has been made about Trump's appeal in rural areas is not necessarily focused on any specific policy, but rather how he was able to appeal to the culture of rural areas. As discussed by Dee Davis, the founder of the nonpartisan organization Center for Rural Strategies from Whitesburg, Kentucky, a Trump supporter stronghold:

> What Trump did in rural areas was try to appeal to folks culturally ... A lot of us in rural areas, our ears are tuned to intonation ... We think people are talking down to us. What ends up happening is that we don't focus on the policy—we focus on the tones, the references, the culture.[19]

And there are two aspects of rural culture that Trump has been particularly adept at addressing among his followers: farmers and hunters.

FARMERS

Trump has found a relatively solid base of support among farmers in the United States, focusing on rhetoric and even policies that appealed to this part of the American population. He focused on issues such as the Waters of the United States rule, an issue Clinton did not engage. It's meant to combat water pollution at its source, but that is controversial among farmers. Many view it as another in a series of land regulations. Trump also focused on other issues that are controversial to many farmers, including the Affordable Care Act and minimum wage for farm workers. Just as he provided the working class with an externalizing rhetoric for their hardships, he has done the same with the American farmer. He appealed to those whose families have been farmers for generations, farmers who have experienced years and even decades of continual economic turmoil, and gave them an external source for their hardships.

In August 2016, Trump announced that he was forming an Agriculture Advisory Council. The council consists of five members of Congress, including members and chairs from the House and Senate agriculture committees, ten former and current governors from farm states, and two former rival Republican presidential nominees, Rick Perry and Jim Gilmore. Following the announcement, Dale Moore, executive director of public policy for the American Farm Bureau, stated, "They pretty much cover what I would consider to be the sweep of agriculture and rural issues we're all working on . . . There's a lot of horse power here that can provide good, solid advice and counsel."[20] The move, however, drew criticism from groups like Rural for Hillary, with organizer Trevor Dean stating: "For a guy who doesn't like politicians, he is sure surrounding himself with them . . . An advisory committee is all well and good, but where's your plan?"

On January 8, 2018, Trump spoke to the American Farm Bureau Federation at the Gaylord Opryland Resort & Convention Center in Nashville, Tennessee, stating that "farm country is God's country."[21] This was the first time an American president has addressed the American Farm Bureau Federation since George H. W. Bush in 1992. Trump said, speaking to the crowd of roughly five thousand: "We're fighting for our farmers and we're fighting for our country and for our great American flag. We want our flag respected . . . And we want our national anthem respected also," which resulted in a standing ovation and chants of "U-S-A."[22] Avoiding ongoing controversies, like the release of Michael Wolff's *Fire and Fury*, Trump focused largely on new tax legislation on farmers and the agriculture industry, stating, "Under this new law, the typical family of four earning $75,000 will see an income tax cut of more than $2,000—slashing their tax bill in half."²³ The new legislation allows farmers to deduct the entire cost of new farming equipment during the first year of the investment. Trump went on to say, "In every decision we make, we are honoring America's proud farming legacy."

During the event Trump, surrounded by most of Tennessee's Republican congressional delegation, plus Tennessee governor Bill Haslam, signed Executive Order 13821, "Streamlining and Expediting Requests To Locate Broadband Facilities in Rural America." The executive order focused on promoting "better access to broadband internet service in rural America." Following the signing, Trump stated that we "should seek to reduce barriers to capital investment, remove obstacles to broadband services, and more efficiently employ government resources . . . Those towers are going to go up and you're going to have great, great broadband." That same day the White House also issued a fact sheet titled "President Donald J. Trump Is Working to Rebuild Rural America," which quotes Trump as saying, "Our farmers deserve a government that serves their interest and empowers them to do the hard work that they love to do so much." The document reads:

> RURAL AMERICA HAS BEEN LEFT BEHIND: President Donald J. Trump has charged the Rural Prosperity Task Force with examining the challenges facing rural America.
>
> BREAKING DOWN BARRIERS TO RURAL PROSPERITY: President Trump's Rural Prosperity Task Force has proposed recommendations to help rural America grow and thrive.
>
> REBUILDING RURAL AMERICA: President Trump's Administration will build on existing projects and efforts to support rural America.²⁴

However, support for Trump from farmers has softened following the government shutdown from December 2018 to January 2019, and his trade war with China. Trump's trade war has actually impacted farmers the most, specifically on soybeans and corn.²⁵ In a survey released on January 9, 2019, by the DTN/

Progressive Farmer, it found that the confidence level of farmers decreased by forty points from the prior year, due to a difficult harvest and concerns over trade issues. In an interview with the Asheboro, North Carolina, *Courier-Tribune*, Roger Cerven, a corn and soybean farmer in Iowa, expressed that while he supports Trump on immigration, he has concerns over his negotiations with China. While he voted for Trump in 2016, he is undecided for 2020. However, in a poll released by Farm Journal Pulse in February 2019, 78% of the 1,043 farmers and ranchers who took part in the poll stated they still strongly or somewhat approve of Trump.

HUNTING

In November 2012, singer Cher tweeted an article from website *Gothamist*, "Photos: Donald Trump's Sons Awesome At Killing Elephants And Other Wildlife," to which Trump tweeted "@cher Old story, one of which I publicly disapproved. My sons love hunting, I don't."[26] While Trump has made comments in the past against hunting, specifically trophy hunting, he has gained quite a bit of support from hunters, especially by highlighting his sons as hunters. In the *Field & Stream* interview of Donald Trump and Donald Trump Jr. by Anthony Licata in January 2016:

> Anthony Licata: Back to . . . access for hunters' rights to get on public land. One of the things that we've found is so much of this . . . election cycle—has talked about cutting budgets and reducing the federal government. And what the budget is for managing public lands right now is at one percent . . . Would you continue to push that number down for wildlife conservation or would you look to invest more?
>
> Donald Trump: I don't think there's any reason to. And I will say—and I've heard this from many of my friends who are really avid hunters and I've heard it from my sons who are avid hunters—that the lands are not maintained the way they were by any stretch of the imagination. And we're going to get that changed; we're going to reverse that. And the good thing is, I'm in a family where I have—I mean, I'm a member of the NRA, but I have two longtime members of the NRA. They've been hunting

from the time they were five years old and probably maybe even less than that. And they really understand it. And I like the fact that, you know, I can sort of use them in terms of—they know so much about every single element about every question that you're asking. And one of the things they've complained about for years is how badly the federal lands are maintained, so we'll get that changed.

Donald Trump Jr.: It's really all about access. I mean, I feel like the side that's the anti-hunting crowd, they're trying to eliminate that access—make it that much more difficult for people to get the next generation in . . . And it's the typical liberal death by a thousand cuts: "We'll make it a little harder here. Make it a little harder here. We won't spend the money there." And it's not just about hunting—it's about fishing; it's about hiking; it's about access . . . those great traditions that are so, you know, so much the foundation of America. And we'd be against anything like that. And frankly, it'd be about refunding those—making sure those lands are maintained properly; making sure they're not going into private hands to be effectively walled off to the general public. And that's something really important to us.[27]

While Trump has made comments at times in opposition to hunting, his presidency has numerous times proposed or enacted policies to ease hunting restrictions. This includes lifting bans on importing big game and elephant trophies from Africa[28] and reversing Obama-era hunting restrictions on national parks in Alaska.[29] In March 2018, an International Wildlife Conservation Council was created by the Trump administration to help advise on revisions for federal laws on importing big game trophies. The council came under heavy criticism for being made up primarily of individuals who are big game hunters, including a number of individuals from pro-hunting organization Safari Club International (SCI). The council also included the NRA's director of hunting policy, Erica Rhoad, as well as Peter Horn, former vice president of the Safari Club International conservation fund and current vice president of Beretta firearms, who co-owns an upstate New York hunting preserve with Donald Trump Jr. and Eric Trump. Trump's appointment on April 11, 2019, of David Bernhardt to secretary of Interior has also received praise from the pro-hunting organization Safari Club International. SCI's president, Paul Babaz, stated, "We have had the privilege of getting to know the secretary through his work at the Interior Department and strongly support his continued efforts to open up America's public lands to the sportsmen and women who love the outdoors."[30]

Trump's sons have also continued to be a major source of support for the hunting community. In September 2018, Donald Trump Jr. found himself in a Twitter war with animal rights organization PETA (People for the Ethical Treatment of Animals). PETA had tweeted a photo of a hunter in camouflage wearing a red MAGA-style cap that said "Donald Trump Jr." being mauled by a leopard, with the following caption, "In a twist on the horrific trophy-hunting photo that showed the Trump brothers grinning while clutching the body of a dead leopard—this time the leopard wins! Pre-order PETA's NEW limited-edition @DonaldJTrumpJr #Halloween costume. http://peta.vg/2bco." Donald Jr. tweeted in response: "Ironically, there are few orgs in world history that have as much animal blood on their hands as PETA. You hypocrites are literally an animal slaughter factory. 'In the last 11 years, PETA has killed 29,426 dogs, cats, rabbits, & other domestic animals,'" followed by a link to a *Huffington Post* article from 2013 on PETA's euthanasia policy.[31] According to Frank Miniter, executive editor of the NRA magazine *American Hunter*, in an opinion piece on Fox News: "The media has mocked President Donald J. Trump's sons for being hunters and has even treated them, and other hunters, as if they are bloodthirsty killers. It is a tragedy that the environmental community, and thus the progressive left, won't treat hunters as the conservationists they are. They don't because they view hunters as a political constituency that more often votes for Republicans."[32]

In February 2019, the advocacy group Hunter Nation announced a raffle contest for a five-day elk-hunting trip with Donald Trump Jr. in Utah in the fall of 2019. The official contest page, which sold the raffle tickets for $10, referred to Donald Trump Jr. as "the modern-day Teddy Roosevelt," going on to say:

> You will have to go a long way to find a bigger advocate for our hunting lifestyle and a more passionate hunter and conservationist than Don, Jr. The opportunity to share a hunting camp with him is truly priceless. Gain a new perspective on real-life conservation

from one of the leading experts on the subject, all while you hunt one of the most prized big game animals on earth.[33]

It is clear, not only by Donald Jr.'s continuation in the spotlight for hunting rights, as well as gun rights, as mentioned in the previous chapter, but by Trump's own actions, that he is keeping up a steady stream of rhetoric aimed toward working-class and rural areas. This is a tactic obviously intended for his 2020 reelection campaign.

11

Permission to Hate

Hate crimes have increased in the United States for the third consecutive year. The Trump presidency has witnessed some of the most horrific hate crimes in our country's history. But how much of this can be attributed to Donald Trump's presidency? The answer to that question can arguably be found in his rhetoric. While Trump has never specifically told his followers to carry out hate crimes, his hateful rhetoric and derogatory language has the power to inspire hate crimes.

The Rhetoric of Trump

Trump has a long history of being accused of racism. As discussed earlier, in the 1970s Trump and his father Fred were sued by the Department of Justice for racial discrimination in their renting practices. Then in the 1980s, Trump was criticized for race-baiting due to a series of full-page ads he paid over $80,000 for in several newspapers. The ads focused on the high-profile Central Park Jogger case, in which Trisha Meili, a twenty-eight-year-old investment banker, was assaulted and raped in Central Park, leaving her in a coma for twelve days. On the night of the attack, five teenagers, four of whom were black and one who was Latino, were arrested for the attack on the young female white jogger. Less than two weeks after the attack, Trump paid for a full-page ad in several newspapers that called for bringing "back the death penalty" for the "savages" who carried out the attack, saying he wanted "criminals of every age" "to be afraid." The ad also read:

> Mayor Koch has stated that hate and rancor should be removed from our hearts. I do not think so. I want to hate these muggers and murderers. They should be forced to suffer . . . Yes, Mayor Koch, I want to hate these murderers and I always will. . . . How can our great society tolerate the continued brutalization of its citizens by crazed misfits? Criminals must be told that their CIVIL LIBERTIES END WHEN AN ATTACK ON OUR SAFETY BEGINS![1]

Trump defended his belief that hate was necessary in an interview with Larry King, saying "maybe hate is what we need if we're gonna get something done." The teenage boys, who came to be known as the Central Park Five, eventually had their convictions overturned in 2002 following the confession of convicted murderer and serial rapist, Matias Reyes, a confession which was confirmed by DNA evidence. That year, Michael W. Warren, a lawyer for the five men, stated, "It was outrageous, the manner that Mr. Trump used to engage in his own personal form of rhetoric. A lot of people felt it colored the eyes of prospective jurors who ultimately sat on the case. Now it's even more appalling, with new evidence that points exclusively to another person. I think Donald Trump at the very least owes a real apology to this community and to the young men and their families." In addition to Warren, protesters gathered outside of Trump Tower chanting "Trump is a chump!" and demanding a public apology, which never came.[2] Trump has continued to state that he believes the Central Park Five are guilty. In 2014, following a $40 million settlement from the City of New York to the five young men, Trump wrote in an op-ed in the *New York Daily News*:

> My opinion on the settlement of the Central Park Jogger case is that it's a disgrace . . . Settling doesn't mean innocence, but it indicates incompetence on several levels . . . As a long-time resident of New York City, I think it is ridiculous for this case to be settled—and I hope that has not yet taken place . . . Forty million

dollars is a lot of money for the taxpayers of New York to pay when we are already the highest taxed city and state in the country. The recipients must be laughing out loud at the stupidity of the city.

Speak to the detectives on the case and try listening to the facts. These young men do not exactly have the pasts of angels.[3]

Trump reiterated his belief that the Central Park Five were guilty during his presidential campaign. In October 2016 on CNN, Trump stated, "They admitted they were guilty. The police doing the original investigation say they were guilty. The fact that that case was settled with so much evidence against them is outrageous. And the woman, so badly injured, will never be the same."[4] It was this belief that was one of the reasons Senator John McCain revoked his endorsement of Trump. McCain said, "I have wanted to support the candidate our party nominated," even as Trump stated that McCain was not a war hero because he had been a prisoner of war. McCain went on to say:

> He was not my choice, but as a past nominee, I thought it important I respect the fact that Donald Trump won a majority of the delegates by the rules our party set. I thought I owed his supporters that deference. But Donald Trump's behavior this week concluding with the disclosure of his demeaning comments about women and his boasts about sexual assaults, make it impossible to continue to offer even conditional support for his candidacy . . . In addition to my well known differences with Donald Trump on public policy issues, I have raised questions about his character after his comments on Prisoners of War, the Khan Gold Star family, Judge Curiel and earlier inappropriate comments about women. Just this week, he made outrageous statements about the innocent men in the Central Park Five case.[5]

Then, in 1991, Trump was accused of making racist and anti–Semitic comments by author John O'Donnell. In his book, with James Rutherford, *Trumped!: The Inside Story of the Real Donald Trump—His Cunning Rise and Spectacular Fall*, O'Donnell quoted Trump as saying:

> I've got black accountants at Trump Castle and at Trump Plaza. Black guys counting my money! I hate it. The only kind of people

> I want counting my money are short guys wearing yarmulkes . . . Those are the only kind of people I want counting my money. Nobody else . . . Besides that, I tell you something else. I think that guy's lazy. And it's probably not his fault because laziness is a trait in blacks.[6]

In an interview with *Playboy* in 1997, Trump told Mark Bowden that this quote was "probably true."[7] However, during his attempt to become the Reform Party presidential nominee two years later, Trump told Tim Russert on *Meet the Press*: "I've never said anything like that."

Since his announcement speech in 2015, in which he referred to Mexicans as criminals and rapists, Trump has continuously and purposefully used rhetoric and derogatory language toward minority groups in the United States. In November 2015, following the terrorist attack in Paris, Trump stated at a rally in Alabama, "I watched when the World Trade Center came tumbling down. And I watched in Jersey City, New Jersey, where thousands and thousands of people were cheering as that building was coming down."[8] When asked later on a political talk show to explain his comments, he said, "There were people cheering on the other side of New Jersey, where you have large Arab populations."[9]

In June 2016, Trump questioned the impartiality of a federal jurist, U.S. District Judge Gonzalo Curiel, who had presided over the Trump University lawsuit, stating that the judge (who was born in Indiana) had an "inherent conflict of interest" because Curiel's family "was of Mexican heritage."[10]

In August 2016, during a rally in Maine, Trump stated, "We've just seen many, many crimes getting worse all the time, and as Maine knows—a major destination for Somali refugees—right, am I right?"[11] During the rally he also alluded to there being a terrorism risk from the Somali community by referring to three young Somali men having been found guilty of planning to join the Islamic State in Syria.

Trump's rhetoric has continued well into his presidency, including the use of hateful tropes and the same derogatory language he used during his campaign. One example of a hateful trope Trump has continued to use is the anti-Semitic term "globalist," including in a speech at the United Nations where he said he rejected "the ideology of globalism" in favor of the "ideology of patriotism." Trump has also consistently stated that he is a "nationalist," not a "globalist."[12]

Then in May 2018, during a roundtable discussion about immigration policy in California, Trump referred to immigrants as "animals," saying, "These aren't people. These are animals and we're taking them out of the country at a level and at a rate that's never happened before. And because of the weak laws, they come in fast. We get 'em. We release 'em. We get 'em again. We bring them out. It's crazy."[13] The following day, Trump explained that he was referring to the gang MS-13.

Trump has also come under heavy criticism for some of the sources he has chosen to retweet on Twitter, as well as other statements he has made on his Twitter account. On January 22, 2016, he retweeted from a Twitter user with the handle @WhiteGenocideTM. The tweet was, "@WhiteGenocideTM: @RealDonaldTrump Poor Jeb. I could've sworn I saw him outside Trump Tower the other day!"[14] The account, which uses the name "Donald Trumpovitz," had roughly 2,300 followers and featured links to a website of a pro–Adolf Hitler documentary. The account included a photo of American Nazi Party founder George Lincoln Rockwell and a background photo for the account contained the phrases "Get the F--- Out of My Country" and "Jewmerica." Trump also came under fire for retweeting alt-right leader, Jack Posobiec, following the rally in Charlottesville. Trump, who had complained that the media would never be satisfied with his commending racist groups, retweeted Posobiec's tweet that read, "Meanwhile: 39 shootings in Chicago this weekend, 9 deaths. No national media outrage. Why is that?"[15] Posobiec in the past has defended white supremacists, including Richard Spencer.

In 2013 Trump tweeted, "Sadly, the overwhelming amount of violent crime in our major cities is committed by blacks and hispanics—a tough subject—must be discussed."[16] Then during his presidential campaign, Trump tweeted an attack ad against Hillary Clinton that featured a picture of Clinton as well as a pile of cash and the words "most corrupt candidate ever" printed in a Star of David. Trump responded to the criticism of the ad by stating, "These false attacks by Hillary Clinton trying to link the Star of David with a basic star, often used by sheriffs who deal with criminals and criminal behavior, showing an inscription that says 'Crooked Hillary is the most corrupt candidate ever' with anti–Semitism is ridiculous."[17] In September 2017, following Hurricane Maria, Trump attacked political leaders and the Puerto Rican community as a whole, writing in a series of tweets, "The Mayor of San Juan, who was very complimentary only a few days ago, has now been told by the Democrats that you must be nasty to Trump. . . . Such poor leadership ability by the Mayor of San Juan, and others in Puerto Rico, who are not able to get their workers to help. They . . . want everything to be done for them when it should be a community effort. 10,000 Federal workers now on Island doing a fantastic job."[18] In August 2018, Trump tweeted, "I have asked Secretary of State @SecPompeo to closely study the South Africa land and farm seizures and expropriations and the large scale killing of farmers. 'South African Government is now seizing land from white farmers.' @TuckerCarlson @FoxNews."[19] In this tweet Trump is referring to the white supremacy conspiracy theory of an ongoing white genocide in South Africa, one that is specifically targeting white South African farmers. A conspiracy theory that has been propagated by Fox News' Tucker Carlson. The South African government responded to Trump's tweet, stating it contained "false information" and that it provided a "narrow perception which only seeks to divide our nation and reminds us of our colonial past."[20]

The Power of Rhetoric

In contrast to "reparative charismatics" who heal their nation's wounds, a hallmark of destructive charismatic leaders is absolutist, polarizing rhetoric, drawing their followers together against the outside enemy. There is the me and the not me, good versus evil, strength versus weakness. Analysis of the speeches of charismatic leaders repeatedly reveals such all-or-nothing polar absolutism. As a destructive charismatic leader, Trump's rhetoric has increased polarization in the United States. And it is this polarization, this use of derogatory language and use of "us versus them," that has encouraged American citizens to carry out hate crimes.

A number of studies have correlated the rhetoric and derogatory language of Trump to hate crimes in the United States. Two separate studies from 2016 found correlations between the rhetoric of Trump against Muslims during his presidential campaign and actual hate crimes carried out against Muslims in the United States. The first report, conducted by the California State University San Bernardino's Center for the Study of Hate and Extremism, noted that hate crimes against Muslims were at the highest they have been since following the September 11 attacks. According to Brian Levin, the director of the Center and the author of the paper, "There's very compelling evidence that political rhetoric may well play a role in directing behavior in the aftermath of a terrorist attack. I don't think we can dismiss contentions that rhetoric is one of the significant variables that can contribute to hate crimes."[21] The second report, conducted at Georgetown University, noted a similar increase in hate crimes against Muslims. Engy Abdelkader, the author of the report, stated, "Trump has seized on people's fears and anxieties. I think that has translated in a number of instances not just to hostility, but acts of violence."[22] In addition, Brian Levin and Jim Nolan, a sociologist with the West Virginia University Research Center on Violence, have noted that the day after Trump's election, November 10, 2016, marked an apex for the single worst month for hate crimes the United States has seen in fourteen years.

A similar correlation has been made between hate crimes and Trump's tweets. In a study conducted at the University of Warwick in the United Kingdom, the authors found that there was a direct correlation between hate crimes against Muslims and Latinos and Trump's derogatory tweets about the two groups. Many of the cases of physical hate crimes were concentrated in parts of the United States were the usage of Twitter is higher.[23] While researchers Karsten Muller and Carlo Schwarz's report did not claim that Trump's tweets caused the hate crimes, Muller stated in an interview with Hatewatch at the Southern Poverty Law Center, "What really stands out to me is just how strong the correlation of Trump's tweets is with future anti–Muslim hate crimes . . . I also found it striking that you see a spike in hate crimes against Muslims in the week of the presidential election, but only in areas where many people use Twitter." Schwarz goes on to say, "We also do not find any evidence that other types of hate crimes increased in areas with many Twitter users around Trump's campaign start—except a small shift for anti–Latino crimes."[24]

A correlation has also been found between Trump's rallies and hate crimes. According to a research study conducted by the political science department at the University of North Texas, counties that hosted Trump rallies in 2016 saw a 226% increase in hate crimes in comparison to comparable countries that did not host a rally. As stated by the authors of the report:

> Our analysis cannot be certain it was Trump's campaign rally rhetoric that caused people to commit more hate crimes in the host county . . . However, suggestions that this effect can be explained through a plethora of faux hate crimes are at best unrealistic. In fact, this charge is frequently used as a political tool to

dismiss concerns about hate crimes. Research shows it is far more likely that hate crime statistics are considerably lower because of underreporting.[25]

This is not surprising given that Trump himself encouraged violence against protesters at his rallies. At a rally on February 1, 2016, in Iowa, Trump stated: "If you see somebody getting ready to throw a tomato, knock the crap out of them, would you? Seriously, okay? Just knock the hell . . . I promise you I will pay for the legal fees. I promise, I promise."[26] At another rally in Oklahoma, Trump suggested that law enforcement should be more violent with protesters, stating: "You see, in the good old days, law enforcement acted a lot quicker than this . . . A lot quicker. In the good old days, they'd rip him out of that seat so fast. But today everyone is so politically correct. Our country is going to hell—we're being politically correct."[27]

Another way in which to understand the power of Trump's rhetoric is to compare it to the role hateful rhetoric has played in America's history. Parallels can be made between Trump's rhetoric and the rhetoric of the KKK in the 1920s. Kelly Baker of *The Atlantic* noted in her article "Make America White Again?" from March 2016 a similarity between Trump's rhetoric and that of the KKK in the 1920s:

> White men and women turned to the Klan for reassurance that America was a nation founded by white people for white people. The Imperial Night-Hawk crafted histories absent of native peoples, African Americans, Catholics, and Jews that confirmed what readers wanted to hear: White Protestants were the creators of America, and the nation would only succeed with their continued dominance. The Klan made enemies of immigrants but also of any people they considered "foreign" who already resided on American soil. Threats appeared everywhere, from newly arrived immigrants to Catholics, Jews, and African Americans who were already citizens—though the order wasn't of the opinion that they should be.[28]

However, the similarities between the rhetoric of Trump and the second KKK are not necessarily in that the rhetoric was identical, but rather in how it appeals to supporters. As discussed by philosopher Eric Hoffer in *The True Believer*:

No matter how vital we think the role of leadership in the rise of a mass movement, there is no doubt that the leader cannot create the conditions which make the rise of a movement possible. He cannot conjure a movement out of the void. There has to be an eagerness to follow and obey, and an intense dissatisfaction with things as they are, before movement and leader can make their appearance.[29]

Neither Trump nor the KKK of the 1920s created hate, rather they appealed to the hate many Americans were already feeling. While the KKK of the 1860s, which was concentrated in the Reconstruction-era South, focused their hate on newly freed slaves, the second revival of the KKK wanted to make a broader appeal to other areas of the country. The founder of the second KKK, William Joseph Simmons, hired public relations specialists Elizabeth Tyler and Edward Young Clarke, to transform the organization. In order to do so, Tyler and Clarke expanded the "enemies" of the Klan:

No longer were blacks the sole objects of the Klan hatred. Now Catholics, Jews, nonwhites, Bolsheviks, and immigrants became targets, a shift that greatly increased the Klan's recruitment in Northern states.[30]

This was a step taken not to create hate for these groups but rather as a PR tactic to appeal to the hate that already existed for them in the United States. Parallels can be drawn between the PR tactics of the second KKK in the 1920s and the rhetoric of Trump's presidential campaign of 2016. Rather than creating hate, using hateful rhetoric toward already discriminated against groups helps make a climate where hate is more acceptable. The 1920s was easily the most successful decade for the KKK, with membership reaching into the tens of thousands. On August 8, 1925, over 50,000 KKK members marched in Washington, D.C., and while they wore the common regalia of robes and hoods, their faces were clearly visible. People felt that they didn't need to hide the fact that they were a part of the KKK; in fact they took pride in it. They weren't alone, they were one of thousands of individuals who felt the same hate toward the same groups of people that they did.

As will be discussed in this chapter, Trump's history of hateful rhetoric and derogatory terms during his campaign and well into his presidency have made right-wing extremists feel emboldened. He has received support from countless such extremists, including white supremacists and neo–Nazis. His presidency has witnessed the highest number of hate crimes and the largest number of hate groups that this country has seen in decades. During the Unite the Right rally in Charlottesville in August 2017, people proudly wore swastikas and other symbols of hate, including the black sun and iron cross. And just like the marches of the 1920s, the faces of the protesters were visible. There is a similar sense of comradery and pride in displaying hate. Trump, like the second KKK of the 1920s, has essentially given the United States permission to hate.

Support from Right-Wing Extremists

Since the announcement of his presidential campaign, Trump has received praise from a number of hate groups and leaders of hate groups. On February 25, 2016, David Duke, former Grand Wizard of the KKK, stated on his radio program:

> Voting for these people [Marco Rubio and Ted Cruz], voting against Donald Trump at this point is really treason to your heritage. I'm not saying I endorse everything about Trump, in fact I haven't formally endorsed him. But I do support his candidacy, and I support voting for him as a strategic action. I hope he does everything we hope he will do.[31]

Trump's responses to David Duke's endorsements included him claiming he didn't know David Duke endorsed him and that he really didn't know anything about David Duke. When asked during a press conference the day following Duke's announcement, Trump responded, "I didn't even know he endorsed me. David Duke endorsed me? Okay, all right. I disavow, okay?"[32] Then two days later, on CNN's *State of the Union*, Trump stated:

> Well, just so you understand, I don't know anything about David Duke. Okay? I don't know anything about what you're even talking about with white supremacy or white supremacists. So, I don't know. I don't know, did he endorse me or what's going on, because, you know, I know nothing about David Duke. I know nothing about white supremacists. And so you're asking me a question that I'm supposed to be talking about people that I know nothing about.[33]

While Trump claimed to not know anything about David Duke or white supremacy, this is not entirely accurate. In 1991, following David Duke's unsuccessful race for governor of Louisiana, Trump discussed Duke with Larry King on *Larry King Live*:

> Larry King: Did the David Duke thing bother you? Fifty-five percent of the whites in Louisiana voted for him.
>
> Donald Trump: I hate seeing what it represents, but I guess it just shows there's a lot of hostility in this country. There's a tremendous amount of hostility in the United States.
>
> Larry King: Anger?
>
> Donald Trump: It's anger. I mean, that's an anger vote. People are angry about what's happened. People are angry about the jobs. If you look at Louisiana, they're really in deep trouble. When you talk about the East Coast, it's not that East Coast. It's the East Coast, the middle coast, the West Coast . . .[34]

On February 13, 2000, in a statement that he would not run to be the Reform Party's nominee for president, Trump stated, "The Reform Party now includes a Klansman, Mr. Duke, a neo–Nazi, Mr. [Patrick] Buchanan, and a communist, Ms. [Lenora] Fulani. This is not company I wish to keep." Then on the following day he was interviewed on NBC's *Today* show:

> Matt Lauer: When you say the party is self-destructing, what do you see as the biggest problem with the Reform Party right now?
>
> Donald Trump: Well, you've got David Duke just joined—a bigot, a racist, a problem. I mean, this is not exactly the people you want in your party.[35]

Since his initial statement in 2016, Duke has continued to voice his support for Trump. In August 2017, Duke explained why white supremacists voted for Trump, stating, "We are going to fulfill the promises of Donald Trump. That's what we believed in. That's why we voted for Donald Trump, because he said he's going to take our country back."[36] Duke has also stated on his podcast on February 20, 2017, that he supports Trump because he believes Trump is an anti–Semite. In his podcast, Duke states, "an anti–Semite is not simply someone who doesn't like Jews, they define an anti–Semite as someone, anyone, who opposes the Jewish agenda." Duke goes on to state that "they see Trump as a huge enemy. They hate Donald Trump because he opposes their agenda."[37]

Trump has received support from other members of the KKK, including Rachel Pendergraft, daughter of the Knights Party's national director Thomas Robb and their current spokeswoman. Pendergraft's Twitter account has made several congratulatory references to Trump, including two from January 2017 that read: "Congradualations Donald Trump from the Christian Revival Center in Harrison, Arkansas @potus" and "What a regal couple, perfect song . . . I did it my way . . . congrats . . . Trump and Milania . . . @potus." Pendergraft's Twitter feed also highlights the KKK's official endorsement of Trump for president in November 2016: "KKK's official newspaper supports Donald Trump for president."[38] The tweet ends with a link to a *Washington Post* article that discusses the KKK's newspaper's, the *Crusader*, endorsement of Trump. With the entire front page of the *Crusader* being devoted to their Trump endorsment, Thomas Robb wrote:

> "Make America Great Again!" It is a slogan that has been repeatedly used by Donald Trump in his campaign for the presidency. You can see it on the shirts, buttons, posters and ball caps such as the one being worn here by Trump speaking at a recent rally. . . . But can it happen? Can America really be great again? This is what we will soon find out! While Trump wants to make America great again, we have to ask ourselves, "What made America great in the first place?" The short answer to that is simple. America was great not because of what our forefathers did—but because of who our forefathers were. America was founded as a White Christian Republic. And as a White Christian Republic it became great.[39]

Shortly after the release of the paper, Trump's campaign criticized the article, issuing a statement that said "Mr. Trump and the campaign denounce hate in any form . . . This publication is repulsive and their views do not represent the tens of millions of Americans who are uniting behind our campaign."[40]

In November 2016, the National Policy Institute, a white supremacist group that describes itself as an "independent organization dedicated to the heritage, identity and future of people of European descent in the United States and around the world," hosted a conference in Washington, D.C.[41] At the conference, Richard Spencer, who is also the institute's president, cheered along with the crowd "Hail Trump! Hail our people! Hail victory!" while giving the Nazi salute. Spencer in the past has stated he wants a "peaceful ethnic cleansing" and that his dream is "a new society, an ethno-state that would be a gathering point for all Europeans." In his speech during the conference, Spencer stated:

> No one mourns the great crimes committed against us. For us it is conquer or die... The mainstream media or perhaps we should refer to them in the original German, Lügenpresse... It is not just they are leftists and cucks, it's not just that many are genuinely stupid, indeed, one wonders if these people are people at all, or instead soulless Golem, animated by some dark power to repeat whatever talking point John Oliver stated the night before... To be white is to be a striver, a crusader, an explorer, and a conqueror. We build, we produce, we go upward. And we recognize the central lie of American race relations. We don't exploit other groups, we don't gain anything from their presence. They need us and not the other way around... Within the very blood in our veins as children of the sun, lies the potential for greatness... We were not meant to beg for moral validation from some of the most despicable creatures to ever populate the planet... The press has clearly decided to double down and wage war against the legitimacy of Trump. And the continued existence of white America. But they are really opening up the door for us. America was, until this past generation, a white country designed for ourselves and our posterity. It is our creation. It is our inheritance. And it belongs to us.[42]

Regardless of what Trump truly believes, it is important to highlight that right-wing extremists, specifically white supremacists like David Duke and Richard Spencer, believe he is one of them. They believe he is racist and anti–Semitic and they believe because they have a president who is one of them that they can operate more freely. Trump's presidency, especially with the rhetoric he uses, has empowered right-wing extremists, a trend that is perhaps most notable in the rise of hate groups in the United States.

Hate Crimes in Trump's America

While reports concerning hate crimes have increased for the third consecutive year, there is still a great deal of debate surrounding hate crimes under Trump's presidency. Trump's supporters argue that hate crimes are not increasing because there is a flaw in the national statistics. And that is true—it is difficult to get an accurate picture of hate crimes in America based on these statistics. The first issue surrounding FBI hate crime statistics is that reporting hate crimes to the FBI is voluntary. And while there was an increase in the percentage of hate crimes reported in 2017, there were also roughly one thousand more law enforcement agencies that reported their information to the FBI than had in previous years. The second issue is that hate crimes are also significantly underreported. Of the law enforcement agencies that did report to the FBI only 12.6% reported having had hate crimes occur in their jurisdictions during 2017. This included law enforcement agencies even for major cities like Miami. However, even though there are issues surrounding national statistics this does not mean that hate crimes have not increased.

One way to better understand the increase in hate crimes in the United States is to examine how hate crimes have increased in major cities that have been consistently reporting them. In a report released by the Center for the Study of Hate and Extremism at California State University San Bernardino, there was a 12.5% increase in hate crime incidents reported to the police in ten major U.S. cities: Chicago; Dallas; Houston; Los Angeles; New York; Philadelphia; Phoenix; San Antonio; San Diego; and San Jose, California. The report found that incidents reported in 2017 reached 1,038, an increase from 923 in 2016. In Washington, D.C., hate crimes reported increased 62% from 104 in 2016 to 169 in 2017, with only 64 reported in 2015. However, D.C.'s criteria for hate crimes differ from other major cities, as it includes both homelessness and political affiliation.

Another way to understand the increase in hate crimes is to examine the countless minority groups who have witnessed an increase in hate crimes in the past two to three years. According to one report released in 2018 by the South Asian Americans Leading Together, violence against Muslims, Sikhs, Arabs, and other south Asians has increased 64% since November 2016. Anti-Arab crimes include the March 2017 attack of an employee at a Middle Eastern restaurant in Salem, Oregon. The employee was assaulted with a pipe by a man, Jason Kendall, who yelled "go back to your country terrorist" and "get out of America (expletive)." Kendall claimed he was on "a warrior's path" when he passed the restaurant and saw a woman inside he thought was a slave because that is "what Arabs do." He then walked into the restaurant, told the woman she was "free to leave" and started yelling at an employee he claimed looked like Saddam Hussein. He returned five minutes later and assaulted one of the employees.[43]

Also in 2017 was an attack on a Portland, Oregon, train, when a man shouted racist and anti–Muslim comments at two Muslim women. The man was confronted by other passengers, at which point he stabbed a number of people, including two men who died from their injuries: Ricky John Best, a technician and U.S. Army veteran, and Taliesin Myrddin Namkai-Meche, a recent university graduate. A third victim who was seriously injured, Micah David-Cole Fletcher, survived the attack.

As for hate crimes against the Sikh community as discussed by the Sikh American Legal Defense and Education Fund: "It is difficult to know the true number of hate crimes against Sikh Americans because many incidents go unreported and because Sikh-specific statistics are currently unavailable."[44] In a number of cases, Sikhs are mistaken for Muslims and attacked. Anti-Sikh attacks include the January 2019 assault of a store clerk in Oregon, a state that saw a 40% increase in hate crimes from 2016 to 2017. The attack was consistent with the way in which physical assaults on male Sikhs take place, which included pulling the man's beard and trying to remove his turban. The Sikh Coalition, the largest Sikh civil rights group in the United States, has stated that Sikhs are often targeted "due to the Sikh articles of faith, including a turban and beard, which represent the Sikh religious commitment to justice, tolerance and equality."[45] Highly visible religious symbols, like a turban, are often a focal point in religious hate crime attacks. Take for instance: Muslim women who are attacked for wearing a *hijab*, a head covering; Orthodox Jewish women who are targeted for wearing a *mitpachat*, a head covering; or Jewish men who are attacked for wearing a *kippah*, a small cap.

Another group to be impacted by increases in hate crimes was the Jewish community. In 2017, anti–Semitic hate crimes increased by an additional

37% from the year prior, accounting for close to 60% of hate crimes based on religion.[46] While predictions for figures on 2018 show that anti–Semitic crimes may have increased by almost 60%. For 2018 over half of the hate crimes in New York City were against Jews, particularly Orthodox Jews who have witnessed a sharp increase in hate crimes perpetrated against them. The predictions for 2018 were not surprising given that 2018 witnessed the largest anti–Semitic attack to ever occur in the United States, the shooting at the Tree of Life synagogue, which took the lives of eleven Jewish people. And while 2019 is not yet over at the time of this writing, there is a strong likelihood that anti–Semitic hate crimes will increase once more. On April 27, 2019, another shooting took place at a Chabad synagogue in San Diego during services for the end of the holiday of Passover. Current reports indicated that one woman was killed and three individuals, including a child and the rabbi, were injured.

Anti-LGBTQ hate crimes have continued to increase as well, including a 5% increase in sexual orientation bias crimes in 2017. This is an increase we will most likely see reported again for 2018. Take for instance, in December 2018, a twenty-year-old woman was attacked on a New York subway by a man shouting anti-gay slurs, resulting in a number of injuries including a broken spine. However, hate crimes motivated by a gender identity bias decreased by 4%, although according to the LGBTQ advocacy group the Human Rights Campaign: "Despite the slight decrease in reported hate crimes motivated by gender identity bias, anti-transgender violence remains an epidemic."[47] According to a Human Rights Campaign report: "Since 2013, at least 128 transgender and gender-expansive individuals have been killed in the U.S. At the end of 2017, we mourned the highest number ever recorded. At the time of publication, at least 22 transgender people have been killed in 2018."[48] Once such incident discussed by the HRC in the report being investigated as a hate crime was the murder of a black transgender woman, Tonya "Kita" Harvey, in Buffalo, New York. It is important to note that in numerous cases, victims of a hate crime can be attacked for more than one reason. Take for instance, the murder of Blaze Bernstein, a Jewish and openly gay sophomore at the University of Pennsylvania. Bernstein was killed in California by a former high school classmate and member of the neo–Nazi group Atomwaffen, Samuel Woodward.

Hate crimes against Asian Americans have been steadily increasing, despite having been on a sharp decline. According to John Yang, the president and executive director of Asian Americans Advancing Justice: "We are seeing quite a number . . . higher than we have seen in the past, and disturbing in terms of the scope, geographically, and the types that we have seen."⁴⁹ The organization has attributed the rise in these hate crimes to the rhetoric of Trump, especially his rhetoric regarding China and North Korea. Yang also stated: "Asian Americans are viewed as foreigners oftentimes, even if they are 100 percent American citizens, and do everything that so-called normal Americans do."⁵⁰ A common thread among a number of hate crime attacks since 2016 has been anti-immigration views. This has resulted in numerous hate crimes targeting individuals who are immigrants or who are believed to be immigrants (i.e., nonwhite-looking individuals). On February 20, 2017, a man shot two Indian engineers at a bar in Kansas, killing one of them, a thirty-two-year-old man by the name of Srinivas Kuchibhotla. The attacker, Adam Purinton, had questioned the two men about whether they had entered the country illegally before he opened fire, shouting, "Get out of my country" and "terrorist." Purinton later bragged in another town to a bartender that he had shot "two Iranians."⁵¹

Then on March 3, 2017, a Sikh man by the name of Deep Rai was shot and injured outside of his home in Seattle by a man who shouted "go back to your country."⁵² Anti-immigration views are also strongly associated with an increase in hate crimes against Latinos. Since 2016, hate crimes against Latinos have increased by more than 50% in California alone.

One of the largest groups to be impacted by hate crimes are African Americans. In 2017, according to national statistics, 48.6% of hate crimes based on "race/ethnicity/ancestry" were "anti–Black or African American." This accounted for roughly 28% of all reported hate crimes that year. And while hate crimes against African Americans have been a longstanding issue in this country, civil rights organizations have noticed a difference since Trump was elected president. As discussed by the president of the Atlanta branch of the NAACP (National Association for the Advancement of Colored People), Richard Rose: "When this president campaigned, it was a campaign of division and bigotry. And so those people who believe in discrimination of any kind gravitated to that campaign. After the election, they feel emboldened to act out these statements that have racial overtones in them."⁵³ Trump's anti-immigrant rhetoric, including comments about the Caribbean and Africa, have also been considered to be a factor in the increase in hate crimes, as discussed by the president of the San Francisco branch of the NAACP: "This president has emboldened those who are perpetrators of hate with his rhetoric, his vulgarity and with his outright abusive language attacking people from Caribbean Islands and from Africa."⁵⁴

In Trump's first year of the presidency hate crimes against Native Americans increased 63%, from 154 incidents in 2016 to 251 incidents in 2017. While speculation was made on whether the increase is due to an increase in disclosure by law enforcement agencies, it is important to note that from 2013 to 2016 hate crimes against Native Americans were relatively steady. In addition, the number of victims, 321, represented a 90% increase in the number of victims from 2016.[55] The Navajo Nation Human Rights Commission held in June 2018 training sessions at Albuquerque Indian Center and City Hall to help raise awareness of hate crimes against Native Americans. The event was sparked by the killing of a homeless man, fifty-year-old Ronnie Ross, who was from the Navajo Nation town of Shiprock, by two teenagers who claimed they carried out the attack "for fun." One of the teenage boys later bragged to a friend that he shot "a hobo in the back." While the attack was not classified as a hate crime due to a lack of evidence that the crime was committed based on racial prejudice, it is just one attack in a series of homicides of homeless Navajos in Albuquerque dating back to 2014. In fact, while only 4% of Albuquerque's population is Native American, roughly 44% of their homeless are Native American and of that 44% about 75% have reported being physically assaulted.[56] Criticism has also been made that "anti–Indian" groups operate with little to no scrutiny and are not counted as hate groups. This includes groups like Citizens Equal Rights Alliance (CERA), whose mission is "to change federal Indian policies that threaten or restrict the individual rights of all citizens living on or near Indian reservations."[57] The group, which claims that tribal sovereignty for Native Americans is a "myth," has been cited by organizations like the Southern Poverty Law Center for pushing conspiracy theories like the one claiming that Agenda 21, a United Nations action plan for sustainable development, is actually a global communist plot.

Hate Groups in Trump's America

In addition to a rise in hate crimes, hate groups have been increasing under Trump, with 1,020 active hate groups in the United States, a 7% increase from 2017 to 2018. The number of hate groups currently active in the United States is at the highest number it has been in decades.[58]

One of the most visible indicators of this increase in hate groups was the Unite the Right rally in August 2017 in Charlottesville, Virginia. The Unite the Right rally essentially did just that; it united right-wing extremists (even momentarily) in a manner that has not been witnessed in the United States in decades. Not since the major law enforcement crackdown of the 1960s and 1970s, in which numerous right-wing extremist groups were infiltrated, causing a shift in tactics by the group to what notorious white supremacist Louis Beam called "leaderless resistance."[59] Right-wing extremists, including white supremacists, neo–Nazis, neo–Pagans, militia members, and more, gathered to protest the removal of a statue of Robert E. Lee and to demonstrate solidarity among white nationalist groups. The rally was truly historic, given the level of infighting that has been present in this movement for decades, with warring Klan websites, each claiming they represent the KKK and that other groups are imposters, or pro–Aryan sites that accuse one another of being corrupted by Jewish influence. What was once a movement that has been weakened and fragmented since the 1960s and 1970s has gained new life and momentum under Trump's presidency.

Overall, the largest spike in hate groups has been among white nationalist groups, which experienced a 50% increase in membership from 2017 to 2018. There is a strong belief among perpetrators of hate crimes, specifically right-wing extremists, that they are protectors, protecting their culture and a way of life that is becoming endangered. This is particularly true among white supremacists who believe that we are undergoing a white genocide or that a white genocide is coming. In their "us vs. them" view of the world, they are not criminals or even terrorists, they are heroes, saviors.

It is important to note, however, that many of these groups have continued to face disfunction even following the Unite the Right rally. Take for instance the formation of the Patriot Front (PF), a white nationalist group which broke off Vanguard America (VA) over disputes between VA's leader Dillon Irizarry and the now founder of PF, Thomas Rousseau. According to the PF's manifesto:

> The time of the Republic has passed in America as the system grows too weak to perform its duty.... The damage done to this nation and its people will not be fixed if every issue requires the approval and blessing from the dysfunctional American democratic system. Democracy has failed in this once great nation.[60]

Following the creation of the PF, infighting continued within the organization, which ultimately ended in the creation of another splinter group, the National Socialist Legion (NSL). While each group shares a similar ideology, that the United States should be solely a white Christian nation, debates over tactics appear to have been one of the causes for the splintering. The VA and PF have disagreed over the effectiveness of public rallies and demonstrations, while the NSL has vowed to set up cells throughout the country "for future white migration and eventual white revolt and secession."

Another set of hate groups that have increased under Trump are militias. The ideas that identify and the social processes that unite organizations can be far more paranoid than their members. The militias demonstrate how unexceptional personal beliefs can be carried to paranoid lengths under the stimulation of a paranoid organization. The right to bear arms is a constitutional right upheld by the courts and adhered to by mainstream political groups. For many of the most active militia members, the advocacy of these established liberties reaches paranoid lengths. There are two themes that militias share: a strong belief in the right to bear firearms and collective paranoia. This phenomenon of paranoia among militia groups can be witnessed today in what has been referred to as "caravan paranoia," which has been running rampant through the border militia movement. "Caravan paranoia" includes beliefs that the members of so-called immigrant "caravans" are really Islamic militants or were secretly trained by the United Nations. Others believe that the caravan is being funded by Jews such as billionaire George Soros.[61] On April 20, 2019, the FBI arrested the commander of a militia group, the United Constitutional Patriots, that was detaining migrants along the border in New Mexico. The commander, Larry Mitchell Hopkins, who calls himself Johnny Horton Jr., has continually spread conspiracy theories about caravans, and in 2018 posted a message on his Facebook page predicting his death, in which he wrote, "i am going to the border when i know the enemy is close to the border, i am going to fight . . . i may give my life . . . if they get me now at least i will die for our country and what keeping America free is all about, GOD WILL GUIDE AND PROTECT ME."[62] The United Constitutional Patriots has been active on Facebook since February 2016, during which time they asked for donations through PayPal and GoFundMe, raising roughly $5,000. The GoFundMe page read: "We are raising money to help finance the various Patriot groups who have volunteered to go to the U.S. Border to help the Border Patrol in securing the Border before the invasion happens. We are doing this by assisting in fuel cards, food and water and various other supplies that are needed. Please give what you can, no amount is too small or too large." According to Horton, the group has detained over 3,500 migrants, of which he claims most were children being trafficked. According to a spokesman for the group, Jim Benvie, they have been camping by the border near El Paso for two months. Benvie defended the group's actions, stating these detentions are "a verbal citizen's arrest" and that the group is there "to support the Border Patrol and show the public the reality of the border."[63]

In addition to a rise in right-wing extremist groups, other hate groups have risen under Donald Trump. This includes a rise in black nationalist organizations that are largely anti–Semitic and anti–LGBTQ, which increased from 233 in 2017 to 264 in 2018. According to the Southern Poverty Law Center, these groups include the Nation of Islam and the New Black Panther Party. In 2018 on the New Black Panther Party podcast, Samir Shabazz, the party's deputy field marshal and minister of defense for the Black Riders Liberation Party, stated: "The white man is the devil. Let's get right down to business. In 2018, any negro coon lips and dares say all white people aren't bad should be sent to a psychiatric hospital and diagnosed with slavery syndrome or you should do the inevitable to yourself."[64] While most of these groups are anti–Trump, leaders like Nation of Islam's Louis Farrakhan have made statements defending some of Trump's actions. Although Farrakhan stated in 2016 that "if Donald Trump becomes president, he will take America into the abyss of hell," he has also offered praise for him. Following Trump's meeting with the Jewish Republican Coalition, Farrakhan stated, "I like what I'm looking at," in reference to Trump saying to Jewish donors, "I don't want your money." In a tweet from May 2018 Farrakhan wrote: "Mr. Trump is destroying every enemy that was an enemy of our rise. Who is the enemy of our rise? Is it the Department of Justice where we get none? Is it Congress where you make a law that favors us and then you turn around and destroy it?"[65] The praise Trump has received by individuals like Farrakhan is eerily similar to the praise he has received from right-wing extremists, including white supremacists, who believe that Trump, like them, is an anti–Semite.

Trump's Reponses to Hate Crimes

For decades, Trump has denied claims that he is racist. During the 2016 presidential campaign, Trump defended himself against racist allegations while also defending the controversial statements he had made about Latinos and immigrants by stating: "I will never apologize for pledging to enforce and uphold every single law of the United States, and to make my immigration priority defending and protecting American citizens above every other single consideration."[66] In

January 2018, following allegations that he referred to certain African countries as "shithole" countries, Trump told reporters: "I am not a racist. I'm the least racist person you have ever interviewed."[67] Trump's children have also come to his defense, including Eric Trump, who has described his father as "the least racist person" he has ever met. Dr. Ben Carson, secretary of housing and urban development, has made a similar claim about Trump on Fox News:

> There is a narrative that's being painted there, but I've had an opportunity to interact with racist people throughout my life. And he is not one . . . And I talked with him early on about the plight of many people, particularly in the inner city, and the compassion that he showed is very impressive. But he doesn't wear it on his sleeve . . . And he doesn't go around playing identity politics. He says, let's just fix this so everybody does well.[68]

White House press secretary Sarah Huckabee Sanders has also defended Trump against allegations of racism, once referring to his hosting *The Apprentice*: "Frankly, if the critics of the president were who he said he was, why did NBC give him a show for a decade on TV?"[69]

Despite numerous attempts to defend himself against allegations of racism, Trump has also come under heavy criticism for his response to hate crimes in the United States. Trump's response to the Unite the Right rally, and the death of Heather Heyer by self-identified white supremacist James Alex Fields Jr., was viewed as defending the actions of the right-wing extremists. Trump had told reporters, "I think there is blame on both sides. You had some very bad people in that group. But you also had people that were very fine people, on both sides."[70] Trump's response to the Pittsburgh synagogue shooting also drew criticism as being "victim blaming" when he stated that the attack wouldn't have happened if the synagogue had had an armed guard.[71] While Trump's responses to hate crimes have been received with less than positive reactions, he did, however, sign into law in October 2018 the Protecting Religiously Affiliated Institutions Act, which expands current hate crime protections to religious institutions. The passing of the law, which had strong bipartisan support, was received with praise. Jason Isaacson, the associate executive director for policy of the American Jewish Committee, stated, "This important law, which provides for new and strengthened measures to deter, as well as punish, perpetrators of attacks on religious institutions, will provide a much-needed sense of comfort and security."[72]

Even when Trump specifically has been cited as an inspiration for hate crime attacks, especially against individuals perceived to be illegal immigrants, his responses have been highly questionable. In August 2015, two men attacked a homeless man they believed to be an illegal immigrant, later telling police: "Donald Trump was right. All these illegals need to be deported." Trump's initial response to the attack was: "I will say, the people that are following me are very passionate. They love this country, they want this country to be great again." However, he would later call the attack "terrible."[73]

Hate Crime Hoax Theories

As hate crimes increase in the United States, so does the belief that most hate crimes are in fact hoaxes. In his 2019 book *Hate Crime Hoax: How the Left is Selling a Fake Race War*, Wilfred Reilly, who describes himself as a "proud black man," argues that only hate crime hoaxes are increasing, not actual hate crimes. Reilly categorizes what he believes to be different types of hate crime hoaxes, one of which he refers to as "'Klan Springs Eternal' (KSE)," in which he writes that KSE hoaxes "involve POC falsely claiming to have been attacked by one or more Caucasian racists in order to conceal their own criminal behavior or mental illness. . . . According to the same Fake Hate Crimes website that I used to calculate the number and frequency of fake collegiate hate crime reports, there have been ninety recent nationally reported hate crime hoaxes involving African Americans and an additional eight involving Hispanics—essentially all of which fell into the KSE category."[74] Reilly's book represents the underlying belief behind hate crime hoax theories, in that hate crimes are largely fabricated by individuals or groups in order to further a personal or political cause.

Hate crime hoax theories largely take root in paranoia. Numerous conservative, right-wing, and alt-right news sources and websites that promote the hate crime hoax theory argue that most hate crimes, which they believe are hoaxes, are an attempt from the left to push their own agenda while suppressing the right. According to the far-right website, *The New American*, "Since the election of Donald Trump, reports of fake hate crimes, meant to make both Trump and his supporters look bad, have increased. The spotlight that the media have given to these made-up hate crimes has helped to reinforce a belief that hate in America is on the rise under Trump."[75] The *American Renaissance*, a white supremacist online publication, features a Hate Hoax Map webpage with an interactive map of the United States. The page includes instances of proven hate crime hoaxes, as well as hate crimes that authors of the page believe are hoaxes. The page states:

> We have done an analysis of recent hate-crime hoaxes with a particular concentration on the period beginning June 2015—the month Donald Trump announced his candidacy—and ending December 2017. We believe there were enough hoaxes in that two-and-a-half year period to provide what we believe are representative data.

The page's "findings" include:

> A few "progressives," for example, have drawn swastikas or written racial slurs in the hope of evoking sympathy for nonwhites or to justify increased anti-racist activity.
>
> Eighty-nine percent of hoaxers tried to convey the false appearance of racial or—in the case of Muslims and Jews—a religious/ethnic bias.
>
> Middle Easterners, at 69 times the white rate, were the group most likely to fabricate hoaxes of this kind, and Hispanics were almost twice as likely as whites to be hoaxers.
>
> Many incidents officially reported to the FBI as hate crimes are never solved because the perpetrator is never identified. A certain number of unsolved hate crimes are likely to be hoaxes like the incidents described in detail in our interactive map.[76]

Numerous conservative and alt-right news outlets have reported similar conspiracy theories regarding hate crime hoaxes. For instance, the conservative website, the *American Spectator*, posted an article on April 1, 2019, titled, "A Real Epidemic of Fake Hate." The author, Robert Stacy McCain, wrote:

> When "a self-described fat-queer activist" claimed on Facebook that her girlfriend "was attacked by 'two young white men' in a maroon SUV"? Portland police don't even have a record of a report

for such an incident, according to Ngo. The good news, then, is that Portland's LGBT community has no reason to fear they're being targeted by an epidemic of hate crimes, but the bad news is, some activists are apparently willing to invent such incidents to support the Left's narrative that President Trump's election has unleashed the forces of "hate." . . . Such hoaxes are self-evidently intended for political propaganda purposes.[77]

Trump's son, Donald Jr., himself has stated on *Fox & Friends*: "There were many more hoax hate crimes than there were actual . . . the problem is, those hate crimes do still exist, racism is still a real problem in this country . . . But it's not the problem for everything, every grievance that you have . . . And so what happens is these things really do a disservice from people who are truly afflicted by this . . . Every grievance, everything that you can't combat with facts, it's 'oh, racist!' It's the easy button for the left, and it's not fair and it's not right."[78]

The perpetuation of the hate crime hoax theory was further fueled in 2019, surrounding the controversy over actor Jussie Smollett. On January 29, Smollett reported to Chicago police that he was attacked by two people who were "yelling out racial and homophobic slurs" and "poured an unknown chemical substance on the victim." As investigations took place into the alleged attack, speculation began to emerge that it had been staged by Smollett himself. Then on February 22, Smollett was indicted for disorderly conduct, alleging that he had paid two brothers from Nigeria to stage a fake hate crime against him. On March 26, all charges against Smollett were dropped, sparking public outrage, as well as causing the FBI to announce the following day an investigation into why the charges were dropped. Regardless of whether Smollett had indeed staged the attack or not, the high-profile case has become a focal point for hate crime hoax theorists. Trump himself has stated: "I think the case in Chicago is an absolute embarrassment to our country and I have asked that it be—that they look at it." He also tweeted: "FBI & DOJ to review the outrageous Jussie Smollett case in Chicago. It is an embarrassment to our Nation!"[79]

It is important to note that the hate crime hoax theory is also used by right-wing extremist groups to support their belief that a "white genocide" is taking place and "so-called" hate crimes are actually an attempt to suppress the white and Christian communities in the United States. In a January 15, 2017, post by the Knights Party's spokeswoman Rachel Pendergraft, she writes:

> It's sickening to see the many politicians, queer lobbies, new age churches, and so-called community leaders scurrying around trying to profit from the young homosexual man's death in Wyoming. It seems they are almost in a sort of competition. Who can express outrage the loudest, who can have the biggest candle light vigil, who can get the first piece of hate speech legislation passed?
>
> Have you noticed who is attempting to destroy the First Amendment? Homosexual groups—minority groups—left wing women's groups—communist groups—Jewish groups. They are, without apology, attempting to silence the protests of the white Christian middle-class. They are quite good at it. All of these anti–Christian groups yield tremendous influence over our governmental leaders and billions are spent to insure that anti–Christian legislation is passed.[80]

The "young homosexual man" to whom Pendergraft is referring in her post is Matthew Shepard, who was beaten, tortured, and left to die by two men in an anti–LGBTQA attack in 1998. Pendergraft continues:

> The proposed hate crime legislation isn't about protecting gay people or minority people. It is about silencing the protests by the Christian middle-class against the politicians. The politicians know they must have a boogey man to protect their special interest groups from and the special interest groups in turn continue their legal bribery via the crooked lobby system. They are both rubbing each others backs and white Christian America is getting squeezed out.[81]

Hate crime hoax theories have a deep-seated root in white supremacy in the United States.

Anti-Trump Hate Crimes?

In addition to the proliferation of hate crime hoax theories, there is also a proliferation in the belief that while hate crimes are not occurring against minority groups, they are occurring against Trump supporters. The *American Renaissance* white supremacist online publication—while denying most hate crimes based on race, ethnicity, sexual orientation, and religion—does feature a map claiming there are hate crimes in the United States based on someone's politician affiliation. This is their Anti-Trump Hate Map. The page containing the interactive map, similar to their Hate Hoax Map, reads, "The Anti-Trump Hate Map is an ongoing project of *American Renaissance* that displays criminal incidents in which Trump supporters were targeted for political reasons. Each marker on the map shows the location of an anti–Trump hate crime."[82]

It is important to note that there have been several cases in which individuals wearing Make America Great Again (MAGA) hats were assaulted. This trend of attacks against individuals wearing MAGA hats was noted by Brian Levin, the director of the Center for the Study of Hate and Extremism at California State University San Bernardino. In an interview with *Newsweek*, Levin stated: "We have a polarized, racially, political infused landscape—this kind of conflict now bleeds over. Unfortunately, we expect to see more of this. We believe that white nationalists and far-right extremists represent the most prominent extremism threats. At a time of intense division, as well as the accession of euro or white nationalism, you're going to get these retaliatory movements to arise as well, even though white nationalism is broadly dispersed and has the most followers."[83] Attacks on individuals wearing MAGA hats include the assault of an elderly man in New Jersey on February 25, 2019, as well as the assault and robbery on April 13, 2019, of an immigrant from Togo who was wearing a MAGA hat in Germantown, Maryland.

While there has been a slight rise in attacks against Trump supporters, the response from Trump's base, the belief that most hate crime against minorities are hoaxes and attacks against Trump supporters are real, is reminiscent of the decades-old white supremacist belief that only whites and Christians face hate crimes. In a post on the KKK website entitled "True Hate Crimes and the Media," Pendergraft writes:

> Blacks commit 90% of the approximately 1,700,000 interracial crimes of violence that occur in the U.S. each year ... My friends, the truth is out there and the fact is there is an ongoing race war in the country and white men, women, and children are the victims. Some mistakenly believe that acts of violence against whites are justified because of past slavery. But the raping of your wife, daughter or sister and the robbery and assault or murder of your son, brother,

father or husband has nothing to do with slavery hundreds of years ago. Blacks still enslave other Blacks in Africa, but who is most often the victim of their savagery—white families butchered by the thousands. Even now, as you are reading this, white children in any part of the world are being mauled, tortured, raped, and murdered! Ahhh—power in the hands of Negroes—Isn't equality great?[84]

This highlights the white supremacist belief that most hate crimes are in fact committed against whites by blacks and that what is reported in mainstream media as hate crime is a fabrication by the Jews to control the white and Christian populations.

Trump, Not Enough

While Trump has received an overwhelming level of support from right-wing extremists in the United States, there has been a contingent of those within the community who opposed Trump. One of the most notable right-wing extremists who have opposed Trump is Robert Gregory Bowers, who carried out the Tree of Life synagogue shooting in Pittsburgh on October 27, 2018. The anti–Semitic attack that cost the lives of eleven Jews took place because Bowers believed Jews were responsible for immigration issues, most notably the immigrant caravans. Prior to the attack he continually posted hateful comments about the Hebrew Immigrant Aid Society (HIAS), a Jewish nonprofit that began in the late 1880s to assist Jewish refugees, and which has since helped to resettle over 4.5 million refugees and immigrants from countless countries. On the social media platform Gab, Bowers wrote: "HIAS likes to bring invaders in that kill our people. I can't sit by and watch my people get slaughtered. Screw your optics, I'm going in."[85] In another post he wrote: "They're committing genocide to my people. I just want to kill Jews."[86] Bowers also believed that Trump was controlled by Jews. In one post he used an anti–Semitic trope for Trump, "globalist," writing: "Trump is a globalist, not a nationalist. There is no #MAGA as long as there is a kike infestation. #Qanon is here to get patriots that were against martial law in the 90's to be the ones begging for it now to drain muh swamp. But go ahead and keep saying you are #Winning."[87] While many white supremacists have followed and supported Trump, for some, he has not done or has not been radical enough.

A number of right-wing extremists have also become increasingly disillusioned by the president they believed would be their champion and savior. Even David Duke has been upset with Trump for not being radical enough. Following a tweet in August 2017, in which Trump wrote, "We ALL must be united & condemn all that hate stands for. There is no place for this kind of violence in America. Lets come together as one!," Duke tweeted, "I would recommend you take a good look in the mirror & remember it was White Americans who put you in the presidency, not radical leftists."[88] This disillusionment became much more apparent around the 2018 midterm elections. The pro–Trump and right-wing men's empowerment blogger Mike Cernovich tweeted in September 2018, "There's no Wall. She's not locked up. But Flynn got fired and sent to wolves. And Sauadi [sic] Arabia sold weapons of murder. I give zero f-cks about Republicans losing the House." Anti-Semitic writer Kevin MacDonald tweeted on November 15, 2018, "Starting to feel swindled by @realDonaldTrump. He will get slaughtered in 2020 unless he does something serious for his base on immigration."[89] And most notably was his loss of support from one of his biggest champions in the white supremacy community, Richard Spencer. Spencer announced to his followers on November 19, 2018, "The Trump moment is over, and it's time for us to move on."

Hate groups like Identity Evropa also expressed anger over Trump's handling of immigration. Group leader, Patrick Casey, said in an interview:

> We don't believe America needs to be 100.00 percent white, but we do think that America isn't going to be America if there isn't a European-American super-majority. So when it comes to policies and so forth we're concerned with reversing these trends. We want to end immigration for the time being. And in the future we would like to have immigration policies that favor high-skilled immigrants from, you know, Europe, Canada, Australia, and so forth. And we also do want to have programs of re-migration wherein people who feel more of a connection to another part of the world, another race, another culture, even another religion in the case of Islam can return to their native homelands essentially.

Twitter pages for various Identity Evropa chapters, such as the one in Massachusetts, continually post articles on immigration in the United States with hashtags like #TrumpAmnesty and #AmnestyDon. In response to one of Trump's tweets from 2017 that read: "Does anybody really want to throw out good, educated and accomplished young people who have jobs, some serving in the military? Really!" The Identity Evropa Twitter page retweeted, stating: "Yes. It's the main reason you were elected. #AmnestyDon #DACADeal #TrumpAmnesty #NoAmnesty."[90] Organizations such as these are clearly dissatisfied with Trump for a number of reasons, including their belief that he has not taken a strong enough stance against immigration. In fact, in October 2018, news stories emerged that Casey and members of Identity Evropa were working to infiltrate the GOP. During an interview with NBC News, Casey even stated that the group's mission is: "to take over the GOP as much as possible."[91] The group, however, was forced to rebrand itself to the American Identity Movement following the March 2019 leak of hundreds of thousands of the group's messages on the platform Discord.

Disillusionment with Trump has also promoted an almost pre-apocalyptic belief by white supremacists that Trump's presidency was the movement's last chance for working within mainstream politics. In response to the 2018 midterm elections, Greg Johnson wrote on the white nationalist website, Counter-Currents:

> We should know by now that we can't depend upon Republicans. And Trump himself is at best on probation. We can only depend on ourselves. . . . Trump is not the last chance for the white race in North America. He is merely the last chance to save the present American system. He is their last chance, not ours. But the establishment is too stupid to realize that, so they want him gone. A lot of them want him dead. By opposing him, they only hasten their own end.[92]

While apocalyptic predictions are not new to the right wing, especially given various beliefs of secret race wars or a "white genocide," the responses some groups have had toward Trump's presidency are somewhat alarming. With many claiming that it is now impossible to work within "the present American system," it is unclear what actions, especially possible violent actions, these individuals or groups may take to further their causes. And what will the right-wing extremist response be in 2020 if Trump loses the election?

12

The Unexpected Followers

Women, minorities, and millennials are almost always characterized as Democrats. And while in all three cases, a majority, even an overwhelming majority, vote Democrat and voted for Hillary Clinton, Trump has been able to carve out a small sect of supporters from each group. So, who are these unexpected supporters and why are they drawn to Trump?

Women for Trump

At a press conference in September 2018, Trump claimed: "You know, I got 52% with women. Everybody said this couldn't happen—52%." However, this statistic is flawed. Trump did not receive 52% of the female vote nor did he receive 52% of the white female vote.[1] While an initial 2016 exit poll survey predicted that he would receive 52% of the female white vote, an analysis conducted by the Pew Research Center found that 47% of white women voted for Trump as opposed to 45% who voted for Clinton. Overall, Trump received closer to 40% of the female vote as opposed to Clinton, who received over 50% of the vote. The largest percentage of women who voted for Trump were white women without college degrees, at 62%. Studies showed many of these women voted on their fears, especially economic fears. The second largest percentage of women who voted for Trump were white women with college degrees, of which 45% voted for him.²

In many cases women voted for Trump for similar reasons as men. As stated by Desiree Zapata Miller, an immigrant from Honduras, in a *Charlotte Observer* column from November 2018 titled, "Why Women Like Me Support Donald Trump":

> I am often questioned about how, as a woman, I could possibly support President Trump. My response is, "Why wouldn't I?" Millions of women support Trump. See for yourself at any Trump rally . . . Republican women focus first on principles, values, and issues. We recognize most Americans agree on certain universal desires and needs, regardless of political affiliation, gender, age, religious affiliation or sexual orientation. We want access to good schools and education for our kids. We want good paying jobs that assure self-sufficiency and income to take care of our families. We want access to quality and timely health care that will not put us in debt and for which we don't have to wait for weeks or months as is the case in single-payer health systems. We want to live in clean and safe neighborhoods.³

In an interview conducted by Caitríona Perry, author of *In America: Tales from Trump Country*, Debbie Elam, a member of the Republican Women of Powhatan County, stated, "My husband and I own a small business and we know there's a lot of challenges with small business and if he has been able to be successful in his career then I think if the country was run more accountable then we may have a better economy as a result."⁴ Another woman, Ann Tackett, the wife of a police officer, stated, "As a woman, I don't know how you could support Hillary Clinton. I'm pro-life, I have children, small children that are in public schools. They don't necessarily always feel safe and I feel that he can bring back some of the order that is missing and that has changed in the last eight years. I'm looking forward to the repeal of the Obamacare that has killed our small businesses. I'm pro-police, and I feel that he is as well."⁵

In Spring 2016, the super PAC, Women Vote Trump, was founded by Kathryn Serkes, Amy Kremer, and Ann Stone. It became the fourth super PAC supporting Trump, despite his claimed denunciation of PACs. Kathryn

Serkes, who also cofounded the Doctor Patient Medical Association, a group that aimed to repeal the Affordable Care Act, stated: "There are so many ad hoc groups of women who back Trump, and what we want to do is harness their energy and give them a home."[6] Among the other cofounders, Kremer is described on the Women Vote Trump website as "one of the founding mothers of the modern day tea party movement," and Stone is the ex-wife of Trump friend and confidant Roger Stone.[7] While the group's initial goal was to help elect Trump, they now work to help support Trump's presidential agenda. According to the group's website:

WOMEN VOTED SMART.
WOMEN VOTED TRUMP.

"They" said that women don't support Donald Trump. "They" said he isn't good for women or our families. "They" said we were supposed to vote for Hillary Clinton because we share the same body parts.

BUT "THEY" WERE WRONG!

There are millions of women who support Donald Trump and we're not standing in the shadows anymore! We won't be pushed around by bullies who tell us who we are "supposed" to like. And we're not going to keep quiet now that he has been elected![8]

The website also includes a pledge for women to sign in support of Trump:

SHOW PRESIDENT TRUMP WE HAVE HIS BACK. Sign the pledge of support:

I support President Trump because . . .
- He thinks outside the box and tells it like it is . . . he's genuine and I think that's a breath of fresh air;
- He has the brains, drive and determination to be successful;
- He takes action, and gets things done in the real world;
- He will keep my family safe from outside threats & illegal immigration;

- And I know he's shaking up the status quo in Washington and putting our country ahead of partisan politics.

He's exactly what our country needs!

Their "Next Steps to *Make America Great Again!*" include: supporting Trump's agenda; help elect new leaders and "drain the swamp"; and "exercise the power of the women's vote."⁹

Minorities for Trump

On September 9, 2016, during a speech in Washington, D.C., Trump stated:

> The African American community has heard my message that I am going to make the inner cities safe again, and I'm going to bring back jobs, and I'm going to bring back the great education. Don't be surprised—because we have been given a lot of support over the last three to four weeks—if on November 8th, I get more African American and Hispanic votes than anyone thought possible about a month ago.

However, in 2016, the black voter turnout rate declined by nearly 7% since 2012. This was the first time the turnout rate has declined in almost twenty years. However, of the 59.6% of black Americans who voted in 2016, less than 10% voted for Trump. And of that amount, over 10% of black men voted for Trump, while less than 5% of black women voted for Trump. Some 2018 polls, however, have shown that Trump's support among black Americans is increasing marginally.¹⁰ While the number of black supporters for Trump are marginal, he has had a number of rather vocal supporters. This includes sister vloggers (video bloggers) Lynnette Hardaway and Rochelle Richardson, commonly known as Diamond and Silk. Diamond and Silk, who were Democrats, say they became Republicans after Trump announced he was running for president. According to Diamond: "When he announced and we heard everything that he stood for, it was on and poppin', and we've been on the Trump train ever since."¹¹ In 2015, they also started their Ditch and Switch Now movement to encourage other Democrats to become Republicans and vote for Trump. According to their website: "While some of our supporters may be surprised to see two American (black) women voicing their opinions about these issues, it's not a racial or cultural thing. It's about doing the right thing when it comes to 'We the American People!'"[12] Since 2015, the two have received a fair amount of news coverage, attending pro–Trump events and due to a controversy with Facebook, eventually becoming contributors on Fox Nation. The two sisters have received a fair amount of criticism and have even been accused of being con artists.

Questions and controversy surrounding black support for Trump was renewed during former Trump lawyer Michael Cohen's hearing before Congress. During his testimony, Cohen claimed Trump was "a racist" who had once said that "black people are too stupid to vote for me."[13] While Cohen provided numerous racist statements that Trump reportedly made to him, another controversy surrounded North Carolina's representative Mark Meadows's decision to invite Lynne Patton. Patton, a black woman, previously worked for the Trump family and now serves as the administrator of the United States Department of Housing and Urban Development for Region II. Patton stood next to Meadows, who defended Trump against Cohen's claims of racism, explaining that Patton would have never worked for a racist. Meadows's decision to have Patton at the hearing drew criticism from other Congressional members, including Representative Rashida Tlaib, who stated: "Just because someone has a person of color, a black person working for them, does not mean they aren't racist. And it is insensitive that someone would . . . actually use a prop, a black woman, in this chamber, in this committee is alone racist in itself."[14] However, in the days that followed, criticism of Meadows and Patton's appearance during the testimony drew considerable backlash. Patton herself posted on social media: "I'm highly educated. I'm not a racist. I'm not low-info. I'm a professional. I'm not brainwashed. I'm not part of a 'cult'. I don't live in a bunker. I hate political correctness. I'm a leader—not a follower. I believe we need a big change. I don't blindly believe the liberal media. I'm tired of politicians who lie & cheat. I support Donald Trump."[15] Then, in a letter to the editor of *USA Today*, Dr. Carol Swain, a black supporter of Trump and host of the podcast "Be the People," wrote:

> Tlaib, a Michigan Democrat, was asked to explain herself by her fellow Democrat, committee Chairman Elijah Cummings, after she

called Patton (a black woman) a "token" and said it was "racist" for Republican Rep. Mark Meadows to invite her to the hearing. Wow!

Then, the left doubled down with more racist attacks. In his column, "Bad move parading black woman to defend Trump," Bennie Ivory argues that Patton's presence was "an obscenely insulting and surreal scene reminiscent of . . . when slaves were put on display on the auction block for inspection." Ivory complains that Patton "stood silently," but neglects to mention that committee rules prevented Patton from speaking.

To the left's race baiters, "racism" is an indefinable yet ever-present specter lurking at the edge of any political debate . . . Racism is alive and well in America, as we saw from Tlaib's baseless attack on a black conservative woman. We can do better in America. We must hold the Democrats to the same standards they apply to Republicans.[16]

Fox Nation hosts Diamond and Silk also called for Representative Tlaib to resign over her remarks.

During a phone call with the president of Mexico Enrique Peña Nieto on January 27, 2017, Trump said, "In the latest election, I won with a large percentage of Hispanic voters. I do not know if you heard, but with Cuba, I had 84 percent, with the Cuban American vote."[17] However, despite Trump's claim, estimates have shown that the Cuban American vote for Trump was closer to 50% and roughly only a third of the entire Latino population voted for him. An area where Trump received a higher percentage of Latino support was in the Cuban American community in Florida, in which 54% voted for him. As discussed by Juan Fiol, who was born in the U.S. to Cuban refugees and was the vice chairman of Miami-Dade County for Trump, "We are not interested in ethnic politics. The media tries to divide people into groups. I am here—we are here because we are Americans first."[18] In September 2018 Trump appointed Mauricio Claver-Carone, a Cuban American lawyer who has served as a close adviser regarding Cuba, to be the new head of western hemisphere affairs on the National Security Council. Claver-Carone, the former executive director of the U.S.–Cuba Democracy PAC, had once reportedly called himself a "Never Trump" Republican when he supported Marco Rubio during the 2016 GOP presidential primary.

In addition to the difference seen between Cuban and non–Cuban Latino voters, another factor that has been noted to make a difference in voting Republican is that nearly a quarter of Latino voters identify as evangelicals. On January 25, 2019, Trump, along with Mike Pence and former secretary of homeland security Kirstjen Nielsen, hosted a roundtable with "Hispanic pastors" whereby he was presented a letter "from 150 Hispanic evangelical leaders, simply saying an expression of gratitude for your good-faith efforts to work with Democrats and try to get everyone to the table to get things moving again." According to the roundtable transcript on the White House website, the pastors in attendance praised Trump, especially in his handling of border security:

> Pastor Pena: One thing you have not done, Mr. President, is manufacture a humanitarian crisis. It's real.
>
> Pastor Norma Urrabazo: . . . I heard a briefing that you were doing . . . about border security and also the humanitarian crisis . . . And I was like, do the American people hear the statistics that the President is saying? . . . what our reality is? . . . I started praying, "Lord, let America have this truth encounter."
>
> Pastor Maldonado: You know, there's misconception in the public, thinking that Spanish community is for illegal immigration . . . also that we want open borders . . . And that . . . they want no laws, that's not true.
>
> Pastor Bramnick: . . . from the times I've had the honor to meet you, I know you have a compassion for the Hispanic people.
>
> Ms. Aguirre: The media gives a major misconception of the Hispanic community . . . I can emphatically say your values stand aligned to the Hispanic community.[19]

Other factors that split Latino votes include whether or not the individual was foreign-born or born in the United States. Gender was also a small factor, with 61% of Latino men voting Democratic in comparison to 69% of Latino women.

In February 2016, the organization Gays for Trump was formed. According to the organization's Facebook page, which has over 2,500 members, Gays for Trump is for "anyone who is Tired of just voting Democrat because they are pro gay... its Time to join a party that has had gays in it the whole time and a party that can make America Great again. Trump is not against the gays like other people. So if you are Gay, Straight, Bi, and all that other stuff and you like Trump JOIN!"[20] The Facebook group also highlights the following quote from Trump: "We need to protect all Americans, of all backgrounds and all beliefs, from Radical Islamic Terrorism—which has no place in an open and tolerant society. Radical Islam advocates hate for women, gays, Jews, Christians and all Americans. I am going to be a President for all Americans, and I am going to protect and defend all Americans. We are going to make America safe again and great again for everyone."[21] Some of Trump's supporters in the LGBTQA community believed that Trump was the better candidate for the community than Clinton. As discussed in an interview with CNN, Chris Barron, the former president of the gay conservative group GOProud and former Trump critic but now supporter, said:

> I have no doubt that Donald Trump would be better for LGBT Americans. Hillary Clinton wants to continue a reckless foreign policy that has made the world less safe for all Americans, including LGBT Americans. She can find plenty of time to crucify Christians in the U.S. for perceived anti-gay bias, but when we've got ISIS throwing gay people off of buildings, when we have Muslim states that are prescribing the death penalty for people who are gay, I would think this would be something that a friend of the LGBT community would be able to speak out on, and Hillary Clinton finds it unable to do so.[22]

Once Trump was elected, Gays for Trump celebrated his inauguration with an Inaugural Deploraball. The theme of having a "deploraball" was inspired by Hillary Clinton's use of the term "deplorable" in describing Trump's supporters, and many of Trump's supporters have come to associate themselves with the term as an act of defiance. One of the attendees of the event was also wearing a mask of Pepe the Frog, a fictional character that has become a symbol for Trump supporters who self-identify as "deplorable." When attendees of the event were asked about their views regarding Mike Pence's stance on gay marriage, Andy Barr from Seattle stated: "He will not be the executive. Let's give Mr. Pence the benefit of the doubt. We saw Mr. Trump holding the LGBT flag. Let's see how it goes in the future." Peter Boykin, president of Gays for Trump, agreed, stating that "people can grow" before also explaining that he has had "Gays for Pence" trademarked.[23]

Trump has also found supporters among religious minorities. While figures surrounding the number of Muslims who support Trump are unclear, a few studies have projected the percentage to be around 10%. In an interview with the BBC, Muslim Trump supporter Mike Hacham stated, "The moment I thought he was you know, capable of becoming president was when I attended his first rally. The atmosphere, you know, just the energy in the crowd, was amazing and you could just feel like this guy was talking to you like he knows you."[24] While in the *Washington Post* opinion piece "I'm a Muslim, A Woman and an Immigrant. I voted for Trump," Asra Q. Nomani, cofounder of the Muslim Reform Movement, wrote:

> . . . as a liberal Muslim who has experienced, first-hand, Islamic extremism in this world, I have been opposed to the decision by President Obama and the Democratic Party to tap dance around the "*Islam*" in Islamic State. Of course, Trump's rhetoric has been far more than indelicate and folks can have policy differences with his recommendations, but, to me, it has been exaggerated and demonized by the governments of Qatar and Saudi Arabia, their media channels, such as Al Jazeera, and their proxies in the West, in a convenient distraction from the issue that most worries me as a human being on this earth: extremist Islam of the kind that has spilled blood from the hallways of the Taj Mahal hotel in Mumbai to the dance floor of the Pulse nightclub in Orlando, Fla.[25]

In its most recent poll, the Institute for Social Policy and Understanding found that 13% of American Muslims approve of the way that Donald Trump is handling his job as president.

In 2016, less than a quarter of Jewish Americans voted for Donald Trump. The Republican Jewish Coalition (RJC) has praised a number of Trump's policy decisions, including the moving of the U.S. Embassy to Jerusalem. However, during his presidential campaign the RJC was wary of Trump, especially following the 2015 RJC candidate forum, in which Trump stated to a Jewish audience that he was "a negotiator like you." Some viewed it as an anti–Semitic trope and only nine of the RJC's fifty-five board members donated to his campaign.[26] In March 2019 on *Fox & Friends*, Trump claimed that "Jewish people are leaving the Democratic Party."[27] However, some studies and polls have shown that Jewish support for Trump is decreasing. In an exit poll following the 2018 midterm elections, it was reported that 72% of Jewish Americans blamed Trump's rhetoric for increasing anti–Semitism and for playing a role in the Pittsburgh shooting. According to the Jewish Democratic Council of America: "Republicans have lost support among Jewish voters since President Trump took office. According to exit polling, support for Trump among the Jewish electorate in 2016 was 24 percent, while support for Republicans among Jewish voters in 2018 fell to 17 percent."[28]

Millennials for Trump

There is an overwhelming misunderstanding that all millennials are liberals. And while a good portion of millennials identify as liberal and voted for Hillary Clinton, a percentage of millennials did in fact vote for Trump. In a survey by the University of Massachusetts Lowell's Center for Public Opinion, they found that of Americans aged eighteen to thirty-seven, 62% disapproved of Trump's performance, while 37% viewed him favorably. According to an analysis conducted by the Center for Information & Research on Civic Learning and Engagement, the major findings for millennial Trump voters were as follows: 57% are men; 84% are white (non–Hispanic); 39% are Protestant (with 21% being Catholic and 23% not affiliated with a religion). In comparison to millennial Clinton supporters, millennial Trump supporters: had a on average higher household income; were less experienced with various types of political engagement; were less likely to be politically engaged whether by volunteering for a campaign or attending a rally; and were slightly less likely to have completed college. One of the starkest differences among millennial supporters was the difference between urban and rural voters. While, according to exit polls, roughly 55% of voters under the age of thirty around the country voted for Clinton, 53% of rural voters under thirty voted for Trump.[29]

Millennials support Trump for many of the reasons discussed in previous chapters. Take, for example, gun rights. During an NRA convention, in which

Trump spoke, Ty Smith, a college student from north Georgia, stated: "I would do anything for this man," and "For me, I feel like he's fighting for me." Smith had help organize students to vote for Trump on his college campus. In fact, Ty was not alone in his attempt to sway college votes for Trump. In 2015, two college students at Campbell University in North Carolina, Ryan Fournier and John Lambert, started the organization Students for Trump (S4T). The organization recruited and trained college students, and even high school students, from across the country to serve as campus ambassadors at their universities or high schools to host events and encourage students to vote for Trump. It was reported that the group had over five thousand volunteers in twenty-five states. One such volunteer, Brittany Brown, at the Miami University of Ohio, discussed with MSNBC her work with the organization, saying: "When Trump says we will lose our country that's not just a . . . I mean maybe he is being a little extreme, but to be quite honest it's just going to get so much worse. And a great analogy is that the world is made up of takers and makers and if you get too many takers on this side it won't balance. Trump is a man who is a maker and he empowers others to be makers."[30] Brown and two of her friends, who were filmed at a rally in Ohio, described Trump as "very entertaining" and smiled as they said that the crowd was "very rowdy."[31] Trump has received praise from another student organization, Students for Life, a pro-life organization.

Trump and His Unexpected Followers

Trump once claimed during a rally in Iowa in January 2016: "I could stand in the middle of Fifth Avenue and shoot somebody and wouldn't lose any voters, okay? It's, like, incredible."[32] This statement accurately describes the charismatic relationship Trump shares with his unexpected followers. Despite any sexist comments he makes, he still has women who vote for him. Despite any racist, anti–Semitic, Islamophobic, anti–LGBTA, or other hateful comments he makes, he still has minorities supporting him. For these unexpected followers, Trump provides them with a reassurance that despite what America or even their own communities expect, it is okay for them to hold conservative views. Trump's posture of total certainty is very attractive to individuals besieged by doubt, including individuals who are told they shouldn't vote Republican or support Trump because they are a woman, or because they are a millennial, or because they are black, or because they are gay, etc.

PART III

Trump's Impact

13

The Mental Health of a Nation

Trump's presidency has had a significant impact on mental health issues in the United States, among not only his non-followers, but his followers as well.

Stress

Over the past two years numerous studies have reported higher levels of stress related to Trump across a broad range of communities in the American public. Through a series of "Stress in America" surveys, the American Psychological Association has found that stress related to American politics has continued to increase since 2016. In their 2016 survey, the American Psychological Association found that 63% of respondents view the future of the country as "a significant source of stress" and 56% "say they are stressed by the current political climate."[1] These percentages have continued to increase, with, in 2018, 63% increasing to 69% and 56% increasing to 62%.[2] A similar finding was found in a 2017 survey by the American Psychiatric Association, which reported two-thirds of Americans seeing the nation's future as a "very or somewhat significant source of stress." Groups that have specifically experienced higher levels of stress include women, minorities, and LGBT communities.

According to Dr. Lindsay Hoyt, lead author of "Young adults' psychological and physiological reactions to the 2016 U.S. presidential election" in *Psychoneuroendocrinology*: "Individual responses to sociopolitical events, like an election, are not distributed evenly across different groups of people. In terms of this study, we found that most individuals reported an increase in negative mood in the days leading up to the election, and a spike on election night, but, overall, emotional and physiological responses were largely dependent upon gender, ethnicity/race, and political attitudes."[3] Adolescents have also felt the impact of the current political climate under Trump's presidency.

A research study conducted by Francis Huang of the University of Missouri and Dewey Cornell of the University of Virginia found that in Virginia, areas that had a higher voter turnout for Trump had higher rates of bullying and teasing in schools than areas that had voted for Clinton, despite the areas showing a similar rate of bullying in 2015. As discussed by Cornell, "Parents should be mindful of how their reactions to the presidential election, or the reactions of others, could influence their children. And politicians should be mindful of the potential impact of their campaign rhetoric and behavior on their supporters and indirectly on youth."[4] Bullying in childhood, especially repetitive bullying, can cause a number of psychological issues, not only during childhood, but can also affect brain development which could affect mental health later in life.[5]

Anxiety and Depression

In many cases the stress caused by Trump's presidency has led to actual cases of anxiety and depression. A survey conducted by the American Psychiatric Association in May 2018 found that 39% of people reported their anxiety level increasing in the past year and 56% were either "extremely anxious" or "somewhat anxious" about "the impact of politics on daily life."[6] Anxiety concerning Trump was characterized by clinical psychologist Jennifer Panning as "Trump Anxiety Disorder," in which symptoms "were specific to the election of Trump and the resultant unpredictable sociopolitical climate." However, Trump supporters, and Trump himself, have mocked this anxiety classification, calling it instead "Trump Derangement Syndrome."[7]

This impact on anxiety and depression, such as stress, has specifically affected a number of groups in the United States. In one study published in *Child & Adolescent Psychiatry & Mental Health*, Melissa DeJonckheere, Andre Fisher, and Tammy Chang found that women and non-white participants are more likely in 2018 to report higher levels of stress, as well as anxiety and depression.[8] In another study published in the *Journal of GLBT Family Studies,* Kirsten A. Gonzalez, Johanna L. Ramirez, and M. Paz Galupo found "higher levels of stress pertaining to sexual orientation rumination, daily experiences of harassment/discrimination, [and] more symptoms of depression and anxiety" following the 2016 election.[9] Trump's policies have had a specific traumatic effect on the transgender community, especially in his two-year attempt to ban transgender individuals from serving in the military, which went into effect in April 2019. On October 21, 2018, the *New York Times* revealed a federal memo that the Trump administration wants to define gender "as a biological, immutable condition determined by genitalia at birth," which is part of an effort to roll back recognition and protection under federal civil rights laws for transgender individuals. In the days following the release of the memo, traffic to the crisis hotline Trans Lifeline quadrupled, with the average number of daily calls increasing from 187 to 471 per day. According to Ashli Owen-Smith, a mental health researcher at Georgia State University, "These types of policies can create a culture in our country whereby transgender individuals may feel even more marginalized, even more at risk for discrimination, thereby increasing their risk of depression, anxiety, and other mental health issues."[10]

Religious minorities have also experienced increases in not only stress, but anxiety and depression. One such religious minority group that has seen such an increase is the Muslim population, who Trump and his administration have continuously equated with terrorism. Michael Flynn, former national security adviser, who has referred to Islam as a "cancer," tweeted in 2016, along with a YouTube video by CleanTV: "Fear of Muslims is RATIONAL: please forward this to others: the truth fears no questions . . ."[11] Trump himself has echoed similar ideas with his Muslim travel ban, which focused on seven predominantly Muslim countries and was rationalized by the September 11 attacks, despite the fact that none of those who committed the 9/11 attacks came from any of those countries. In addition, an analysis by the Cato Institute found that between 1975 and 2015 no one from any of those countries committed a single U.S. terrorist attack. According to Dr. Goleen Samari, in an article published in the *American Journal of Public Health*: "Islamophobia can negatively influence health by disrupting several systems—individual (stress reactivity and identity concealment), interpersonal (social relationships and socialization processes), and structural (institutional policies and media coverage)."[12]

Divided

Another psychological impact of Trump's presidency has been the effect it has had on American families, and even friendships, that include both Trump supporters and non-supporters. In the three months following the election, polls demonstrated the number of Americans who argued with families and friends over politics increased by 6% from prior to the election, which had already been at a high for the American population. According to the poll, 16% of Americans have stopped talking to a family member or friend because of the election and 13% said they have ended a relationship with a family member or friend because of the election. In addition to emotional fractures among families and friendships, romantic relationships have also been highly affected by the Trump presidency. A survey conducted by Wakefield Research in 2017 found that one in ten Americans have ended a romantic relationship, including marriages, over political differences, a number that rises to over two in ten for millennial Americans. According to Linda Skitka, a psychology professor at the University of Illinois at Chicago who conducted a study with two other academic psychologists on people's willingness to listen to individuals with opposing views, "The idea of actually entertaining the other's point of view is about as adverse as going to the dentist. We're are a point in history in which it's not so much about politics. It's about our hatred of the other side."

Paranoia

The psychological impact that Trump has made on his followers can largely be summed up by one word: paranoia. Trump has long prized paranoia as being a positive attribute, as discussed in the "King Donald" chapter. (In *The Art of the Comeback*, one of "Trump's Top Ten Comeback Tips" is "Be Paranoid": "I have noticed over the years that people who are guarded or, to put it coldly, slightly paranoid, end up being the most successful. Let some paranoia reign! You've got to realize that you have something other people want. Don't let them take it away."[13]) This paranoid tone is also noted in his book *Think Big*. Trump has turned his long-held belief of paranoia being positive into a political strategy.

Increasingly the term paranoia has been used to refer not only to clinical paranoia but also more broadly to a personality trait and a personality style characterized by guardedness, suspiciousness, hypersensitivity, and isolation. An important aspect of this style is a pattern of disowning uncomfortable personal feelings and attributing them to others, the psychological defense mechanism known as projection. Although the paranoid outlook affects many areas of human affairs, it is most evident in the adversarial world of politics, where it is a constant feature. At its extreme, the paranoid style is more destructive than any other political style. Paranoids do not have adversaries or rivals or opponents; they have enemies, and enemies are not to be simply defeated and certainly not to be compromised with or won over. Enemies are to be destroyed. Consider Trump's presidential race against Hillary Clinton, whereby he didn't just want to defeat her in the election, but wanted to destroy her. Take for instance his rhetoric of "Crooked Hillary" and "Lock her up!" which continued after the election and into his presidency in his tweets and at his rallies.

What makes political paranoia so difficult to define and understand is that it begins as a distortion of an appropriate political response but then far overshoots the mark. Like fever in cases of disease, a certain amount of suspicion in politics is a necessary, even healthy, defense. Lyndon Johnson, though not a paranoid leader, once noted that everyone in politics needs to be able to walk into a room full of people and sense who is for him and who is against. But where Trump has largely overshot the mark of political paranoia is in regards to the media. The media has perhaps become to Trump his biggest enemy. And while misinformation in the media is an issue, especially in the age of social media, Trump's constant rants of "fake news" and that the media is the "enemy of the people" is a defense mechanism against any negative coverage, specifically the Mueller investigation. And Trump's paranoia of the media has had a strong effect on his followers. In February 2019 at a rally in El Paso, Texas, a Trump supporter attacked a BBC cameraman as he shouted "fuck the media."[14] Another example of the extremes to which Trump's rhetoric of the media being the enemy can draw his followers is Cesar Altieri Sayoc Jr., who orchestrated the October 2018 attempted mail bombings. Sayoc mailed sixteen packages of pipe bombs to critics of Donald Trump, including Barack Obama, Joe Biden, Hillary Clinton, and one addressed to CNN. Once he was arrested it was discovered that Sayoc had a van covered in stickers, including anti-media stickers such as "CNN Sucks," as well as pictures of Donald Trump and Mike Pence.[15] Video footage also surfaced of Sayoc at a Trump rally among other Trump supporters as they chant "CNN Sucks" and shout "shame" at the group of journalists and cameramen filming the rally. Sayoc was also holding a sign that had a sticker that said "CNN Sucks" along with an image of a casket with funeral flowers and two signs depicted above the casket that read "CNN" and "BuzzFeed."[16] Paranoid rhetoric, such as Trump's, can have a major impact on followers, especially those who have a history of instability. Sayoc himself had an extensive criminal history, including bomb threats, theft, battery, and drug possession.

Trump's paranoia has expanded beyond the media to beliefs of conspiracies against him within the U.S. government. Since January 2019, Trump has increasingly used the term "coup," including numerous retweets of his supporters claiming Trump is facing attempted coups. However, a coup is derived from the French word *coup d'état* and is largely used to describe a sudden, violent and also illegal seizure of government by a smaller group. Trump has supported his followers in referring to the Russian investigation and actions taken by the Democratic party, including calls for impeachment, as attempted coups on his presidency. Trump himself has referred to the 2016 text exchange between former FBI lawyer Lisa Page and former FBI agent Peter Strzok as evidence of an attempted "coup" against his administration. The text exchange included a message from Strzok saying "we will stop it," referring to the possibility of Trump being elected as president. During a congressional testimony, Strzok stated: "In no way, unequivocally, any suggestion that me, the FBI, would take any action whatsoever to improperly impact the electoral process, for any candidate." Trump has referred to this incident as a "coup" and that "this was an attempted overthrow of the United States government." Trump has similarly referred to the Russian investigation as an "attempted takeover of our government," also referring to the investigation as "treasonous." The belief that attempted coups have been made on his administrations ties into the paranoid idea of the "deep state" working against him, which has included accusations of the Justice Department being a part of the "deep state." Much of this paranoia has strongly resonated with his followers as well.

Trump has also largely given a voice to the paranoia that was already present in the United States concerning immigration, terrorism, and American jobs. One area that Trump has given credence to, as discussed in the "Permission to Hate" chapter, is caravan paranoia. Along with other conspiracy theories popular among white supremacists, Trump has propagated conspiracy theories regarding illegal immigration, specifically with migrant caravans. In January 2018, Trump tweeted: "Border rancher: 'We've found prayer rugs out here. It's unreal.'—Washington Examiner. People coming across the Southern Border from many countries, some of which would be a big surprise."[17] The article Trump is quoting provided absolutely no proof of its claim, only the testimony of one anonymous rancher. The rancher who stated: "There's a lot of people coming in not just from Mexico . . . People, the general public, just don't get the terrorist threats of that . . . That's what's really scary. You don't know what's coming across. We've found prayer rugs out here. It's unreal," also claimed that Border Control caught "Czechoslovakians."[18] However, Czechoslovakia is no longer a country and hasn't been since 1993.

Trump's Views on Mental Health

While Trump has said he wants to focus on mental health in the United States, his actions and especially his rhetoric tell a different story. In personal attacks against other politicians, Trump has used derogatory language about mental illness, including calling Jeb Bush a "basket case;" Bernie Sanders a "wacko;" Lindsey Graham a "nut job;" and Ted Cruz "nuts" and "unstable." The federal website, MentalHealth.gov, has even cautioned individuals against using stigmatizing labels like "crazy."[19] Trump himself has made very negative comments about mental health, making allegations that people with mental health issues are violent. Following the Parkland, Florida, school shooting, Trump referred to the shooter, Nikolas Cruz, who struggled with depression, attention-deficit hyperactivity disorder, and autism, as a "savage sicko." However, numerous mental health experts have stated that using terms like "sicko" will not help mental health in this country nor will it stop school shootings. According to Ron Honberg, senior policy adviser with the National Alliance on Mental Illness: "When it comes to mental health, language really matters. This is not about being politically correct. It's about wanting to do everything we can to encourage people to get health treatment that works . . . Hearing language like this is a punch to the gut, particularly if we have a goal as a nation to increase access to mental health care. This is about the worst thing you can do."[20] And, in fact, implying that individuals with a DSM-5 diagnosis are more likely to be dangerous or violent is statistically incorrect. Not only are they less likely to be violent, unless it is a specific diagnosis that includes symptoms of aggression and/or violent outbursts, but individuals who have mental health issues are more likely to be victims of violence.

14

The Left's Reaction

In 2016, many political pundits, politicians, professional pollsters, and even everyday Americans predicted that Hillary Clinton would defeat Donald Trump. Trump's victory shocked the nation, especially the left, but what has been the effect of Trump's victory and his presidency on the left and the Democratic Party?

Trump's History with the Democratic Party

As discussed in the chapter "A Divided Republican Party," since the 1980s Trump has been at times a registered Democrat. In addition to having spent a number of years as a Democrat, Trump has donated a significant amount of money to Democrats.[1] When asked about his donations to Democrats, Trump has stated: "So, what am I going to do, contribute to Republicans? . . . I mean, one thing I'm not stupid. Am I going to contribute to a Republican for my whole life when . . . the most they can get is one percent of the vote?" Democrats whose campaigns Trump has donated to include Chuck Schumer up until 2010 and John Kerry. In an interview with Fox News's Sean Hannity, Trump stated: "I mean, I've contributed to Schumer, I contribute—I've known Schumer for many,

many years. And I have a good relationship with him. The fact is, that I think it is time maybe that we all do get along." Trump also defended his donations to New York Democrats, stating that in New York "everyone is Democratic" and for him to have donated his money to Republican candidates would have been a waste of money. Aside from New York Democrats, Trump has donated to other Democratic candidates, including a number who are now 2020 contenders, including Kamala Harris, Cory Booker, Kirsten Gillibrand, and Joe Biden.[2]

Trump was also relatively close to the Clintons in the 1990s and early 2000s. In his 1997 book *Trump: The Art of the Comeback* Trump features a picture of himself, Donald Jr., and Eric Trump with Hillary Clinton, accompanied by the following quote: "Hillary Clinton, Donny Jr., Eric, and me. The First Lady is a wonderful woman who has handled pressure incredibly well." Both Trump and his son Donald Jr. donated to Hillary Clinton's campaigns in 2002, 2005, 2006, and 2007. Trump has also donated at least $100,000 to the Clinton Foundation. However, his relationship to the Clintons expanded outside of just political donations. During his 2005 wedding to Melania at Mar-a-Lago in Florida, Hillary sat in the front pew, with both her and Bill attending the reception. In 2008, Trump even blogged: "I know Hillary and I think she'd make a great president or vice-president."[3] And following her loss of the Democratic nomination to Obama, Trump stated: "I think she's going to go down, at a minimum, as a great senator. I think she is a great wife to a president, and I think Bill Clinton was a great president."[4] Trump has later claimed he was only nice to the Clintons because they were "bigwigs" and he was a businessman.

From Defeat in 2016 to the 2018 Midterms

In the days and even months that followed the November 2016 election, headlines about the Democratic Party contained words like disarray; defeated; leaderless; abandoned; lost; finished; division; and collapse. The presidency wasn't the only loss the Democrats faced after 2016. At the start of Obama's presidency, the country had twenty-nine Democratic governors and controlled 59% of state legislatures. By 2017, the number of Democratic governors dropped to sixteen, the lowest number since 1920, and controlled only 31% of state legislatures, the lowest since before 2000.

Since then the Democratic Party has undergone a number of changes. One is the structure of the party. As described by Democratic pollster Geoff

Garin: "In 2015, the Republicans were not the party of Trump, and now they are wholly that. In 2015, the Democrats were more of a top-down party. The party of 2019–2020 is much more driven at the grass-roots level."[5]

A major turning point for the Democratic Party was the 2018 midterm elections. While for his presidency Trump enjoyed a Republican-dominated Congress, following the midterm elections Democrats gained control of the House of Representatives. However, some have argued that the Democratic Party has become defined by their opposition to Donald Trump. In a 2019 article in the *San Francisco Chronicle*, Andrew Malcolm wrote: "What was not expected was how dramatically the leader of the Republican Party would change the Democratic Party. In many ways, it has forsaken traditional liberal tenets to become not so much a party in opposition to the country's other major party. It is now the party of opposition to one man, Donald Trump . . . Deep party fissures between the . . . establishment and youthful progressives will likely grow more apparent during fractious primaries."[6] And just as we have seen a new Republican Party under Trump, there has also been a change in the Democratic Party between establishment Democrats and some of the new members of Congress who have been deemed progressive Democrats. As described on the *FiveThirtyEight* website by ABC News, there are now six wings in the Democratic Party: the Super Progressives; the Very Progressives; the Progressive New Guard; the Progressive Old Guard; the Moderates; and the Conservative Democrats.[7] Overall the Democratic Party has changed rather dramatically in recent decades. During the Bill Clinton administration of the 1990s, only 25% of Democrats identified themselves as liberal, with 25% identifying as conservative and 48% identifying as moderates. As for the Democratic Party in 2018, 51% now identify as liberal, with 13% identifying as conservative and only 34% identifying as moderates.[8]

Conflicted Over How to Deal with Trump

While the left and the Democrats are in agreement on wanting to end Trump's presidency, debate remains on how this should be achieved. As there are those focused on defeating Trump in 2020, there are also calls to have him impeached or indicted. House Speaker Nancy Pelosi has stated that she wants the Democratic Party to focus on the 2020 elections, as opposed to impeaching Trump: "I'm not for impeachment. This is news. I'm going to give you some news right now because I haven't said this to any press person before. But since you asked, and I've been thinking about this: Impeachment is so divisive to the country that unless there's something so compelling and overwhelming and bipartisan, I don't think we should go down that path, because it divides the country."[9] Pelosi went on to state that although she doesn't believe Trump is "fit to be president" she also doesn't believe he is "worth it" to look into impeachment. This has come in sharp contrast to other Democrats, like Representative Rashida Tlaib, who has promised "we're going to impeach the motherf*****." Tlaib, following Pelosi's remarks, stated: "I'm going to move forward, obviously. It's important that there is a transparent process. No one, not even the President, should be above the law."[10] Representative Al Green has also stated that he plans to push for another vote on impeachment in the House.

And it's not only Democratic politicians who are conflicted over how to deal with Trump, members of the Democratic Party are divided as well. Those who wish to impeach Trump argue that there is more than enough reason and evidence to have the president impeached. According to the Need to Impeach website, Trump has committed a number of impeachable offenses, including: obstructing justice; violating the emoluments clause of the U.S. Constitution; conspiring with others to commit crimes against the U.S. and attempting to conceal those violations; advocating violence and undermining equal protection under the law; abusing the pardon power; engaging in conduct that grossly endangers the peace and security of the U.S.; directing law enforcement to investigate political adversaries for improper and unjustifiable purpose; undermining the freedom of the press; and cruelly and unconstitutionally imprisoning children and their families.[11] And in fact the 2019 release of the Mueller investigation report has furthered Democratic views on impeachment. According to an NPR/PBS News/Marist poll, seven out of ten Democrats believe Congress should start impeachment hearings for Donald Trump. However, of the entire U.S. population, including Democrats, Republicans, and Independents, only 39% believe that impeachment is the proper course of action.[12]

Controversy on the Left

While the Republican Party, and Trump in particular, faces constant controversies and accusations of racism, the Democratic Party has not been free of its own controversies and allegations. This includes a number of Democratic politicians in the state of Virginia, including Governor Ralph Northam and Attorney General Mark R. Herring. In 2018, a copy of Northam's 1984 medical school yearbook surfaced, featuring a page with a picture of one person in blackface and another in a Ku Klux Klan robe. Numerous Democrats ended up calling for Northam to resign, including a number of 2020 Democratic presidential nominee contenders. Following the controversy surrounding Northam, Herring, who plans to run for governor in 2021, admitted that he had also worn blackface in college. This was followed by Lieutenant Governor Justin Fairfax facing allegations of sexual assault.[13] Tulsi Gabbard, a representative from Hawaii who is running to be the Democratic Party's 2020 nominee, has faced criticism for her past support of anti–LGBTQ groups and anti–Muslim Hindu nationalists. Before she was elected in 2012, Gabbard apologized for her past views, but she has come under even more criticism while in Congress. This includes her dubbing herself a "hawk" on terrorism and for meeting with the Syrian dictator Bashar al-Assad. Gabbard has defended both her position on terrorism, saying we need to respond to the serious threat from jihadism, and for advocating peace with Assad.[14] A number of Democrats have also faced accusations of anti–Semitism, including Representative Rashida Tlaib and Representative Ilhan Omar. Tlaib has been criticized for following an anti–Semitic Instagram page that refers to Jews as vermin, claims Israel is responsible for 9/11 and supports the Islamic State.[15] Omar has been cited for using anti–Semitic tropes such as accusing Israel of hypnotizing the world and American Jews of having dual loyalty.

2020 Elections

As the Democratic Party is preparing for primary elections ahead of the 2020 elections, Democratic candidates (of which there are twenty-five at the time of writing this) are in a battle not only to become the Democratic Party's presidential nominee, but they are in a battle against Trump. Trump has begun using his own personalized nicknames for the various Democratic nominees, an obvious attempt to begin undermining and belittling his opponents in the 2020 elections. This includes: "Sleepy Joe Biden" (and "SleepyCreepyJoe"); "Crazy Bernie;" and calling Elizabeth Warren "Pocahontas." It is a similar tactic he deployed against not only Hillary Clinton, whom he still refers to as "Crooked Hillary," but also against his fellow Republicans in the 2016 nominee race. While Trump has continued to make his attacks against the Democratic nominees a priority, especially in his Twitter storms, many Democratic candidates have had to focus portions of their campaign on opposing Trump. Comments from primary nominees on Trump have included:

Joe Biden: Trump is an "existential threat" to the United States.

Bernie Sanders: "We have a president who is a racist, who is a sexist, who is a homophobe, who is a xenophobe and he is a religious bigot."

Kamala Harris: "He has engaged in a cover up. He's obstructed justice. He openly welcomes foreign collusion . . ."

Kirsten Gillibrand: "President Trump is weak. He is a coward."

With defeating Trump as a focal point for the Democratic Party, the race for a Democratic nominee will focus on not only who is the best candidate for the party, but who is the best candidate to defeat Trump. As for Trump, he continues to mount personal attacks against the various candidates, a tactic that will most likely increase as we get closer to the 2020 elections. Following the second round of Democratic candidate debates, of which he stated he only watched part, Trump tweeted about what he considered to be low ratings for the debate and that he believed it was evident the U.S. public wants to reelect him.

15

Foreign Affairs

Trump's Foreign Policy

Donald Trump's foreign policy is centered around his motto of "America First," whether it is in regard to dealing with our allies or adversaries. Trump laid out his foreign policy views of "America First," in his 2011 book, *Time to Get Tough*:

> I believe that any American foreign policy doctrine should be defined by at least seven principles:
>
> 1. American interests come first. Always. No apologies.
> 2. Maximum firepower and military preparedness.
> 3. Only go to war to win.
> 4. Stay loyal to your friends and suspicious of your enemies.
> 5. Keep the technological sword razor sharp.
> 6. See the unseen. Prepare for threats before they materialize.
> 7. Respect and support our present and past warriors.[1]

Trump wrote this book at a time he was becoming increasingly vocal about America's foreign policy, specifically in criticizing the foreign policy decisions of Barack Obama. This focus culminated in a Twitter storm in September and October 2012 leading up to the election between Obama and Mitt Romney. His tweets focused on Libya, Egypt, Iraq, and Afghanistan, referring to Obama's foreign policy as being a "disaster," a "failure," and "dangerous." One tweet from October 11, 2012, read: "Our foreign policy decisions are dumbest in U.S. history."[2] During an October 2012 interview with *Fox & Friends*, Trump stated:

> Our foreign policy is a total disgrace. I guess you would have to say it's a joke. It's so bad. So out of control. Nobody has ever seen anything like it. Everything that we've touched has turned to garbage . . . We have no foreign policy. This has been the worst foreign policy president in the history of the country. Without question.

And it would appear that going into the presidency one of Trump's goals has been to dismantle all of Obama's foreign policy. However, Trump's criticism of American foreign policy has also focused on State Department diplomats. In his 2016 book *Crippled America*, he wrote:

> The career diplomats who got us into many foreign policy messes say I have no experience in foreign policy. They think that successful diplomacy requires years of experience and an understanding of all nuances that have to be carefully considered before reaching a conclusion . . . Some of these so-called "experts" are trying to scare people by saying that my approach would make the world more dangerous . . . My approach to foreign policy is built on a strong foundation: Operate from strength . . . If we're going to continue to be the policemen of the world, we ought to be paid for it.[3]

Trump himself stated when he was asked who he consults about foreign policy on MSNBC's *Morning Joe*: "I'm speaking with myself, number one, because I have a very good brain and I've said a lot of things . . . I know what I'm doing and I listen to a lot of people, I talk to a lot of people and at the appropriate time I'll tell you who the people are. But my primary consultant is myself and I have a good instinct for this stuff." This attitude toward foreign policy has altered the way foreign leaders interact with the United States, as discussed in a report by the *Wall Street Journal*: "Increasingly, savvy leaders are bypassing the standard protocols and government processes of American diplomacy to go directly to President Trump himself, according to current and former officials, allies, and foreign-policy experts. North Korea's Kim Jong-un, Turkey's Recep Tayyip Erdogan, and Russia's Vladimir Putin are among the heads of state who have cut out the middle layers of aides and agency officials to talk to Mr. Trump."[4]

Trump and Europe

Along with many of the other controversies that surround Trump's presidency is his foreign policy. Critics are arguing that he treats the United States' allies as if they are enemies and vice versa. Following Trump's first overseas trip, European Council president Donald Tusk stated that he and Trump don't "have a common position, a common opinion on Russia."[5] Since becoming president, Trump has placed tariffs on European imports like steel and aluminum, which has resulted in the Europeans placing retaliatory tariffs on American products like motorcycles and orange juice. In an interview on *60 Minutes* in October 2018, Trump replied to questions regarding his stance toward U.S. allies:

> Lesley Stahl: You have also slapped some tariffs on our allies.
>
> Donald Trump: I mean, what's an ally? We have wonderful relationships with a lot of people. But nobody treats us much worse than the European Union. The European Union was formed in order to take advantage of us on trade, and that's what they've done.
>
> Lesley Stahl: But this is hostile.
>
> Donald Trump: And yet, they—it's not hostile.
>
> Lesley Stahl: It sounds hostile.
>
> Donald Trump: You know what's hostile? The way they treat us. We're not hostile.

Trump has often acted as though he is alone in making foreign policy decisions, as he even stated he "consults" himself first. Take for instance the breakdown of the relationship between Trump and former Secretary of State Rex Tillerson, which resulted over a number of issues, including contradictions over North Korea and Trump wanting to increase the U.S. nuclear arsenal. Following his dismissal, Tillerson stated: "It was challenging for me coming from the disciplined, highly process-oriented ExxonMobil corporation . . . to go to work for a man who is pretty undisciplined, doesn't like to read, doesn't read briefing reports, doesn't like to get into the details of a lot of things, but rather just kind of says, 'This is what I believe.'"[8] Tillerson was then replaced in April 2018 by former CIA director Mike Pompeo, who has been viewed as one of Trump's most loyal cabinet members—far from contradicting Trump, he is viewed as Trump's "mouthpiece." It is almost as important to point out the important role John Bolton, the current national security adviser, has played in Trump's foreign policy. Bolton, who has been referred to as a "war hawk," has been a major advocate for regime change in numerous countries, including in the ongoing conflict in Venezuela. Trump even joked in May 2019 that Bolton wants to get him "into a war" in Venezuela.

Trump has continued to have an unsteady relationship with a number of European leaders. For instance, while Trump has called the German Chancellor Angela Merkel "possibly the greatest world leader," he has also attacked Merkel and Germany over his attitudes toward NATO. Following the NATO leaders' summit in 2017, Trump stated: "The Germans are bad, very bad . . . Look at the millions of cars they sell in the US. Terrible. We'll stop that."[9] He has also heavily criticized Merkel for Germany's refugee policy: "I think she made one very catastrophic mistake and that was taking all of these illegals (sic), you know taking all of the people from wherever they come from."[10] In an attack on Germany he also tweeted: "The people of Germany are turning against their leadership as migration is rocking the already tenuous Berlin coalition. Crime in Germany is way up. Big mistake made all over Europe in allowing millions of people in who have so strongly and violently changed their culture!"[11]

Trump has had a similar relationship with the leaders of France. Following his first phone call with the former French president François Hollande, Trump told him that France is "beautiful" and how much he "loved France." Then, in 2017, Trump stated to a group of his supporters during his speech at the Conservative Political Action Conference that "France is no longer France" due to issues of terrorism. Hollande criticized Trump for these remarks in that it was no way for allies to speak about one another.[12] Trump's relationship with France's next president, Emmanuel Macron, has also been frayed. While the two leaders at first had a good rapport following Macron's election in 2017, Trump's announcement of his intention to withdraw American troops from Syria damaged their relationship. Macron was informed of Trump's decision by a White House official one day in advance, called and reminded Trump of his pledge to fight alongside the United States' allies against terrorism, as well as his responsibility to Europe. The next day Trump tweeted his decision, which caused backlash not only from European allies, but also within his own administration.

Trump's stance toward U.S. allies has drawn criticism from other U.S. politicians, including Mitt Romney. Romney wrote in an op-ed:

> Trump's words and actions have caused dismay around the world. In a 2016 Pew Research Center poll, 84 percent of people in Germany, Britain, France, Canada and Sweden believed the American president would "do the right thing in world affairs." One year later, that number had fallen to 16 percent. This comes at a very unfortunate time. Several allies in Europe are experiencing political upheaval. Several former Soviet satellite states are rethinking their commitment to democracy. Some Asian nations, such as the Philippines, lean increasingly toward China, which advances to rival our economy and our military. The alternative to U.S. world leadership offered by China and Russia is autocratic, corrupt and brutal.

Trump has also been criticized for how his rhetoric toward the United States' allies has impacted the American population and how it may be changing the American public's perception of its allies. As discussed by former secretary of state Madeleine Albright in her book *Fascism: A Warning*:

> The commander in chief's swaggering disregard for how his words are perceived has at times stunned the world, including allies of long standing in Europe and Asia. Our shared interests are so deep that I expect alliance members to continue working with America when possible. However, many of them fear—as I do—that the unilateralist mind-set espoused by Trump will endure in the United States even after the man himself has retired.[13]

Trump's presidency is affecting Americans' views of our allies, and also our allies' views of the United States. In Western European countries, such as the U.K., Spain, France, and Germany, confidence that the president of the United States "will do the right thing regarding world affairs" is at an all-time low. And while opinions of the United States are still relatively favorable, at 50% in the twenty-five countries surveyed by the Pew Research Center, a majority of those surveyed has no confidence in Trump. In addition, 70% believe that the United States doesn't really take into account the interests of other countries when making foreign policy decisions.[14]

Trump and Russia

There is arguably not any country with which Trump's name graces headlines more than Russia. Trump has continually claimed that he has "nothing to do with Russia," tweeting in January 2017: "Russia has never tried to use leverage over me. I HAVE NOTHING TO DO WITH RUSSIA—NO DEALS, NO LOANS, NO NOTHING!"[15] However, Trump has attempted to create business deals in Russia for decades. Trump even tried striking business deals in Moscow before the collapse of the Soviet Union, as mentioned in his 1987 book *The Art of the Deal*, in his chapter "Dealing: A Week in the Life":

> A prominent businessman who does a lot of business with the Soviet Union calls to keep me posted on a construction project I'm interested in undertaking in Moscow. The idea got off the ground after I sat next to the Soviet ambassador, Yuri Dubinin, at a luncheon . . . Dubinin's daughter, it turned out, had read about Trump Tower and knew all about it. One thing led to another, and now I'm talking about building a large luxury hotel, across the street from the Kremlin, in partnership with the Soviet government. They have asked me to go to Moscow in July.[16]

Although Trump did end up traveling to the Soviet Union, the business deal fell apart, with Trump stating: "In the Soviet Union, you don't own anything. It's hard to conjure up spending hundreds of millions of dollars on something and not own."[17] Trump attempted another business deal in Russia in the late 1990s, a plan he discussed with Russian politician Aleksander Lebed in 1997, stating: "We are actually looking at something in Moscow right now . . . Only quality stuff. And we're working with the local government, the mayor of Moscow, and the mayor's people. So far, they've been very responsive . . ."[18] This plan also failed. Trump's attempts to make business deals in Russia continued into the 2000s, with Trump stating during the Miss Universe pageant in Moscow: "I have plans for the establishment of business in Russia. Now, I am in talks with several Russian companies to establish this skyscraper."[19] Reportedly, Trump's discussions for building a Trump Tower in Moscow continued until June 2016, following him becoming the GOP presidential nominee.

As president, Trump's relationship with Russia, and particularly Putin, has come into question. Trump was questioned in an interview on *60 Minutes* in October 2018 why he has never publicly criticized Putin, especially given how he criticizes so many other political leaders.

> Donald Trump: I think I'm very tough with him personally. I had a meeting with him. The two of us. It was a very tough meeting and it was a very good meeting.
>
> Lesley Stahl: Do you agree that Vladimir Putin is involved in assassinations? In poisonings?
>
> Donald Trump: Probably he is, yeah. Probably. I mean, I don't—
>
> Lesley Stahl: Probably?
>
> Donald Trump: But I rely on them, it's not in our country.
>
> Lesley Stahl: Why not—they shouldn't do it. This is a terrible thing.
>
> Donald Trump: Of course they shouldn't do it . . .[20]

However, Trump has long praised Putin, even prior to his presidency. During an interview with Larry King in 2007, Trump stated: "Look at Putin—what he's doing with Russia—I mean, you know, what's going on over there. I mean this guy has done—whether you like him or don't like him—he's doing a great job in rebuilding the image of Russia and also rebuilding Russia, period."[21] In his 2011 book, *Time to Get Tough*, Trump wrote:

Russian Prime Minister Vladimir Putin, of whom I often speak highly for his intelligence and no-nonsense way, is a former KGB officer ... Putin has big plans for Russia. He wants to edge out its neighbors so that Russia can dominate oil supplies to all of Europe. Putin has also announced his grand vision: the creation of a "Eurasian Union" made up of former Soviet nations that can dominate the region. I respect Putin and the Russians but cannot believe our leader allows them to get away with so much—I am sure that Vladimir Putin is even more surprised than I am. Hats off to the Russians.[22]

Trump tweeted in 2013, prior to the Miss Universe pageant in Moscow: "Do you think Putin will be going to the Miss Universe Pageant in November in Moscow—if so, will he become my new best friend?"[23] Following his decision to run for president in 2015, Trump stated: "I think I'd get along very well with Vladimir Putin. I just think so."[24] Trump also commented that Putin was a better leader than Obama. In an interview on *Morning Joe,* Trump stated when discussing allegations that Putin had ordered the killings of journalists: "He's running his country and at least he's a leader, unlike what we have in this country. I think our country does plenty of killing also."[25] As president, Trump has continued to praise Putin. Trump even met with Putin in Finland in July 2018, during which the two leaders spoke alone for two hours with only two translators and no aides. To some it has seemed as if Putin has something on Trump. In the steel dossier that was circulating among journalists, it was suggested that: 1) He was indebted to Russian banks to the tune of $600 to $800 million; and 2) It was rumored that there were comprising images of Trump from an earlier trip to Russia with Russian prostitutes partaking in "golden showers." To better understand Trump's relationship with Putin, it is important to have an understanding of Putin and how Putin may continue to interact with Trump.

Vladimir Putin: A Mini Political Personality Profile

While President Vladimir Putin has not designated himself President for life, he is behaving as if he believes he is indispensable to the leadership of his country and the Russian-speaking peoples. Putin is driven by a strong need for power and control. Since becoming president in 2000, he has engineered elections to perpetuate his rule; quelled opposition and critics with imprisonment, exile, or death; and mercilessly suppressed the rebellion in Chechnya. A brutal, ruthless dictator masquerading as a principled democrat, Putin is determined to defend his power—so long as it does not damage his international image and reputation. To achieve these two conflicting goals, Putin relies on his legal training and extremely calculating nature to fabricate meticulous pseudo-legal justifications for his actions.

In his autobiography, Putin describes himself as selfless and indifferent to power—governed instead by patriotism and a desire to serve his country. But his actions say otherwise. Reflecting his high self-esteem and drive for power, Putin appears to believe that only he can lead the former superpower. Putin has been at the helm since 2000 and sees himself and Russia as one and the same. Putin created a political machine to ensure the survival of his rule for decades. In 2008, when he "stepped down" as president, his successor, Dmitry Medvedev, increased the presidential term to six years. Medvedev then resigned after one term, paving the way for then–Prime Minister Putin to regain the presidency in 2012, with the possibility of retaining power until 2024.

From childhood on, Putin has been intensely ambitious, setting his sights on becoming a KGB spy and staying doggedly focused on the path to achieve this. Putin explains that he was drawn to this career by the realization that "one spy could decide the fate of thousands of people"—reflecting his narcissistic dreams of glory. Bullied in school, in response to any insults or criticism, Putin immediately responded viciously to his tormentors. This was an early example of narcissistic dynamics—an exaggerated defense overcompensating for his underlying insecurity. Putin was also incapable of handling criticism from teachers, openly expressing outrage at being reprimanded. Now, as president, Putin continues to react intensely to criticism, as any oligarch or journalist who criticizes or opposes him could find themselves in prison or dead.

Putin is obsessed with masculinity, size, strength, and power, as evidenced by bare-chested photos of him with guns, and with a tranquilized tiger. These arranged stunts and photos convey the image of Putin as fearless, powerful, and in control. It also is notable that these photo shoots increased dramatically in 2008 when Putin became prime minister and was replaced by Medvedev. It appears this was a carefully calculated move to remind the Russian people and the world who was really in charge. Putin's preoccupation with size and strength is overcompensation for his underlying insecurity—which may be over his small stature and his need to prove he cannot be pushed around. Standing 5'6", he was often bullied as a kid and picked on for his slight build.

While Putin has publicly acknowledged that he does not want to restore the former Soviet Union, he does appear to view himself as a modern-day czar leading the Russian-speaking people. (A portrait of Peter the Great is prominently displayed in his office.) He thus finds threats to his crumbling empire intolerable. So when Ukraine turned to the European Union, and the prospect of the West settling into his backyard became a genuine possibility, Putin acted quickly to forestall further erosion of his empire. He seized Crimea first and then orchestrated violence and unrest in southern and eastern Ukraine.

The quintessential narcissist, Putin is consumed with his image and how others perceive him. As evidenced by the extravagance of the Olympic Games in Sochi, Putin yearns to be respected as a first-tier world leader and he understands that to earn this respect, his actions must appear reasonable and legitimate.

However, Putin's two goals are difficult to pursue simultaneously. On the one hand, Putin yearns to be viewed as a respected world leader. On the other hand, "Putin the Great" views any potential loss of influence as an intolerable threat to Russian preeminence. Putin has continuously demonstrated his willingness to defend his power and influence at any cost. He believes the loss of Ukraine would be a death knell for his Russian empire, yet his aggressive, destabilizing actions threaten to oust him from the community of respected world leaders. At present there are no other military or political leaders of note in Putin's leadership circle to constrain him; it is truly a leader-dominant society.

Putin's ruthless brutality was plainly exhibited in his handling of the situation in Chechnya in 1999. The western Russian province had become ungovernable with Chechen rebels executing attacks in major Russian cities. When then–Prime Minister Putin was named acting president after the resignation of President Boris Yeltsin, Russian forces had begun to bring the Chechen situation under control. However, instead of implementing an armistice Putin embarked on a plan of total warfare with large-scale combat operations. Putin indicates in his autobiography that he equated the loss of the Chechen conflict with the collapse of Russia. This outlook would also underlie his brutal response to the short-lived uprising in Georgia.

Putin's tendency to see a challenge to his control in such apocalyptic terms can be traced back to his time serving as a KGB officer in Dresden, East Germany, when he was witness to the fall of the Berlin Wall. This signified the beginning of the end for the Soviet Union and the country's subsequent demise in what Putin understood to be a consequence of Moscow's inaction, "a paralysis power." It appears that, in his view, had there been decisive action, the USSR could still be around today. It is this bitter memory that prompted such swift action with Ukraine to forestall further erosion of his empire. He would not let Ukraine fall as the Soviet Union had.

Trained as a lawyer, Putin understands full well the commitments Russia made in the 1994 Budapest Memorandum—to respect the territorial integrity of Ukraine in exchange for relinquishing their significant nuclear arsenal. This is why Putin has been carefully crafting a justification for occupation of Crimea as "absolutely legitimate" and a response to the "official request" for help from Ukrainian president Viktor Yanukovych, whom he considers to characterize the legitimate president. He has been careful to characterize the present occupying forces as "local militias" who do not answer to Moscow. Most recently, the newly appointed and compliant Crimean Parliament has unanimously voted for a referendum for Crimea to split from Ukraine and rejoin Russia—a move that Europe, the U.S., and the new Ukrainian president characterized as unconstitutional. Clearly arranged by Putin, the referendum appears to be another pseudo-legal justification for his aggressive land grab, as Putin has stated that he cannot "ignore calls for help" and will "act accordingly, in full compliance with international law." This is a remarkable example of "Putin speak"—justifying his aggression as a necessary response to what he calls the "rampage of reactionary, nationalist, and anti–Semitic forces" going on in Ukraine. It is this reversal of reality that has led Merkel to conclude that Putin is "living in another world."

It is the political personality of Putin described above that colors his response to sanctions from the West—he has not flinched and he will not be bullied. In fact, Putin could actually capitalize domestically on Western sanctions by citing these as the cause of any future Russian economic woes. Putin refuses to be pushed around or controlled—*he* will be the one in control. It appears Putin has a deep-seated need to not capitulate to outside attempts at controlling him. In the face of control and criticism, he cannot be seen as backing down. Putin may only respond to force and likely adheres to the Leninist maxim: *If you strike steel, pull back; if you strike mush, keep going*.

Putin has been fostering cleavage in the U.S.-European alliance and is not deterred by the fragmented Western response. In responding to Putin's current and future actions, it is imperative that there be a unified voice from the West. The U.S. cannot assume a unilateral leadership role, as it is too easy for Putin to single out one country and demonize it. He did this in a March 18, 2014, speech, saying, "Our western partners, led by the United States of America, prefer not to be guided by international law" and "have come to believe in their exclusivity and exceptionalism, that they can decide the destinies of the world, that only they can ever be right." He also argues that Crimea's separation from Ukraine follows the Kosovo precedent, but that the U.S. and Western Europe regard it as "some special case." Putin critically states, "One should not try so crudely to make everything suit their interests."

Putin has a remarkable capacity to accuse his adversary of exactly what he is doing. Consider the following backward logic: "[The West and the U.S.] act as they please: here and there, they use force against sovereign states, building coalitions based on the principle, 'If you are not with us, you are against us.' To make this aggression look legitimate, they force the necessary resolutions from international organizations, and if for some reason this does not work, they simply ignore the UN Security Council and the UN overall." Putin cites Yugoslavia, Afghanistan, Iraq, and Libya as situations where the U.S. and the West ignored the UN Security Council. In effect, Putin makes the United States the main aggressor and portrays himself as righteously defending the Russian-speaking people. This has played well in Russia where Putin has enjoyed a surge in popularity.

Putin will continue to try to create splits in the western alliance through economic blackmail. If he is successful in maintaining the fractures, he will continue to surge forward. Putin will only be deterred from his forward march if he meets a strong and steely response from a unified West.

Trump and the Middle East

IRAQ

During the 2016 presidential campaign, Trump stated repeatedly that the United States should "take Iraq's oil as the spoils of war." Whether Trump actually believed this is possible or not, or if it was just another one of his countless rhetorical phrases to appeal to his base, "taking Iraq's oil" would involve not only a continued invasion of Iraq, but as many legal experts pointed out would be a war crime under the Geneva Conventions. Trump has defended his statements, citing concern that Iraq's oil could fall under the control of the Islamic State.[26] However, Trump's rhetoric of the "spoils of war" began before 2016, in which he argued that the United States should take Iraq's oil before Iran did. In *Time to Get Tough*, in a section titled "To the Victor Go the Spoils," he wrote:

> We've spent blood and treasure defending the people of the Middle East, from Iraq to Kuwait to Saudi Arabia and the small Gulf states. And if any country in the Middle East won't sell us their oil at a fair market price—oil that we discovered, we pumped, and we made profitable for the countries of the Middle East in the first place—we have every right to take it . . . We should take the oil. And here's why: because the Iraqis won't be able to keep it themselves. Their military . . . is incompetent, and the minute we leave, Iran will take over Iraq . . . If we protect and control the oil fields, Iraq will get to keep a good percentage of its oil—not to mention its independence from Iran—and we will recoup some of the cost of liberating the Iraqis . . . Call me old school, but I believe in the old warrior's credo that "to the victor go the spoils." In other words, we don't fight a war, hand over the keys to people who hate us, and leave. We win a war, take the oil to repay the financial costs we've incurred, and in so doing, treat Iraq and everybody else fairly.[27]

Even as president, Trump reportedly brought up the issue of Iraq's oil twice to the Iraqi prime minister Haider al-Abadi, which caused issues among members of his administration. Former national security adviser H. R. McMaster was described as saying to Trump: "We can't do this and you shouldn't talk about it. Because talking about it is just bad . . . It's bad for America's reputation, it'll spook allies, it scares everybody."[28] Former secretary of defense James Mattis also had to publicly state that the United States has no intentions "to seize anybody's oil." Iraq was also one of the countries Trump targeted in his Muslim travel ban.

SYRIA

Trump's stance on Syria has been divided by his changing views of the Syrian regime under Bashar al-Assad and the U.S. effort to combat the Islamic State.

During his presidential campaign, Trump suggested he would not involve the United States in the Syrian civil war. In an interview on *The O'Reilly Factor*, Trump said to Bill O'Reilly: "Iran and Russia are protecting Syria and it's sort of amazing that we're in there fighting ISIS in Syria so we're helping the head of Syria Bashar al-Assad who is not supposed to be our friend although he looks a lot better than some of our so-called friends." As president, Trump initially condemned the Assad regime for chemical weapons attacks on Syrian civilians, including ordering military strikes against Assad targets in response to the 2017 Khan Shaykhun chemical attack and the 2018 Douma chemical attack, but he has since appeared to have backtracked on his position. In his tweet from the end of 2018, announcing the withdrawal of U.S. troops from Syria, Trump wrote: "We have defeated ISIS in Syria, my only reason for being there during the Trump Presidency."[29] Trump's tweet signaled to many that he may no longer have any intention of opposing Assad's regime, which has been accused of war crimes and crimes against humanity against its own civilians. As for the Islamic State, Trump has maintained a strong position against the terrorist organization. Even calling for actions during his presidential campaign that many pointed out amounted to war crimes under the Geneva Convention, Trump said: "You have to take out their families, when you get these terrorists, you have to take out their families. . . . When they say they don't care about their lives, you have to take out their families."[30] Despite backlash from some of his supporters, Trump maintained U.S. involvement in both Iraq and Syria to combat the Islamic State. While Trump declared in December 2018 that "we have won against ISIS," followed by his tweet that the U.S. would be withdrawing from Syria, the Islamic State has continued to carry out terrorist attacks not only in the Middle East, but in western countries.

ISRAEL AND THE PALESTINIAN AUTHORITY

Throughout his presidency, and even prior, Trump has demonized the Obama administration for their handling of the Israeli-Palestinian conflict, boasting that as a businessman he could get the "deal of the century" and have the Israelis and Palestinians agree to a peace plan. Since coming into office, Trump has met with both the Israeli leadership, President Benjamin Netanyahu, and the Palestinian leadership, Palestinian Authority President Mahmoud Abbas. In December 2017, Trump recognized Jerusalem as the capital of Israel and announced plans to move the U.S. Embassy from Tel Aviv to Jerusalem. Trump has also recognized Israel's claim of sovereignty over the Golan Heights. As for his "deal of the century," the Trump administration has continued to push back the release of the peace plan. The Palestinian Authority under Abbas has already started making efforts to ensure that major Arab countries oppose the peace plan, including Saudi Arabia and Egypt. However, according to the Lebanese newspaper, *Al Akhbar*, Saudi Arabia offered Abbas $10 billion to accept Trump's peace plan. Abbas reportedly declined the deal, stating it would "mean the end of my political life."[31]

SAUDI ARABIA

In *Time to Get Tough*, Trump wrote: "Saudi Arabia funnels our petro dollars—our very own money—to fund terrorists that seek to destroy our people, while the Saudis rely on us to protect them!"[32] Trump echoed a similar sentiment during his campaign, focusing on Saudi Arabia paying for the cost of American troops stationed in the country and arguing for the U.S. to halt the sales of oil unless Saudi Arabia provided ground troops for fighting the Islamic State. However, while initially critical of Saudi Arabia, Trump has defended the United States's relationship with the country as president. Trump continued to defend his strong ties with Saudi leadership even following international outcry over the murder of journalist Jamal Khashoggi in the Saudi Arabian Embassy in Turkey. While a number of countries placed arms embargoes on Saudi Arabia, the United States did not, with Trump stating: "If we foolishly cancel these contracts, Russia and China would be the enormous beneficiaries, and very happy to acquire all of this newfound business. It would be a wonderful gift to them directly from the United States."[33] And while the State Department condemned the murder, Trump defended Saudi crown prince Mohammad bin Salman, stating the prince told him that he knew nothing about the murder. Even following a CIA conclusion that Saudi Arabia's leadership, including the crown prince, knew of the attack, Trump has maintained his position. In November 2018, Trump further suggested that even if the crown prince had lied to him, it is something he could live with, stating: "We do have an ally, and I want to stick with an ally that in many ways has been very good . . . I don't know. Who could really know? But I can say this, he's got many people now that say he had no knowledge."[34] Trump also declined to listen to the tape of the murder provided by Turkish president Erdogan, saying: "Because it's a suffering tape, it's a terrible tape. I've been fully briefed on it. There's no reason for me to hear it. . . . It was very violent, very vicious and terrible." Trump's support of Saudi Arabia is perhaps best explained by comments he made to supporters at a rally in Wisconsin in April 2019: "They have nothing but cash, right? They buy a lot from us, $450 billion they bought . . . You had people wanting to cut off Saudi Arabia . . . I don't want to lose them."[35]

IRAN

Trump has long focused on Iran as an "enemy" of the United States and the "biggest terrorist supporter" in the world. During his presidency, his main focus with Iran has been the Joint Comprehensive Plan of Action (JCPOA), commonly known as the "Iran Deal," which was negotiated under the Obama administration.[36] The deal, which was agreed upon by Iran, the United States, France, Russia, China, the United Kingdom, Germany, and the European Union, pressures Iran to eliminate and reduce parts of its nuclear program in exchange for relief from sanctions imposed by the United States, the European Union, and the United Nations. While Trump has said from the beginning that the deal was "terrible," he stated in 2015 he would attempt to enforce it. However, he later in 2016 focused on his plan to dismantle the deal, which he eventually did with the United States' withdrawal from the agreement in May 2018. In 2019, Trump has also labeled the branch of the Iranian armed forces, the Islamic Revolutionary Guard, a terrorist organization.[37] This is the first time in U.S. history that the military of another country has been labeled a terrorist organization. While some of his supporters have applauded his stance toward Iran, declaring that the Islamic Revolutionary Guard is a terrorist organization contradicts widely held academic definitions of terrorist organizations as being non-state actors. Tensions between Iran and the United States continue to increase under Trump's administration. While members of Trump's administration have pushed for possible military action against Iran, Trump himself has seemed to waiver. Following accusations that Iran both attacked two oil tankers in the Strait of Hormuz and shot down a U.S. drone in June 2019, Trump ordered an airstrike against Iran. However, he reportedly called off the attack after planes had been dispatched.

Trump and Africa

Trump and his administration have largely been accused of overlooking Africa in their foreign policy. A number of times Trump has been accused of making racist comments about African countries, including reportedly saying in 2017 that once Nigerians come to the United States they will never "go back to their huts." In 2018, Trump reportedly also asked why the United States would want immigrants from "all these shithole countries," referring to African countries, as well as Haiti.[38] This comment sparked backlash from numerous African countries, including the government of Botswana, which called the comments "reprehensible and racist." The government of Botswana also summoned the U.S. ambassador to Botswana to clarify if Trump considered their country to be one of the "shithole countries."[39] The statement also drew criticism from the African Union, with Ebba Kalondo, the group's spokeswoman, stating: "Given the historical reality of how many Africans arrived in the United States as slaves, this statement flies in the face of all accepted behavior and practice . . . particularly surprising as the United States of America remains a global example of how migration gave birth to a nation built on strong values of diversity and opportunity."[40] Trump, as noted in the "Permission to Hate" chapter, has also faced criticism for sharing white supremacy theories about South Africa.

Trump and China

As president of the United States, Trump's relations with the People's Republic of China have resulted in a trade war between the two countries. However, Trump's attitude toward China, specifically his belief that China is an enemy of the United States, has been a long-held conviction. In his 2000 book, *The America We Deserve*, Trump wrote:

> Our biggest long-term challenge will be China. The Chinese people still have few political rights to speak of . . . Our China policy under presidents Clinton and Bush has been aimed at changing the Chinese regime by incentives both economic and political. The intention has been good, but it's clear that the Chinese have been getting far too easy a ride . . . Why am I concerned with political

rights? I'm a good businessman and I can be amazingly unsentimental when I need to be. I also recognize that when it comes down to it, we can't do much to change a nation's internal policies. But I'm unwilling to shrug off the mistreatment of China's citizens by their own government. My reason is simple: These oppressive policies make it clear that China's current government has contempt for our way of life.[41]

From 2011 to 2013, Trump tweeted numerous times that China was America's enemy. In his 2011 book *Time to Get Tough*, while criticizing Obama's foreign policy, Trump again paints China as an enemy of the United States:

There are four Chinese people for every American. China's population is massive, and its economic power is huge and growing. China is now the second-largest economy in the world. We are building China's wealth by buying all their products, *even though we make better products in America*. I know. I buy a lot of products . . . I buy American whenever I can. Unfortunately, a lot of times American businesses can't buy American products because, with the Chinese screwing around their currency rates, American manufacturers can't be competitive on price . . . The Chinese cheat with currency manipulation and with industrial espionage—and our alleged commander in chief *lets them cheat*.[42]

Trump echoed his accusation of currency manipulation by China during his presidential candidacy. And while Trump inveighed that American businesses should be buying American products, data collected regarding various Trump products, like his apparel, household goods, hotel items, and beverages, from 2007 to 2016, were largely made in other countries. Twelve countries to be exact, including China, Bangladesh, Honduras, Vietnam, the Netherlands, Mexico, India, Turkey, Slovenia, Germany, Indonesia, and South Korea.[43]

Following the November 2016 election, Trump accepted a congratulatory phone call from the Taiwanese president Tsai Ing-wen. This marked the first time contact was made between Taiwanese leadership and a U.S. president (or president-elect) since 1979, sparking backlash from China for violating the "One China Policy." And while in 2016, Trump stated he did not feel bound by the traditional American acceptance of the "One China Policy," by February 2017 he reaffirmed the United States' commitment to the policy during a phone call with Chinese president Xi Jinping.[44]

Trump and the Philippines

President Trump has formed a relationship with the president of the Philippines, Rodrigo Duterte. Duterte, who once called Obama a "son of a whore" who could "go to hell,"[45] believes that the relationship between the Philippines and the United States has improved because of Trump, describing Trump as a "good friend" who "speaks my language."[46] In the past Duterte has been noted for such controversial language as comparing himself to Adolf Hitler and joking with his troops that rape is an acceptable tool of war. Trump has applauded Duterte's efforts in combating drugs in the Philippines, which has included thousands of extrajudicial killings. In a 2017 phone call with Duterte, Trump stated: "I just wanted to congratulate you because I am hearing of the unbelievable job on the drug problem. Many countries have the problem, we have a problem, but what a great job you are doing and I just wanted to call and tell you that." During this phone call Trump also discussed North Korean leader Kim Jong-un with Duterte:

> Donald Trump: What's your opinion of him, Rodrigo? Are we dealing with someone who [is] stable or not stable?
>
> Rodrigo Duterte: He is not stable, Mr. President, as he keeps on smiling when he explodes a rocket . . . He is laughing always and there's a dangerous toy in his hand, which could create so much agony and suffering for all mankind.
>
> Donald Trump: Well he has got the power but he doesn't have the delivery system. All his rockets are crashing. That's the good news . . . We have a lot of firepower over there. We have two submarines—the best in the world—we have two nuclear submarines—not that we want to use them at all. I've never seen anything like them but we don't have to use this but he could be crazy so we will see what happens.

> Rodrigo Duterte: Every generation has a mad man—in our generation it is Kim Jong-un—you are dealing with a very delicate problem.
>
> Donald Trump: We can handle it.

One of Trump's last remarks to Duterte during the phone call was: "Just take care of yourself, and we will take care of North Korea."

Trump and North Korea

Prior to announcing his presidential candidacy in 2015, Trump has had a history of voicing his opinion on the Democratic People's Republic of Korea (North Korea), especially in 1999 before he first attempted to run for president. In an interview with Tim Russert on *Meet the Press* in 1999, Trump said:

> First, I'd negotiate. I would negotiate like crazy and I'd make sure we tried to get the best deal possible . . . The biggest problem this world has is nuclear proliferation. I mean we have a country out there, North Korea, which is sort of wacko. Which is not, it's not a bunch of dummies and they are going out and they are developing nuclear weapons. And they are not doing it because they are having fun doing it, they are doing it for a reason. And wouldn't it be good to sit down and really negotiate something and I do mean negotiate. Now, if negotiation doesn't work you better solve the problem now than solve it later. And you know Tim and every politician knows it, but no one wants to talk about it. Jimmy Carter who I really like, I mean he went over there and was so soft, these people were laughing at him.[47]

Trump made a similar comment that year in an interview with CNN's Wolf Blitzer, adding that the United States shouldn't rule out any options against North Korea, which he characterized along with Russia as "unstable," including military strikes.[48] In his 2000 book *The America We Deserve*, Trump further explained his views not only on North Korea but the Kim family:

Look at our policy toward North Korea, an outlaw, terrorist state run by a family of certifiable loons. If these guys don't scare you, you've been playing too many interactive games. North Korea has an army of goose-stepping maniacs, and they're building nuclear bombs while most of the population is starving to death. Think it through. What does it mean when the leadership of a country spends money on weapons instead of food for a starving population? Remember, starving populations have toppled more than one regime. If the North Korean rulers are exposing themselves to this kind of risk, you can be sure they're not building these weapons just for the hell of it. They're going to use them if they can.

We discovered this arms-building plan a couple of years ago. What did we do? We offered to build the North Korean government two light-water nuclear reactors and supply them with heating oil if they'd promise to be good. Am I the only one who thinks it might make more sense to disarm the North Korean nuclear threat before it shows up in downtown Seattle or Los Angeles?[49]

Now, with Trump as president of the United States, there is concern that the United States will stumble into an inadvertent war with Kim Jong-un. This is particularly worrisome when one considers that both Trump and Kim are unseasoned in crisis decision-making, and both are under extreme stress now. Declaring it had nuclear weapons in 2003, the DPRK has conducted six nuclear tests since 2006. They have been developing a long-range missile program in parallel, intensifying under Kim Jong-un's leadership, with a total of fourteen solid-fuel rocket tests with twenty-one missiles since February 2017. In July, North Korea successfully launched a solid-state intercontinental ballistic missile which they claimed "could reach anywhere in the world." (United States defense experts estimated that it could reach targets in this country, including Los Angeles, Chicago, and Denver.) In August 2017 President Trump escalated the war of words, warning that "North Korea best not make any more threats to the United States. They will be met with fire and fury like the world has never seen." But a trio of missiles was test-fired on that August 26. In an act of further defiance, on August 29, an intermediate-range ballistic missile (IRBM) was fired over Japan.

One cannot understand and estimate North Korean political behavior without putting it in the context of the Kim dynasty. The founding father of the modern state of North Korea, Kim Il-sung, was a larger-than-life figure. A heroic guerilla fighter who rose to power under the patronage of Stalin, he was given almost godlike stature by his son, Kim Jong-il; in his first position as director of propaganda and agitation he was responsible for burnishing the image of his father. The charismatic Kim Il-sung was responsible for developing the doctrine of *juche* (self-reliance) and the goal of reunification of the Korean peninsula. As he aged, he wisely designated his son as successor, and for the last twenty-five to thirty years of his life, Kim Jong-il was running the day-to-day government under the public face of his father's heroic image.

But Kim Jong-il was *not* a heroic guerrilla fighter, *not* the charismatic founder of his nation, and *not* an ideology creator. It is always difficult psychologically to succeed a successful father. But to be the son of God, as he was depicted, is an overwhelming, impossible challenge. Nevertheless, Kim fostered the myth of continuity between father and son. Having led the Democratic People's Republic of Korea since 1980, Kim Jong-il had a finely tuned set of political antennae, and was always able to pull back from the edge and avoid conflict. Convinced that a nuclear shield was necessary for defensive purposes, Kim continued to develop both a nuclear capability as well as weaponizing them with increasingly sophisticated and powerful rockets. Demonstrating no empathy for his starving people, Kim regularly called for sacrifices from them, while lavishing 40% of the budget on the military and weapons research.

Unlike his father, Kim Jong-il did not designate a successor until he suffered a major stroke in August 2008. Then he designated his third son, Kim Jong-un, as successor. The aggressive acts by the DPRK—the attack on a South Korean frigate, leading to forty-six deaths, and the military shelling of Yeonpyeong Island—were probably designed to prove Kim Jong-un's chops with the DPRK military. He was soon to be promoted to general. His tutelage was cut short by Kim Jong-il's death on December 11, 2011. In vivid contrast to his father, Kim Jong-un was not seasoned and is inexperienced in crisis management.

Moreover, Kim Jong-un, no longer appreciating the continuing guidance and criticism of his uncle and regent Jang Song Thaek, had him killed in 2013. In 2014 he killed his relatives as well, including grandchildren, and in February

2017 ordered his half-brother Kim Jong-nam assassinated in Malaysia with the nerve agent VX.

When President Trump is under extreme stress and subject to heavy criticism, as has often been the case, his tendency is to go on the offensive. Despite President Trump's bellicose words, Kim Jung-un continues his provocative escalation. The death of Otto Warmbier, the twenty-two-year-old student at the University of Virginia who returned home in a coma after a year and half of detention by North Korea, led to pressures for a strong response from President Trump. Trump later responded to the controversy surrounding Warmbier's death, saying that when he questioned Kim about it: "He tells me he didn't know about it and I will take him at his word . . . I don't believe that he would have allowed that to happen. It just wasn't to his advantage. Those prisons are rough, rough places and bad things happen." Trump also stated, referring to Kim as a "friend," that Kim "feels very badly" about what happened.[50] In April 2019 it was reported that Trump may have approved of a $2 million payment in 2017 to North Korea to cover the medical care of Warmbier.

On July 4, 2018, an ICBM was successfully tested, capable of reaching Alaska. This led Kim Jong-un to state that the conflict between North Korea and the U.S. had entered a new phase. On July 28 another ICBM test traveled 2,300 miles, capable of reaching Chicago. Kim Jong-un declared this demonstrated the DPRK now has the capability of mounting a surprise attack. The successful testing of a hydrogen bomb will make Kim Jong-un more confident in his deterrent capabilities. North Korea's accelerating progress toward nuclear-armed intercontinental missiles could offer President Trump an irresistible opportunity to demonstrate his strong, bold leadership in international affairs, and deflect attention from the domestic chaos.

This is reminiscent of President Nixon under the stress of Watergate, when concern was raised about his unilateral control of the nuclear codes, and provisions were made to guard against rash decision-making. There is heightened concern of stumbling into inadvertent war, as both Kim Jong-un and President Trump, neither experienced in crisis management, seem to be locked in a mutually provocative spiral.

President Trump eagerly and unilaterally, in the sense of without consultation with our allies or without being staffed out with the Department of State and Defense, accepted Kim Jong-un's invitation to a summit meeting. While response to the first summit, which occurred in June 2018 in Singapore, was relatively positive, the manner in which President Trump approaches negotiation is apparently based on his individualistic style of decision-making as he functioned in his role as CEO of a major real estate company. In the months following the first summit, when Trump was asked whether he believed he deserved the Nobel Peace Prize, he responded: "Everyone thinks so, but I would never say it."[51] Later on, Trump stated that the prime minister of Japan nominated him for the award, a claim never confirmed by the prime minister. However, according to a report from a Japanese newspaper, Japan only nominated Trump for the award after the White House requested them to do so.[52] Trump also continued to boast about this relationship with Kim Jong-un following the first summit. At a rally in West Virginia, Trump stated: "I was really tough and so was he, and we went back and forth. And then we fell in love, okay? No, really, he wrote me beautiful letters, and they're great letters. We fell in love."[53]

While Trump's first summit meeting with Kim was met with a positive response, the second summit in February 2019 in Vietnam ended abruptly and without any resolution. The summit ended during the second day of negotiations, even prior to the scheduled lunch and agreement signing, over a disagreement regarding the lifting of current sanctions against North Korea. While Kim wanted all international sanctions lifted in exchange for the dismantling of the Yongbyon nuclear complex, Trump would not agree to lifting sanctions unless an entire inventory of nuclear weapons was provided, as well as the dismantling of other sites outside of Yongbyon. In regard to the quick end to the summit, Trump stated: "Sometimes you have to walk."[54] In April 2019, North Korea's vice foreign minister stated on North Korean state media that "if the United States fails to reestablish its position within the timeline we gave, it will see truly undesired consequences."[55]

In fact, the negative results of the second summit between Trump and Kim prompted Kim to hold a similar summit with Vladimir Putin. Russia reportedly extended the invitation for a summit over a year ago, but it was not until the breakdown in talks between Trump and Kim in February 2019 that Kim finally agreed to meet with Putin. The purpose of the summit was to set up Russia as an intermediary between North Korea and the United States, with Kim believing that current intermediaries to Trump, including the current U.S. secretary of state Michael Pompeo, were not properly representing North Korea's message. Putin stated of the summit: "We are all pleased with the outcome of the talks—both I and my colleagues. Chairman Kim Jong-un is a fairly open person, leading a free discussion on all issues that were on the agenda," and that "Chairman Kim Jong-un himself asked us to inform the American side about his position."[56] Another sign of the failing relationship between Kim and Trump is the Pentagon's announcement on May 8 that North Korea has halted the war dead program. The program, which was a sign of improved relations between the two countries following the first summit, focused on the returning of the remains of U.S. servicemen killed during the Korean War. In 2018, fifty remains were returned to the United States. There are most likely a great deal more remains, as 7,700 of the 36,000 American servicemen who died during the war are still unaccounted for, and roughly 5,300 of those were lost in North Korea. It is important, as with Putin, to understand not only the relationship between Kim and Trump, but the psychology of Kim and how he may continue to react toward Trump and the United States.

Kim Jong-un: A Mini Political Personality Profile

Unlike Kim Jong-il, who was designated as successor some thirty years before his father's death and held significant positions in his father's government—indeed probably running North Korea for the last fifteen years of his father's life—Kim Jong-un, who is his father's third son, was only designated as successor after Kim Jong-il suffered a stroke in August 2008. Indeed, there had been great uncertainty as to who would succeed Kim Jong-il. The initial favorite of the Kim sons was the eldest, Kim Jong-nam, who faced a great deal of public embarrassment in 2001 after being caught trying to enter Japan with a fake Dominican Republic passport in order to visit Tokyo's Disneyland. Kim Jong-il's second son Kim Jong-chul was reportedly passed over due to being considered "too effeminate," a euphemism for being gay.

Kim Jong-un has had virtually no experience, but nevertheless was named Kim Jong-il's successor. Despite no military experiences, he was named a four-star general in the People's Army, deputy chairman of the military commission of the Workers' Party, member of the party's Central Committee, and deputy chairman of the party's military commission in 2010. It is widely speculated that North Korea's attack on the South Korean frigate in March 2010, and the more recent artillery shelling of Yeonpyeong, are indications that Kim Jong-un had to earn his stripes with the North Korean military, and that Kim Jong-il was helping to build the credentials of his son.

His father was well seasoned, and while there have been provocative actions for two decades and frequent belligerent rhetoric, he always showed restraint and pulled back from the brink. In vivid contrast, Kim Jong-un is unseasoned and inexperienced, and we cannot be confident of the degree to which he is exerting control of his wisdom and judgment. Especially with the climate in South Korea having changed under President Park Guen-hye, who came to office in 2008 vowing to end the decade-long "sunshine policy" of her two predecessors. There is widespread support in South Korea for a strong response to North Korea's provocations, but there is a significant possibility of one side or another going too far and precipitating conflict.

Recognizing his son's youth and inexperience, Kim Jong-il appointed Choe Ryong-hae and his sister's husband Jang Song-thaek as co-regents. It is not clear how disabled Kim Jong-il was from his stroke in terms of his leadership functioning. What is clear is that Jang Song-thaek was exercising close control over the leadership of Kim Jong-un and probably was the source of increasing resentment by him. When Kim Jong-il died at the end of 2011, never having fully recovered from his stroke, the influence of the uncle began to decline toward the end of 2012. We can infer that Kim Jong-un was feeling increasingly confident of his own leadership, and resenting the control of his uncle. Moreover, the relationship between Kim's aunt Kim Kyong-hui and her husband became estranged, and she was apparently accusing him of forming a plot. Following the arrest and execution of Jang's two deputies in November 2013, he was secretly detained until his staged public arrest and then executed in December of that year. Reports later came out that following the execution of his uncle, Kim Jong-un ordered the execution of not only Jang's followers, but his extended family as well. Thus, he had fully consolidated his power with the elimination of the challenges or constraints to his leadership.

The first recorded nuclear test for North Korea was in 2006, with Kim Jong-il fully in charge. The second test, which occurred in 2009 after Kim Jong-il's stroke, may have represented the military's commitment to a long-planned operation. Despite active warnings against another test by China, Russia, European nations, and the United States, the third test occurred in February 2013 after Kim Jong-il's death, when Kim Jong-un was in place as his successor. This came after the decline of Kim Jong-un's uncle Jang Song-thaek's influence at the end of 2012. Ongoing decisions in the nuclear program were now solely in the hands of Kim Jong-un.

Trump's Followers and Foreign Policy

While Trump's foreign policy decisions have appeared to some as being almost chaotic, with his stances toward various countries changing continually, in many ways his foreign policy has focused on appeasing his base. Trump declared that as president he would keep "America First," especially in terms of foreign policy decisions, and for the most part he has maintained that promise. From berating the United States' European allies over NATO to starting a trade war with China and even supporting regimes that have been cited for numerous human rights violations because "they have money," Trump is only focused on American money and preserving his image to his base. And many of his foreign policy decisions have been supported not only by his base, but by non-followers as well. Trump has long declared that he is a president against humanitarian interventions and it is a position that many Americans, both Republican and Democrat, agree on. In the study, *Worlds Apart: U.S. Foreign Policy and American Public Opinion*, conducted by the Eurasia Group Foundation (EGF), the organization found that most Americans do not want the United States to become entangled abroad. Whether or not someone is a Trump supporter, or even supports his foreign policy decisions, his actions represent a larger portion of American public opinion than most other U.S. politicians.[57]

16

What Does the Future Hold?

> *"Do not go gentle into that good night*
> *But rage, rage against the dying of the light"*
> —Dylan Thomas, 1947

One of our favorite poems by Welshman Dylan Thomas is this marvelous poem about confronting dying, written while he was attending to his dying father. In this, the most famous of Thomas's poems, he was urging his dying father not to accept death but to vigorously resist it. And we thought how well it summarized questions being asked about how Donald Trump will accept possible defeat in the 2020 elections.

Joshua Geltzer explores the provocative question, "What if Trump refuses to accept defeat in 2020?" As Geltzer noted in exploring why this question needed to be answered, overstepping presidential authority is increasingly Trump's way as he displayed his "willingness to overstep unprecedented presidential power" as evidenced by his declaring, with no foundation, a national emergency at the southern border with Mexico.[1]

As a presidential candidate in 2016, Trump stated that he would refuse to commit, that he would honor the results of the election if he lost. Attempting to discredit Clinton's popular victory in the 2016 election, he claimed massive voter fraud by illegal aliens. As the 2018 midterms approached Trump expressed his concern that the "Russians would be fighting very hard for a Clinton victory." So in his fevered imagination, there was a real basis for voter fraud. And this suggests, given his reliance on the defense mechanism of projection, that he would consider implementing voter fraud. Now with the 2020 elections looming, Trump refuses to accept any poll that does not show him in the lead. On June 17, 2019, he tweeted: "Only Fake Polls show us behind the Motley Crew. We are looking really good, but it is far too early to be focused on that. Much work to do! MAKE AMERICA GREAT AGAIN!" Trump is even refusing to accept polls from his favorite news source, Fox News, that do not show him in the lead, also tweeting in June 2019: "@FoxNews Polls are always bad for me. They were against Crooked Hillary also. Something weird going on at Fox. Our polls show us leading in all 17 Swing States . . ."

The consistency of Trump's attacks on the media and on the intelligence community is impressive and adds to the impression that he might well not accept the election results if they documented his loss.

Geltzer suggests four steps that could be utilized should Trump lose the election and refuses to accept defeat:

1. Electoral college. Geltzer recommends that electors pledge that they will not withhold, delay, or alter their vote based on the claims or protestations of any candidate, including President Trump.
2. Congress. It is the newly elected representatives who on January 21, 2020, meet to receive the electoral votes. They, too, should pledge in the manner suggested for the electoral college not to alter their votes.
3. Among governors, thirty-nine of fifty will not be up for reelection in 2020. They can play a useful role should there be controversy over accepting the electors' ballots, as exemplified by Governor Mike Huckabee's constructive role in resolving the controversy concerning the special election for senate seat in December 2017.
4. There is potentially a constructive role for senior military executives, in particular the secretary of defense and chairman of the joint chiefs, if Congress certifies a Trump loss, and Trump refuses to step down on January 21, 2020.

Journalist Robin Wright has raised the provocative question: Is America headed for a new kind of civil war? Referring to the violence in

Charlottesville and the deadly episodes in Ferguson, Missouri, Charleston, Dallas, St. Paul, Baltimore, Baton Rouge, and Alexandria, Virginia, she asks: Where is the country going? In a discussion with Keith Mines, who spent his career dealing with civil wars on five continents, he provides his definition of civil wars, which is of large-scale violence that includes a rejection of traditional political authority and requires the National Guard to deal with it. Writing her essay after the tragic and deadly violence in Charlottesville, she tellingly observed that Virginia Governor Terry McAuliffe had put the National Guard on alert and declared a state of emergency.

Mines was one of the authors asked by *Foreign Policy* to estimate the likelihood of America descending into a civil war. He estimated there was a 60% chance! Other experts indicated from 5% to 95%. The consensus was 35% and as Wright emphasizes, this was before Charlottesville. And it was during the fatal violence in Charlottesville between the neo–Nazis and counter-protesters that Trump made the troubling relativistic observation that "there were fine people on both sides." And whether or not Trump wins the election of 2020, the divisions his presidency has caused while likely take years if not decades to mend.

Trump thrives on conflict. He very skillfully exploits fault lines at his rallies, encouraging his base to engage violently against any counter-demonstrators, saying he will pay any of their legal fees. In his inaugural address, the typical call to come together as one nation and talk of healing after a contentious campaign was not in evidence. Rather, he was the jubilant victor.

Should Trump succeed in winning the 2020 election, we can expect a triumphant cry of vindication, with little attention paid to being president for all the people. He will seem almost high. In addition, Trump has continued to make "jokes" about expanding his presidency past two terms, despite it being unconstitutional. This has included comments of praise for China's "president for life" Xi Jinping and a recent tweet that stated: ". . . after America has been made GREAT again and I leave the beautiful White House (do you think the people would demand that I stay longer? KEEP AMERICA GREAT) . . ." On the other hand, should he lose, it will not be gracefully accepted. Rather he will "rage, rage, at the passing of the light," for the loss of the limelight which has been such a rewarding accompaniment of the presidential role will be very difficult for him to tolerate.

The interregnum between the election and the inauguration will be a time of particular vulnerability. Should they be President Trump's last months in power, it could well add to pressure to act with reference to the failing state of Venezuela, or to counter Kim Jong-un's short-range missile tests. The 2019 summit between Kim Jong-un and Vladimir Putin adds an additional level of complexity to this fragile region. This frequently observed tendency for Donald Trump to take bold actions when he has suffered reverses can be anticipated as his way of regaining the feeling of being in charge.

And it is not only Trump who may not accept defeat in 2020, but his supporters as well. One is reminded of the trending hashtag prior to the 2016 election, #repealthe19th, whereby some Trump supporters actually advocated for the repeal of the Nineteenth Amendment to the U.S. Constitution, which gave women the right to vote. This social media movement was in response to a finding that was posted on *FiveThirtyEight*, which argued that if only men voted Trump would win by a large margin and that if only women voted Hillary Clinton would win by an enormous margin. While this social media movement was not supported by a majority of his followers, it demonstrates the extremeness of some of his supporters, and raises red flags regarding their possible reaction to the 2020 election. Trump's rhetoric has already inspired violent actions by a number of supporters, including attacks at his rallies and the 2018 attempted mail bombings. If Trump loses in 2020 and he chooses to call foul play or tout conspiracy theories, it is unclear just how extreme the reaction of some of his supporters may be.

Until 2020 we will expect to see bold actions taken by Trump to restore his sense of strong leadership, especially if his poll numbers fall. And if he feels his grip on popular support faltering, he assuredly will not "go gentle into that good night, but will rage, rage at the passing of the light."

EPILOGUE

One of the most difficult aspects of writing this book was the feeling that we were chasing history, as with each passing day President Donald Trump continued to dominate media headlines both at home and abroad. Though this book in no way was meant to capture every moment of Trump's life or of his presidency, it is meant to provide the readers with a clearer understanding of both the political personality of Trump and that of his followers. But as we draw closer the end of Trump's term and the impending 2020 elections, we see a man who continues to rile up his supporters. This section of the book will highlight some of the events that have occurred since the completion of this book to further emphasize a number of the issues that have been discussed:

Gun Rights, Hunting, and Environmentalism

Trump is continuing to focus on issues that have been important to his followers, including gun rights and hunting rights, as well as weakening U.S. environmental protection laws. On August 1, 2019, the White House released an official statement from Trump honoring National Shooting Sports month, a major recruitment month for the National Rifle Association (NRA), in which Trump praises the right to keep and bear arms as one of the United States' "most-cherished liberties." In the statement, he also boasts about the June 2019 plan which will open an additional 1.4 million acres of wildlife refuges and fish hatcheries for hunting and fishing. Then on August 12, 2019, the Trump administration announced rules to further weaken the Endangered Species Act. The new rules will reduce the amount of land set aside for wildlife and removes the tools used by officials to predict harm to species caused by climate change. In addition, these rules will scale back regulations placed on corporations, including granting more access to the gas and oil industry who wish to drill on protected land.

Immigration

Stemming the tide of immigrates has been and continues to be a major focal point not only for Trump, but for his followers as well. In addition to his efforts to increase security along the southern border, including his desire to build a wall, Trump has encouraged and applauded raids on undocumented immigrants in the United States by the U.S. Immigration and Customs Enforcement (ICE). On July 12, 2019, Trump announced that up to 2,000 undocumented immigrants would be detained by ICE, stating a few days later: "they're going to bring them back to their countries or they're gonna take criminals out, put them in prison, or put them in prison in the countries they came from…We're focused on criminals as much as we can…we're taking them out by the thousands, we're getting them out." In August 2019, ICE carried out one of the largest immigration raids in U.S. history, arresting 680 workers from seven food processing plants in Mississippi. Trump hailed the raid, stating: "I want people to know that if they come into the United States illegally, they're getting out. They're going to be brought out. And this serves as a very good deterrent."

Drain the Swamp

The June 2019 public announcement of the move of researchers from two wings of the U.S. Department of Agriculture, the Economic Research Service and the National Institute of Food and Agriculture, to Kansas City is being viewed by proponents of the decision as an attempt to drain the swamp. In fact, following reports that up to 2/3 of the researchers will resign, acting White House chief of staff Mick Mulvaney joked: "what a wonderful way to streamline the government!" Proponents of the move have also argued that this will weaken the role scientific research has on policy making decisions, including research on climate change. The move has also encountered criticism from employees due to the short amount of time given to relocate, as well as waivers for special consideration due to medical treatment or familial circumstances being denied. The Trump administration argues, however, that the move will not only be cost-saving, but that it will also allow the researchers to have easier access to rural areas.

Lack of Empathy

In addition, we see a man who is consistently exemplifying the quintessential narcissist, showing time and time again his inability to empathize with others. For instance, on July 17th in the White House Trump met with victims of religious persecution, including individuals from Iraq, China, Myanmar, and North Korea, as well as a Holocaust survivor. During the meeting, Trump claimed that he doesn't think that any president has taken religious freedom abroad as seriously as he. Despite this claim, Trump went on to question Yazidi human rights activist Nadia Murad on why she won the Nobel Peace Prize. Murad, who lost most of her family during the Islamic State's attempt to ethnically cleanse the Yazidi people, has been an advocate not only for the Yazidi victims of the Islamic State, but also for women who have suffered sexual violence. Personal experiences she had explained to him prior to his questioning her about winning the Noble Peace Prize. Then only two days after this meeting, it was reported that the Trump administration is considering not allowing any refugees to enter the United States in 2020.

Paranoia

Trump's relentless focus on conspiracy theories of a "deep state coup" against him was further intensified by Robert Mueller's testimony before Congress on July 24, 2019. This resulted in further accusations by Trump that the investigation was "treasonous" and a "witch hunt", continuing his claims that there was no obstruction of justice and no collusion with Russia. Painting himself as a victim Trump has repeatedly claimed that he has been persecuted and treated worse than any other president in U.S. history. In a tweet from July

31, Trump even went so far to invoke the language of "never again" a phrase commonly used for Holocaust remembrance. While Trump has asserted that Mueller's investigation exonerated him, during his testimony Mueller himself stated that the report did not exonerate Trump. Mueller additionally said that there is a possibility Trump could be prosecuted for obstruction of justice following the end of his presidency. As the 2020 election approaches, it is likely his paranoid reactions to the media and to his critics will magnify.

Rhetoric

On the weekend of August 4, 2019, two mass shootings took place, one in El Paso, Texas and one in Dayton, Ohio, within a matter of 14 hours, leaving 31 dead and dozens injured. While the motive of Connor Betts, the Dayton shooter, appears at this time to be based on an obsession with violence and mass shootings, the motive of Patrick Crusius, the El Paso shooter, appears to be based upon hatred for the Latinx community and the attack itself is being investigated as an act of domestic terrorism. Crusius, who opened fire at a Walmart, told the authorities that he was targeting "Mexicans." He is also reportedly a Trump supporter. His social media presence has included praises of Trump and Trump's attempt to build a wall, as well as a photo of guns spelling out "Trump."

In addition, a manifesto, which was posted an hour prior to the shooting on 8chan, an online message board popular for the far right, is believed to be have been authored by Crusius. The 2,300-word screed discusses the "Hispanic invasion of Texas," expresses support for the March 2019 New Zealand mosque shooting and warns that white Americans are being replaced by foreigners. Aspects of the manifesto, including the use of the term "invasion," is reminiscent of Trump's own rhetoric. A recent analysis of Facebook's political ad archive conducted by CNN found that Trump has run nearly 2,200 ads with the word "invasion" at the U.S. border. Maria Teresa Kumar, the CEO of the organization Voto Latino, has characterized the El Paso shooting as a "resounding accumulation" of Trump's rhetoric.

Shortly after the shooting Trump tweeted: "Today's shooting in El Paso, Texas was not only tragic, it was an act of cowardice. I know that I stand with everyone in this Country to condemn today's hateful act. There are no reasons or excuses that will ever justify killing innocent people." The Wednesday following the shooting, August 7th, Trump traveled to El Paso to meet with first responders, survivors and families of the victims. After reportedly getting upset with his aides that his visit to Dayton earlier that day was not receiving positive press, Trump demanded proof that people in El Paso were happy to see him. Trump's social media director, Dan Scavino, subsequently tweeted following the El Paso hospital visit: "The President was treated like a Rock Star inside the hospital, which was all caught on video. They all loved seeing their great President!" During Trump's visit to the hospital, Trump was caught on camera boasting about the rally he held in El Paso a few months ago, stating: "That place was packed. ... That was some crowd. And we had twice the number outside. And then you had this crazy Beto. Beto had like 400 people in a parking lot, they said his crowd was wonderful." In fact, El Paso has been mentioned in a number of tweets by Trump since that rally in February 2019. Trump's last tweet regarding El Paso, prior to the shooting, was on May 30th in which he wrote: "Yesterday, Border Patrol agents apprehended the largest group of illegal aliens ever: 1,036 people who illegally crossed the border in El Paso around 4am. Democrats need to stand by our incredible Border Patrol and finally fix the loopholes at our Border!"

While Trump's recent political behavior is consistent with the portrait we have drawn, there is evidence he is under increasing pressure, pressure that will continue to mount as the 2020 election approaches.

ENDNOTES

PREFACE

1. This was a notable occasion for the discipline of political psychology, being the first time that a political personality profile of a foreign leader was presented in testimony to Congress. The testimony can be found in the *Congressional Record*, December 5 and 12, 1990, under the title "Saddam Hussein of Iraq: A Political Psychology Profile." It has also been printed in *Political Psychology* (Post, 1991).
2. The Tarasoff principle derives from a controversial case (Tarasoff v. State of California) in which a client in counseling told his therapist that he was obsessed with a coed and that if she would not go out with him, he would kill her. She would not, and he killed her. In the trial, the therapist claimed that he could not warn her because to do so would violate confidentiality. The California Supreme Court overruled this previously all-encompassing principle of confidentiality, indicating that when specific danger emerged in the course of counseling, there was a "duty to warn."
3. Allen Dyer, who served on the original commission that formulated the ethical principles applicable to psychiatrists, has noted that originally these were intended to be ethical principles, to serve as guidelines, where what is now referred to as the Goldwater Rule has become a prohibition in the sense of "Thou shalt not."

INTRODUCTION

1. This chapter is drawn from Post, Jerrold (1986), "Narcissism and the Charismatic Leader-Follower Relationship," *Political Psychology*, vol. 7, no. 4, pp. 675–688, and chapter 6 in Dr. Post's book *Narcissism and Politics: Dreams of Glory* (New York: Cambridge University Press, 2015).
2. A few words about the psychoanalytic concept of transference are in order. As originally conceptualized by Freud, transference refers to the feelings that develop between the client and the psychoanalyst during psychoanalytic treatment, in

which the client *transfers* feelings that originated in his childhood to the psychoanalyst. Thus the client with a highly authoritarian father is apt to relate to the psychoanalyst as if he is authoritarian. But the term has been broadened in its contemporary applications so that it now refers to any distortion of a relationship wherein the individual relates to individuals in his current interpersonal surround as if they are ghosts from the past. Thus the individual referred to earlier who had been raised by a highly authoritarian father may relate to authority figures—bosses, teachers—with anxiety. Indeed the reason for seeking psychoanalytic treatment may well be because of recognition of this long-standing anxiety concerning authority. Interpreting and resolving the transference is at the very heart of psychoanalytic therapy.

In the earliest stage of development—the stage of primary narcissism—the infant does not distinguish between himself and others. He experiences the external world—his mother—as part of himself. He is not just the center of the universe—he is the universe. As the young child experiences the frustrating reality of the external world's less-than-perfect response to his needs, he begins to differentiate himself from it. He is demoted from being the universe to becoming merely its center. Two psychological constellations develop as ways of restoring a sense of completeness.

The first is the ideal or grandiose self. The "mirroring" responses of the mother—her admiration and attention—allow the child to feel special and highly valued. This treasured position is maintained by an important psychological mechanism called "splitting." The very young child is unable to tolerate the bad aspects of himself and his environment and to integrate them with the good ones into a realistic whole. He splits the good and the bad into the "me" and the "not me." Thus, by rejecting all aspects of himself and his situation that do not fit his ideal or grandiose self, the child attempts to maintain it.

The child's second mechanism for remedying frustration and incompleteness is to attach himself to an ideal object (Kernberg), or idealized parental image (Kohut), which derives particularly from the father. This is the fantasized image of the all-powerful, all-knowing, all-giving, all-loving parent. The child gains his own sense of being complete and worthwhile by experiencing himself as connected to, united with, his idealized object. In Crayton's (1983) formulation, "If I am not perfect, I will at least be in a relationship with something perfect."

If the child is traumatized during this critical period of development, his emerging self-concept is damaged, leading to the formation of what Kohut calls "the injured self." Such damage can occur in several ways. Children rejected by cold and ungiving mothers may be left emotionally hungry, with an exaggerated need for love and admiration. A special form of rejection is overprotection by the intrusive narcissistic mother. She cannot let her child individuate because she sees him as an extension of herself. Her own sense of perfection seems to depend on her child's perfection. (This mechanism has been discussed in the chapter "Entrepreneurial Provenance," with the examples of the mothers of General Douglas MacArthur, Woodrow Wilson, and Australian Prime Minister Bob Hawke, among others, who groomed their sons to be the vehicle of their own success in this world.)

3   I had a colleague whose father was a diplomat in Germany in the 1930s, during the rise of Hitler. As a boy of eight, he accompanied his father to a Hitler Youth rally and was transfixed by the experience. He described the theatrical spectacle, the solitary figure walking alone, the spotlight on him, the stadium in darkness. At times, Hitler's voice dropped to a whisper, and the stadium was so quiet one could hear a pin drop as the adoring crowd strained to hear his every word. At other times, his voice was an exultant roar. "I didn't understand a word of German, but I would have followed him anywhere."

4   Using carefully designed questionnaires together with structured interviews, Dr. Galanter, then with the Department of Psychiatry, Albert Einstein College of Medicine, has systematically studied the social psychology of the members of charismatic religious cults (1978, 1979, 1980, 1983, 1986).

5   The observations of Wilfred Bion (1961) concerning repetitive patterns of group behavior add further to our understanding of the forces mobilized in followers by charismatic leaders. Bion's work has been elaborated by the Tavistock Institute in Great Britain and the A. K. Rice Institute in the United States through their Human Relations Conferences on the roles of leadership, authority, and responsibility in organizations. Working with psychologically healthy executives, educators, and health care professionals, the staffs of these organizations continue to reconfirm the observations Bion first made with psychiatric inpatients in military hospitals in Great Britain. He noted that no matter how healthy the individuals, when they come together in a group they behave as if they are acting on the basis of shared basic assumptions. He described three psychological states that regularly come into play—three emotional states by which group members act as if they are dominated. He calls these three "basic assumption" groups: the dependency group, the pairing group, and the fight-flight group. The dependency group turns to an omnipotent leader for security. Acting as if they do not have independent minds of their own, the members blindly seek directions and follow orders unquestioningly. They tend to idealize and place the leader on a pedestal, but when the leader fails to meet the standards of omnipotence and omniscience, after a period of denial, anger and disappointment result. In the pairing group, the members act as if the goal of the group is to bring forth a Messiah, someone who will save them. There is an air of optimism and hope that a new world is around the corner. And the fight-flight group organizes itself in relationship to a perceived outside threat. The group itself is idealized as part of a polarizing mechanism, while the outside group is regularly seen as malevolent in motivation. The threatening outside world is at once a threat to the existence of the group, and also the justification for its existence.

1: THE QUINTESSENTIAL NARCISSIST

1   Alex Horton, "'Give it hell, John': Washington reacts to Sen. McCain's cancer diagnosis," *Washington Post*, July 20, 2017, https://www.washingtonpost.com

/news/powerpost/wp/2017/07/19/tougher-than-a-2-steak-washington-reacts-to-john-mccains-tumordiagnosisnoredirect=on&utm_term=.ad707cf7c0ee.

2. Kevin Breuninger, "Trump aide reportedly said John McCain's view on CIA pick 'doesn't matter' because 'he's dying anyway'," CNBC, May 11, 2018, https://www.cnbc.com/2018/05/11/wh-aide-dismissed-mccain-view-saying-hes-dying-sources.html.

3. "Donald Trump full interview," *This Week with George Stephanopoulos*, video, 20:21, https://www.youtube.com/watch?v=hhy-xQbQ14s.

4. Jenna Johnson, "Even in hurricane-ravaged Texas, Trump keeps the focus on himself," *Washington Post*, August 29, 2017, https://www.washingtonpost.com/politics/even-in-visiting-hurricane-ravaged-texas-trump-keeps-the-focus-on-himself2017/08/29/3037a4a6-8cc3-11e7-84c0-02cc069f2c37_story.html?utm_term=.f2a7f786064e.

5. Donald J. Trump, Twitter, June 29, 2017, 8:52 A.M., https://twitter.com/realdonaldtrump/status/880408582310776832?lang=en.

6. "President Trump Bashes Senator As 'Phony Vietnam Con Artist'," *Time*, video, 2:10, https://www.youtube.com/watch?v=1A_aerHucEY.

7. Donald J. Trump and Kate Bohner, *Trump: The Art of the Comeback* (New York: Times Books, 1997).

8. Donald J. Trump, *Crippled America: How to Make America Great Again* (New York: Simon & Schuster, 2011).

9. Donald J. Trump, Twitter, June 15, 2017, 4:57 A.M., https://twitter.com/realdonaldtrump/status/875321478849363968?lang=en.

10. Donald J. Trump, Twitter, January 11, 2017, 7:48 A.M., https://twitter.com/realdonaldtrump/status/819164172781060096?lang=en.

11. Donald J. Trump and Kate Bohner, *Trump: The Art of the Comeback* (New York: Times Books, 1997).

12. Donald J. Trump, Twitter, December 15, 2014, 4:53 A.M., https://twitter.com/realdonaldtrump/status/544611347255013376?lang=en.

13. "Trump Warns GOPers 'Anybody Who Hits Me, We're Gonna Hit Them 10 Times Harder'," *Fox News Insider* (blog), video, 11:25, https://www.youtube.com/watch?v=aG87U_VSg9w.

14. Donald J. Trump and Bill Zanker, *Think Big: Make It Happen in Business and Life* (New York: HarperBusiness, 2008).

15. Donald J. Trump, Twitter, November 27, 2016, 3:30 P.M., https://twitter.com/realdonaldtrump/status/802972944532209664?lang=en.

16. Alex Wigglesworth, "Trump on new poll results: 'Would still beat Hillary'," *Los Angeles Times*, April 23, 2017, https://www.latimes.com/politics/la-pol-updates-everything-president-trump-shares-poll-1492981332-htmlstory.html.

17. Donald J. Trump, Twitter, January 22, 2017, 7:51 A.M., https://twitter.com/realdonaldtrump/status/823151124815507460?lang=en.

18. The authors wish to acknowledge the contribution of Sheldon Roth, M.D. and psychiatrist, in calling their attention to Donald Trump identifying the Orson Welles film *Citizen Kane* as his favorite film.

ENDNOTES

2: ENTREPRENEURIAL PROVENANCE

1. Gwenda Blair, *The Trumps: Three Generations of Builders and a President* (New York: Simon & Schuster, 2001).
2. Mike Pearl, "About Fred Trump's Alleged Involvement with the KKK," *Vice*, March 10, 2016, https://www.vice.com/en_us/article/mvke38/all-the-evidence-we-could-find-about-fred-trumps-alledged-involvement-with-the-kkk.
3. *Papers of Woodrow Wilson*, Vol. 1, JWW to WW, May 20, 1974 (Princeton, NJ: Princeton University Press).
4. Michael Kruse, "The Mystery of Mary Trump," *Politico*, 2017, https://www.politico.com/magazine/story/2017/11/03/mary-macleod-trump-donald-trump-mother-biography-mom-immigrant-scotland-215779.
5. Donald J. Trump, *Crippled America: How to Make America Great Again* (New York: Simon & Schuster, 2011).
6. "Inside Donald Trump's military school," CNN, video, 3:12, 2016, https://www.cnn.com/videos/politics/2016/04/12/donald-trump-military-school-sanchez-pkg-ebof.cnn.

3: SEEKING THE SPOTLIGHT

1. Marie Brenner, "How Donald Trump and Roy Cohn's Ruthless Symbiosis Changed America," *Vanity Fair*, June 28, 2017, https://www.vanityfair.com/news/2017/06/donald-trump-roy-cohn-relationship.
2. Michael Kruse, "I Need Loyalty," *Politico*, April 28, 2018, https://www.politico.com/magazine/story/2018/03/06/donald-trump-loyalty-staff-217227.
3. Donald J. Trump and Meredith McIver, *Trump: Think Like a Billionaire: Everything You Need to Know About Success, Real Estate, and Life* (New York: Ballantine Books, 2005).
4. Tony Schwartz, "I wrote *The Art of the Deal* with Trump. His self-sabotage is rooted in his past," *Washington Post*, May 16, 2017, https://www.washingtonpost.com/posteverything/wp/2017/05/16/i-wrote-the-art-of-the-deal-with-trump-his-self-sabotage-is-rooted-in-his-past/?noredirect=on&utm_term=.223e583cd3eb.
5. "Donald Trump: GOP Takes Me Seriously," CNN, video, 01:46, https://www.youtube.com/watch?time_continue=1&v=AbdE1GNy7pQ.
6. James Barron, "In Trump, the Game, The Object is Money," *New York Times*, February 8, 1989, https://www.nytimes.com/1989/02/08/nyregion/in-trump-the-game-the-object-is-money.html.
7. Christopher Lasch, *The Culture of Narcissism: American Life in an Age of Diminishing Expectations* (New York: W.W. Norton & Company, 1991).
8. Glenn Plaskin, "The 1990 *Playboy* Interview with Donald Trump," *Playboy*, March 1, 1990, https://www.playboy.com/read/playboy-interview-donald-trump-1990.
9. Emily Nussbaum, "The TV That Created Donald Trump," *New Yorker*, July 24, 2017, https://www.newyorker.com/magazine/2017/07/31/the-tv-that-created-donald-trump.
10. David Hochman, "The 2004 *Playboy* Interview with Donald Trump," *Playboy*, October 01, 2004, https://www.playboy.com/read/donald-trump-interview.

11   Patrick Radden Keefe, "How Mark Burnett Resurrected Donald Trump as an Icon of American Success," *New Yorker*, December 27, 2018, https://www.newyorker.com/magazine/2019/01/07/how-mark-burnett-resurrected-donald-trump-as-an-icon-of-american-success.

4: THE RELATIONSHIPS OF A NARCISSIST

1   Donald J. Trump and Charles Leerhsen, *Trump: Surviving at the Top* (New York: Random House, 1990).
2   Evgenia Peretz, "Inside the Trump Marriage: Melania's Burden," *Vanity Fair*, April 21, 2017, https://www.vanityfair.com/news/2017/04/donald-melania-trump-marriage.
3   Donald J. Trump and Kate Bohner, *Trump: The Art of the Comeback* (New York: Times Books, 1997).
4   "Watch Donald Trump Tell Oprah in 1988 That Ivana Does Whatever I Say," *Inside Edition*, video, 1:30, March 25, 2016, https://www.youtube.com/watch?v=aHpJUD_X_mE.
5   Donald J. Trump and Kate Bohner, *Trump: The Art of the Comeback* (New York: Times Books, 1997).
6   Ibid.
7   "Interview: Donald Trump on The Howard Stern Show—November 9, 1999," *Factbase*, 2019, https://factba.se/transcript/donald-trump-interview-howard-stern-show-november-9-1999.
8   Ibid.
9   "Melania Trump: The unusual, traditional First Lady," BBC, February 9, 2017, https://www.bbc.com/news/election-us-2016-37256893.
10   Lauren Effron, "Why You Don't See Donald Trump's Wife Melania Out on the Campaign Trail," ABC News, November 20, 2015, https://abcnews.go.com/Politics/donald-trumps-wife-melania-campaign-trail/story?id=35309120.
11   "US child migrants: First ladies speak out on Trump separation policy," BBC, June 18, 2018, https://www.bbc.com/news/world-us-canada-44515123.
12   Chris Cillizza, "Melania Trump totally changed her story on the 'I really don't care' jacket," CNN, October 14, 2018, https://www.cnn.com/2018/10/13/politics/melania-trump-jacket-i-really-dont-care-do-u/index.html.
13   Donald J. Trump, *Crippled America: How to Make America Great Again* (New York, Simon & Schuster, 2011).
14   Michele Gorman, "Transcript: Donald Trump's Family Town Hall with CNN," *Newsweek*, April 13, 2016, https://www.newsweek.com/donald-trump-cnn-family-town-hall-full-transcript-new-york-city-447144.
15   Jonathan Van Meter, "Did Their Father Really Know Best?," *New York Magazine*, December 4, 2004, http://nymag.com/nymag/features/10610/.
16   Ibid.
17   Tim Elfrink, "Miami DJ Says He Watched Donald Trump Brutally Slap His Son in College," *Miami New Times*, November 4, 2016, https://www.miaminewtimes

ENDNOTES

.com/news/miami-dj-says-he-watched-donald-trump-brutally-slap-his-son-in-college-8900500.

18 Robert Slater, *No Such Thing as Over-Exposure: Inside the Life and Celebrity of Donald Trump* (Upper Saddle River, NJ: Prentice Hall, 2007).

19 Maxwell Tani, "Donald Trump Jr. says media would be 'warming up the gas chamber" if his dad acted like Clinton," *Business Insider*, September 15, 2016, https://www.businessinsider.com/donald-trump-warming-up-gas-chamber-holocaust-2016-9.

20 Robyn Barry, "Donald Trump Jr. compares Syrian refugees to Skittles," BBC, September 20, 2016, https://www.bbc.com/news/election-us-2016-37416457.

21 Rebecca Leung, "Eric Trump: American Royalty," CBS News, June 9, 2003, https://www.cbsnews.com/news/eric-trump-american-royalty/.

22 Ibid.

23 Ibid.

24 Ivanka Trump, *The Trump Card: Playing to Win in Work and Life* (New York: Touchstone, 2010).

25 Ivanka Trump, *Women Who Work: Rewriting the Rules for Success* (New York: Portfolio, 2017).

26 Jia Tolentino, "Ivanka Trump Wrote a Painfully Oblivious Book for Basically No One," *New Yorker*, May 4, 2017, https://www.newyorker.com/books/page-turner/ivanka-trump-wrote-a-painfully-oblivious-book-for-basically-no-one.

27 Annalisa Quinn, "Many Working Women Won't See Themselves In 'Women Who Work'," NPR, May 3, 2017, https://www.npr.org/2017/05/03/526580960/many-working-women-wont-see-themselves-in-women-who-work.

28 Jodi Kantor, Rachel Abrams and Maggie Haberman, "Ivanka Trump Has the President's Ear. Here's Her Agenda," *New York Times*, https://www.nytimes.com/2017/05/02/us/politics/ivanka-trump.html.

5: KING DONALD

1 Daniel G. Hall, "The King of New York," *BELLA*, https://bellanyc.com/the-king-of-new-york-donald-trump/.

2 "The Story Behind TIME's Trump 'King Me' Cover," *Time*, June 7, 2018, http://time.com/5303844/donald-trump-king-cover/.

3 Kyle Cheney and Elana Schor, et al., "Democrats warn Trump on pardon powers: 'You are not a king'," *Politico*, June 4, 2018, https://www.politico.com/story/2018/06/04/trump-pardon-tweet-620658.

4 Ian Schwartz, "Trump on Border: We'll Call It 'The Great Wall of Trump'," *Real Clear Politics*, August 20, 2015, https://www.realclearpolitics.com/video/2015/08/20/trump_on_border_well_call_it_the_great_wall_of_trump.htm.

5 Donald J. Trump and Tony Schwartz, *Trump: The Art of the Deal* (New York: Random House, 1987).

6 Ibid.

7   Donald J. Trump and Kate Bohner, *Trump: The Art of the Comeback* (New York: Times Books, 1997).
8   Donald J. Trump, *Think Big: Make It Happen in Business and Life* (New York: HarperBusiness, 2008).
9   Ibid.
10 "Top US general: Wasn't consulted on Syria announcement," CNN, video, 01:43, February 5, 2019, https://www.cnn.com/videos/politics/2019/02/05/joseph-votel-trump-syria-starr-sot-ath-vpx.cnn.
11 General James Mattis to Donald Trump, December 20, 2018, https://d3i6fh83elv35t.cloudfront.net/static/2018/12/ mattis-letter2.pdf.
12 Brent Bambury, "How Donald Trump lied his way onto the Forbes 400 richest people list," CBC Radio, May 10, 2019, https://www.cbc.ca/radio/day6/gig-economy-workers-unite-trump-s-billion-dollar-con-hatari-vs-eurovision-ramadan-in-xinjiang-and-more-1.5126682/how-donald-trump-lied-his-way-onto-the-forbes-400-richest-people-list-1.5126688.
13 Donald J. Trump and Tony Schwartz, *Trump: The Art of the Deal* (New York: Random House, 1987).

6: POLITICAL PERSONALITY

1   "Donald Trump's campaign strategy," Fox News, January 24, 2017, https://www.foxnews.com/transcript/donald-trumps-campaign-strategy.
2   Jeremy Diamond, "Trump on looking presidential: 'How handsome am I?'," CNN, April 25, 2016, https://www.cnn.com/2016/04/25/politics/donald-trump-how-handsome-am-i/index.html.
3   Emily Nussbaum, "The TV That Created Donald Trump," *New Yorker*, July 24, 2017, https://www.newyorker.com/magazine/2017/07/31/the-tv-that-created-donald-trump.
4   Lawrence K. Altman MD, "Donald Trump's Longtime Doctor Says President Takes Hair-Growth Drug," *New York Times*, February 1, 2017, https://www.nytimes.com/2017/02/01/us/politics/trump-prostate-drug-hair-harold-bornstein.html.
5   Donald J. Trump, Twitter, April 24, 2013, 11:10 A.M., https://twitter.com/realdonaldtrump/status/327077073380331525?lang=en.
6   Donald J. Trump and Meredith McIver, *Trump: How to Get Rich* (New York: Random House, 2004).
7   "Trump: 'Look at Those Hands! Are They Small Hands?'," Fox News, March 3, 2016, https://insider.foxnews.com/2016/03/03/look-those-hands-are-they-small-hands-donald-trump-defends-himself-gop-debate.
8   Bruce Handy, "Donald Trump's Short Fingers: A Historical Analysis," *Vanity Fair*, February 23, 2016, https://www.vanityfair.com/news/photos/2016/02/donald-trumps-short-fingers-a-historical-analysis.
9   General James Mattis to Donald Trump, December 20, 2018, https://d3i6fh83elv35t.cloudfront.net/static/2018/12/ mattis-letter2.pdf.

10   Ibid.
11   Donald J. Trump, *Crippled America: How to Make America Great Again* (New York: Simon & Schuster, 2011).
12   Donald J. Trump, *Think Big: Make It Happen in Business and Life"* (New York: HarperBusiness, 2008).
13   Byron Spice, "LTI Analysis Finds Most Presidential Candidates Speak at Grade Levels Six Through Eight," Carnegie Mellon University, March 16, 2016, https://www.lti.cs.cmu.edu/news/lti-analysis-finds-most-presidential-candidates-speak-grade-levels-six-through-eight.
14   Philip Rucker and Ashley Parker, "How President Trump consumes or does not consume—top-secret intelligence," *Washington Post,* May 29, 2017, https://www.washingtonpost.com/politics/how-president-trump-consumes--or-does-not-consume--top-secret-intelligence/2017/05/29/1caaca3e-39ae-11e7-a058-ddbb23c75d82_story.html?noredirect=on&utm_term=.391c794c2390.
15   Eliza Collins, "Trump: I consult myself on foreign policy," *Politico,* March 16, 2016, https://www.politico.com/blogs/2016-gop-primary-live-updates-and-results/2016/03/trump-foreign-policy-adviser-220853.
16   "Donald Trump: My Primary Consultant Is Myself," *Morning Joe,* MSNBC, video, 3:11, March 16, 2016, https://www.youtube.com/watch?v=W7CBp8lQ6ro.
17   Melanie Bencosme, "Macy's Cuts Ties with Trump: 'No Tolerance for Discrimination'," NBC News, July 1, 2015, https://www.nbcnews.com/news/latino/macy-s-cuts-ties-trump-n385131.
18   "Transcript: Donald Trump's Taped Comments About Women," *New York Times,* October 8, 2018, https://www.nytimes.com/2016/10/08/us/donald-trump-tape-transcript.html.

7: THE CHARISMATIC LEADER-FOLLOWER RELATIONSHIP

1   Garrett Fagan, *The Lure of the Arena: Social Psychology and the Crowd at the Roman Games* (Cambridge, UK: Cambridge University Press, 2011).
2   David Gura, "Pres. Trump: 'Any guy who can do a body slam he's my guy'," MSNBC, October 20, 2018, https://www.msnbc.com/david-gura/watch/pres-trump-any-guy-who-can-do-a-body-slam-he-s-my-guy-1348951619822.
3   Richard Spencer, Twitter, January 30, 2018, 10:22 P.M., https://twitter.com/RichardBSpencer/status/958540973780254721.
4   Grace Sparks, "Majority oppose policy that causes family separation, but Republicans approve," CNN, June 18, 2018, https://www.cnn.com/2018/06/18/politics/immigration-trump-approval/index.html.

8: THE TEA PARTY

1   Rebecca Ballhaus, "A Short History of the Tea Party Movement," *Wall Street Journal,* February 27, 2014, https://blogs.wsj.com/washwire/2014/02/27/a-short-history-of-the-tea-party-movement/.

ENDNOTES

2   "About Us," Tea Party, Inc., 2019, https://www.teaparty.org/about-us/.
3   Amanda Fallin, Rachel Grana, and Stanton A. Glantz, "'To quarterback behind the scenes, third-party efforts': The tobacco industry and the Tea Party," National Institutes of Health, February 8, 2013, https://www.ncbi.nlm.nih.gov/pmc/articles/PMC3740007/.
4   Jeff Nesbit, *Poison Tea: How Big Oil and Big Tobacco Invented the Tea Party and Captured the GOP* (New York: Thomas Dunne Books, 2016).
5   Amanda Fallin, Rachel Grana, and Stanton A. Glantz, "'To quarterback behind the scenes, third-party efforts': The tobacco industry and the Tea Party," *National Institutes of Health*, February 8, 2013, https://www.ncbi.nlm.nih.gov/pmc/articles/PMC3740007/.
6   Jeff Nesbit, *Poison Tea: How Big Oil and Big Tobacco Invented the Tea Party and Captured the GOP* (New York: Thomas Dunne Books, 2016).
7   Brian Montopoli, "Tea Party Supporters: Who They Are and What They Believe," CBS News, December 14, 2012, https://www.cbsnews.com/news/tea-party-supporters-who-they-are-and-what-they-believe/.
8   Kate Zernike and Megan Thee-Brenan, "Poll Finds Tea Party Backers Wealthier and More Educated," *New York Times*, April 14, 2010, https://www.nytimes.com/2010/04/15/us/politics/15poll.html.
9   Chris Good, "Who Are the Tea Partiers?," *The Atlantic*, April 5, 2010, https://www.theatlantic.com/politics/archive/2010/04/who-are-the-tea-partiers/38510/.
10 Ibid.
11 Elizabeth Price Foley, *The Tea Party: Three Principles* (Cambridge, UK: Cambridge University Press, 2012).
12 Bryan T. Gervais and Irwin L. Morris, "How the Tea Party Paved the Way for Donald Trump," *Washington Post*, September 7, 2018, https://www.washingtonpost.com/news/monkey-cage/wp/2018/09/07/how-the-tea-party-paved-the-way-for-donald-trump/?noredirect=on&utm_term=.1a086eb666d9.
13 David Brody, *The Teavangelicals: The Inside Story of How the Evangelicals and the Tea Party Are Taking Back America*, (Grand Rapids, MI: Zondervan, 2012).
14 "The Wall Street Journal/NBC News Poll—Archive and Details," *Wall Street Journal*, April 1, 2019, https://www.wsj.com/articles/the-wall-street-journalnbc-news-poll-1378786510.
15 "Trump on the 'Today' show: I'm with the 'tea party'," *Los Angeles Times*, April 7, 2011, https://latimesblogs.latimes.com/showtracker/2011/04/trump-on-the-today-show-im-with-the-tea-party.html.
16 Juana Summers, "Trump: I stand with tea party," *Politico*, April 7, 2011, https://www.politico.com/story/2011/04/trump-i-stand-with-tea-party-052723.
17 Chris Cillizza, and Aaron Blake, "Donald Trump. Seriously?," *Washington Post*, April 7, 2011, https://www.washingtonpost.com/blogs/the-fix/post/donald-trump-seriously/2011/04/06/AF0481rC_blog.html?utm_term=.b79c3f352155.
18 Ibid.
19 "Donald Trump To Obama: Show The Birth Certificate," *Real Clear Politics*,

March 23, 2011, https://www.realclearpolitics.com/video/2011/03/23/donald_trump_to_obama_show_the_birth_certificate.html.

20   Kathleen Foster, "Donald Trump Proves He Was Born in Queens," Fox News, December 23, 2015, https://www.foxnews.com/politics/donald-trump-proves-he-was-born-in-queens.

21   Laura Ingraham, "Laura Ingraham Show—Donald Trump 'proud' to be a birther," Video, 05:59, March 30, 2011, https://www.youtube.com/watch?v=WqaS9OCoTZs.

22   "Trump on the 'Today' show: I'm with the 'tea party'," *Los Angeles Times*, April 7, 2011, https://latimesblogs.latimes.com/showtracker/2011/04/trump-on-the-today-show-im-with-the-tea-party.html.

23   Evan McMorris-Santoro, "Trump Promises to Reveal Secrets of Obama's Birth Before Summer," *Talking Points Memo,* Video, April 7, 2011, https://talkingpointsmemo.com/dc/trump-promises-to-reveal-secrets-of-obama-s-birth-before-summer-video.

24   "Donald Trump Announces He Won't Run for President," *South Florida Sun Sentinel*, May 16, 2011, https://www.sun-sentinel.com/news/fl-xpm-2011-05-16-sfl-donald-trump-president-link-20110516-story.html.

25   Shannon Travis, "Trump bashes, boasts, and curses in first major Tea Party speech," CNN, April 16, 2011, http://politicalticker.blogs.cnn.com/2011/04/16/trump-bashes-boasts-and-curses-in-first-major-tea-party-speech/.

26   Bryan T. Gervais and Irwin L. Morris, "How the Tea Party Paved the Way for Donald Trump," *Washington Post*, September 7, 2018, https://www.washingtonpost.com/news/monkey-cage/wp/2018/09/07/how-the-tea-party-paved-the-way-for-donald-trump/?noredirect=on&utm_term=.1a086eb666d9.

27   Elizabeth A. Yates, "How the Tea Party Learned to Love Donald Trump," *Washington Post*, December 1, 2016, https://www.washingtonpost.com/news/monkey-cage/wp/2016/12/01/how-the-tea-party-learned-to-love-donald-trump/.

28   Vanessa Williamson, "What the Tea Party Tells Us about the Trump Presidency," Brookings, November 9, 2016, https://www.brookings.edu/blog/fixgov/2016/11/09/tea-party-and-trump-presidency/.

29   Lisa Mascaro, "Donald Trump's Campaign Might Break Apart the Tea Party," *Los Angeles Times*, March 18, 2016, https://www.latimes.com/politics/la-na-trump-tea-party-divide-20160318-story.html.

30   Joshua Green, *Devil's Bargain: Steve Bannon, Donald Trump, and the Storming of the Presidency* (London: Penguin Press, 2017).

31   Connie Bruck, "How Hollywood Remembers Steve Bannon," *New Yorker*, April 24, 2017, https://www.newyorker.com/magazine/2017/05/01/how-hollywood-remembers-steve-bannon.

32   "Evolution of Anger: The Tea Party in the Age of Trump," NBCNEWS.com, August 18, 2018, Video, 5:15, https://www.nbcnews.com/video/evolution-of-anger-the-tea-party-in-the-age-of-trump-1310621251792.

ENDNOTES

33 Josh Sanburn, "Meet the Tea Partiers Behind the Rallies President Trump around the U.S.," *Time*, March 2, 2017, http://time.com/4688825/donald-trump-rallies-tea-party-spirit-america/.
34 Julian Zelizer, "Trump throws down a challenge to the tea party," CNN, February 28, 2017, https://www.cnn.com/2017/02/28/opinions/trumps-challenge-to-tea-party-conservatives-zelizer/index.html?no-st=1547334507.
35 Jennifer Stefano, "This Isn't What the Tea Party Fought For," *New York Times*, February 17, 2018, https://www.nytimes.com/2018/02/17/opinion/sunday/tea-party-trump-budget.html.

9: A DIVIDED REPUBLICAN PARTY

1   Ashley Parker and Jeremy W. Peters, "Dueling Town Hall Meetings Add Distance to Jeb Bush-Donald Trump Gulf," *New York Times*, August 19, 2015, https://www.nytimes.com/2015/08/20/us/politics/dueling-town-halls-add-distance-to-jeb-bush-donald-trump-gulf.html.
2   Chris Moody, "Trump in '04: 'I probably identify more as Democrat'," CNN, July 22, 2015, https://www.cnn.com2015/07/21/politics/donald-trump-election-democrat/index.html.
3   These numbers do not represent any donations made to super PACs, which can be anonymous.
4   Danielle Kurtzleben, "Most of Donald Trump's Political Money Went To Democrats—Until 5 Years Ago," NPR, July 28, 2015, https://www.npr.org/sections/itsallpolitics/2015/07/28/426888268/donald-trumps-flipping-political-donations.
5   "About," Reform Party National Committee, 2019, http://www.reformparty.org/about/.
6   Donald J. Trump and Dave Shiflett, *The America We Deserve* (Kent, OH: Renaissance Books, 2000).
7   Al Kamen, "Sunday in The Loop," *Washington Post*, January 23, 2000, https://www.washingtonpost.com/archive/lifestyle/magazine/2000/01/23/sunday-in-the-loop/f851630a-be02-4a47-b94a-de2e009dd672/?utm_term=.a6c2855008cc.
8   Adam Nagourney, "Reform Bid Said to Be A No-Go For Trump," *New York Times*, February 14, 2000, https://www.nytimes.com/2000/02/14/us/reform-bid-said-to-be-a-no-go-for-trump.html.
9   "Here's Donald Trump's Presidential Announcement Speech," *Time*, June 16, 2015, http://time.com/3923128/donald-trump-announcement-speech/.
10 "Donald Trump's *New York Times* Interview: Full Transcript," *New York Times*, November 23, 2016, https://www.nytimes.com/2016/11/23/us/politics/trump-new-york-times-interview-transcript.html.
11 Mike Huckabee, Twitter, December 26, 2017, 11:34 A.M., https://twitter.com/govmikehuckabee/status/945739713138315264?lang=en.
12 Benjamin Fearnow, "Mike Huckabee Says Donald Trump Has Stamina, Vigor, of 32-Year-Old in Defense of High Administration Turnover," *Newsweek*, December 17, 2018, https://www.newsweek.com/mike-huckabee-trump-vigor-health-turnover-cult-personality-physical-fitness-1262246.

ENDNOTES

13   Mike Huckabee, Twitter, August 3, 2018, 1:07 A.M., https://twitter.com/GovMikeHuckabee/status/1025291947467059200.

14   *Good Morning America*, "White House press secretary responds to report," Video, 06:10, https://www.goodmorningamerica.com/news/video/white-house-press-secretary-responds-report-62503956.

15   Nick Gass, "Dick Cheney Will Support Trump," *Politico*, May 6, 2016, https://www.politico.com/story/2016/05/dick-cheney-support-donald-trump-222907.

16   Ryan Struyk, "Bobby Jindal Slams Donald Trump As 'Egomaniacal Madman' and 'Non-Serious Carnival Act'," *Politico*, September 10, 2015, https://abcnews.go.com/Politics/bobby-jindal-slams-donald-trump-egomaniacal-madman-carnival/story?id=33666609.

17   "Remarks by President Trump at the 2019 Conservative Political Action Conference," White House, March 3, 2019, https://www.whitehouse.gov/briefings-statements/remarks-president-trump-2019-conservative-political-action-conference/.

18   Ibid.

19   Paige Cowett, ed., "What Happened to Lindsey Graham?," *The Daily* (podcast), *New York Times*, 27:44. March 5, 2019, https://www.nytimes.com/2019/03/05/podcasts/the-daily/lindsey-graham-trump.html.

20   Monica Langley, "Behind Mitt Romney's Increasingly Lonely Challenge to Donald Trump," *Wall Street Journal*, May 28, 2016, https://www.wsj.com/articles/behind-mitt-romneys-increasingly-lonely-challenge-to-donald-trump-1464354734.

21   Mitt Romney, "Mitt Romney: Where I Stand on the Trump Agenda," *Salt Lake Tribune*, June 25, 2018, https://www.sltrib.com/opinion/commentary/2018/06/24/mitt-romney-where-i-stand-on-the-trump-agenda/.

22   Mitt Romney, "Mitt Romney: The president shapes the public character of the nation. Trump's character falls short," *Washington Post*, January 1, 2019, https://www.washingtonpost.com/opinions/mitt-romney-the-president-shapes-the-public-character-of-the-nation-trumps-character-falls-short 2019/01/01/37a3c8c2-0d1a-11e9-8938-5898adc28fa2_story.html.

23   Jeff Mason, "Republican Romney says he is 'sickened' by Trump's behavior during Russia probe," Reuters, April 19, 2019, https://www.reuters.com/article/us-usa-trump-russia-romney/republican-romney-says-he-is-sickened-by-trumps-behavior-during-russia-probe-idUSKCN1RV1AR.

24   Mike Huckabee, Twitter, April 19, 2019, 1:45 P.M., https://twitter.com/govmikehuckabee/status/1119341155450224640?lang=en.

25   Reena Flores, "Former GOP Sen. John Warner endorses Hillary Clinton," CBS News, September 28, 2016, https://www.cbsnews.com/news/former-gop-sen-john-warner-endorses-hillary-clinton/.

26   Garrett Haake, "Clinton camp hopes for Virginia boost from Warner endorsement," WUSA9, September 28, 2016, https://www.wusa9.com/article/news/politics/clinton-camp-hopes-for-virginia-boost-from-warner-endorsement/327554849.

27   Heidi Przybyla, "Virginia GOP dean John Warner endorses Democrats for Congress," NBC News, November 2, 2018, https://www.nbcnews.com/card/virginia-gop-dean-john-warner-endorses-democrats-congress-n930381.

28 Ibid.
29 John Cassidy, "The Problem With the 'Never Trump' Movement," *New Yorker*, March 3, 2016, https://www.newyorker.com/news/john-cassidy/the-problem-with-the-never-trump-movement.
30 "'Our Principles' Super PAC Spreads Anti-Donald Trump Message," NPR, March 8, 2016, https://www.npr.org/2016/03/08/469692183/our-principles-superpac-spreads-anti-donald-trump-message.
31 Chris Cillizza, "Donald Trump's amazing 'cease and desist' letter, annotated," *Washington Post*, September 22, 2015, https://www.washingtonpost.com/news/the-fix/wp/2015/09/22/donald-trumps-cease-and-desist-letter-annotated/?utm_term=.7439961d551b.
32 Lauren R. Johnson, Deon McCray, and Jordan M. Ragusa, "#NeverTrump: Why Republican members of Congress refused to support their party's nominee in the 2016 presidential election," *Sage Journals*, January 11, 2018, https://doi.org/10.1177/2053168017749383.
33 Ryan Westerdahl, "'Make America Great Again'—A History," *Medium*, November 8, 2018, https://medium.com/@ryanwesterdahl/make-america-great-again-a-history-68a791f0b87a.
34 Gregory Krieg, "Donald Trump reveals when he thinks America was great," CNN, March 28, 2016, https://www.cnn.com/2016/03/26/politics/donald-trump-when-america-was-great/index.html.
35 Ryan Moore, "Why I Proudly Wear My Make America Great Again Hat: Opinion," *Tennessean*, January 30, 2019, https://www.tennessean.com/story/opinion/2019/01/30/why-proudly-where-my-make-america-great-again-hat/2716182002/.
36 Ibid.
37 Kristan Hawkins, "Why I wear a MAGA hat these days (and I didn't start out as a Trump fan)," Fox News, February 2, 2019, https://www.foxnews.com/opinion/why-i-wear-a-maga-hat-these-days-and-i-didnt-start-out-as-a-trump-fan.
38 Margot Sanger-Katz, "When Was America Greatest?," *New York Times*, April 26, 2016, https://www.nytimes.com/2016/04/26/upshot/when-was-america-greatest.html.
39 Carroll Doherty, "5 facts about Trump supporters' views of immigration," Pew Research Center, August 25, 2016, https://www.pewresearch.org/fact-tank/2016/08/25/5-facts-about-trump-supporters-views-of-immigration/.
40 Laura Finley and Luigi Esposito, "The Immigrant as Bogeyman: Examining Donald Trump and the Right's Anti-immigrant, Anti-PC Rhetoric," *Sage Journals*, April 7, 2019, https://doi.org/10.1177/0160597619832627.
41 Stephen Hawkins and Daniel Yudkin, et al., "Hidden Tribes: A Study of America's Polarized Landscape," 2018, https://static1.squarespace.com/static/5a70a7c3010027736a22740f/t/5bbcea6b7817f7bf7342b718/1539107467397/hidden_tribes_report-2.pdf.
42 Ibid.

43 Eric Garcia, "A History of 'Draining the Swamp,'" *Roll Call*, October 18, 2016, http://www.rollcall.com/news/politics/history-of-draining-the-swamp.
44 Peter Overby, "Trump's Efforts to 'Drain the Swamp' Lagging Behind His Campaign Rhetoric," NPR, April 26, 2017, https://www.npr.org/2017/04/26/525551816/trumps-efforts-to-drain-the-swamp-lagging-behind-his-campaign-rhetoric.
45 Russell Berman, "Donald Trump's Last-Ditch Plan to 'Drain the Swamp,'" *The Atlantic*, October 18, 2016, https://www.theatlantic.com/politics/archive/2016/10/donald-trumps-plan-to-drain-the-swamp/504569/.
46 Ibid.
47 Eric Bolling, *The Swamp: Washington's Murky Pool of Corruption and Cronyism and How Trump Can Drain It* (New York: St. Martin's Press, 2017).
48 Ken Buck, *Drain the Swamp: How Washington Corruption Is Worse than You Think* (Washington, DC: Regnery Publishing, 2017).
49 Donald J. Trump and Dave Shiflett, *The America We Deserve* (Kent, OH: Renaissance Books, 2000).
50 Lee Horwich, Beryl Love, John Brecher, Amalie Nash, eds., "Trump Nation," *USA Today*, 2016, https://www.usatoday.com/pages/interactives/trump-nation/#/?_k=1w2iy6.
51 Ibid.
52 Ibid.
53 John Fea, *Believe Me: The Evangelical Road to Donald Trump* (Grand Rapids, MI: Eerdmans, 2018).
54 "Remarks by Vice President Mike Pence at a Reception Honoring March for Life Participants," White House, January 18, 2018, https://www.whitehouse.gov/briefings-statements/remarks-vice-president-mike-pence-reception-honoring-march-life-participants/.
55 Trump's full 2019 State of the Union Address, CNN, Video, 1:26:30, February 5, 2019, https://www.cnn.com/videos/politics/2019/02/06/trump-entire-2019-state-of-the-union-full-speech-cnngo-sot.cnn.
56 McKay Coppins, "God's Plan for Mike Pence?," *The Atlantic*, January/February 2018, https://www.theatlantic.com/magazine/archive/2018/01/gods-plan-for-mike-pence/546569/.
57 Donald J. Trump, *Crippled America: How to Make America Great Again* (New York: Simon & Schuster, 2011).
58 Anthony Licata, "Q&A: Donald Trump on Guns, Hunting, and Conservation," *Field & Stream*, January 21, 2016, https://www.fieldandstream.com/articles/hunting/2016/01/qa-donald-trump-on-guns-hunting-and-conservation.
59 SilencerCo, "One on One: Donald Trump Jr. Uncut," Video, 38:14, September 26, 2016, https://www.youtube.com/watch?v=0vlu2G5UkXk.
60 Ibid.
61 Chris Cillizza, "The 40 most breathtaking lines from Donald Trump's NRA speech," CNN, May 5, 2018, https://www.cnn.com/2018/05/04/politics/donald-trump-speech-nra/index.html.

62 AWR Hawkins, "Trump at CPAC: Democrat Gun Control Will Not Get Past My Desk," *Breitbart*, March 2, 2019, https://www.breitbart.com/politics/2019/03/02/trump-at-cpac-democrat-gun-control-will-not-get-past-my-desk/.

63 John Bowden, "Mueller asked Trump campaign about ties to NRA: CNN," *The Hill*, January 22, 2019, https://thehill.com/policy/national-security/426481-mueller-asking-about-trump-campaigns-ties-to-nra-cnn.

64 Ann Coulter, *In Trump We Trust* (New York: Sentinel, 2016).

65 Edward-Isaac Dovere, "'This Is the New Republican Party'" *Politico*, June 13, 2018, https://www.politico.com/story/2018/06/13/trump-republicans-sanford-resistance-644721.

10: THE WORKING CLASS AND RURAL AREAS

1 Donald J. Trump and Tony Schwartz, *Trump: The Art of the Deal* (New York: Random House, 1987).

2 Newt Gingrich and Eric Trump, *Understanding Trump* (New York: Center Street, 2017).

3 Jared McDonald, David Karol, and Lilliana Mason, "'An Inherited Money Dude from Queens County': How Unseen Candidate Characteristics Affect Voter Perceptions," *Political Behavior*, January 9, 2019, https://doi.org/10.1007/s11109-019-09527-y.

4 Joan C. Williams, "What So Many People Don't Get About the U.S. Working Class," *Harvard Business Review*, November 10, 2016, https://hbr.org/2016/11/what-so-many-people-dont-get-about-the-u-s-working-class.

5 Ibid.

6 "President Donald J. Trump is Delivering Results for American Workers," White House, September 4, 2018, https://www.whitehouse.gov/briefings-statements/president-donald-j-trump-delivering-results-american-workers/.

7 "Trump: 'The greatest jobs producer the God ever created'," *USA Today*, Video, 00:43, January 11, 2017, https://www.youtube.com/watch?v=jElcJsZhjxY.

8 Ahiza Garcia and Chris Isidore, "Trump: Companies will be punished for leaving U.S.," CNN, December 1, 2016, https://money.cnn.com/2016/12/01/news/companies/trump-carrier-visit-us-jobs/index.html.

9 Daniel Politi, "Donald Trump in Phoenix: Mexicans are 'Taking our Jobs' and 'Killing Us'," *Slate*, July 12, 2015, https://slate.com/news-and-politics/2015/07/donald-trump-in-phoenix-mexicans-are-taking-our-jobs-and-killing-us.html.

10 "Trump's full 2019 State of the Union Address," Video, 1:26:30, February 5, 2019, https://www.cnn.com/videos/politics/2019/02/06/trump-entire-2019-state-of-the-union-full-speech-cnngo-sot.cnn.

11 Ben Adler and Rebecca Leber, "Donald Trump Once Backed Urgent Climate Action. Wait, What?," *Grist*, https://grist.org/politics/donald-trump-climate-action-new-york-times/.

12 Scott Peters, "The Politics of Climate Change," *Medium*, November 14, 2017, https://medium.com/@Rep.ScottPeters/the-politics-of-climate-change-706941147857.

ENDNOTES

13   Howard Gleckman, "What's Up With the No Climate Tax Pledge?," Tax Policy Center, June 2, 2015, https://www.taxpolicycenter.org/taxvox/whats-no-climate-tax-pledge.

14   Adriana Belmonte, "America is running low on blue-collar workers," *Yahoo Finance*, December 31, 2018, https://finance.yahoo.com/news/america-running-low-blue-collar-workers-181206902.html.

15   Molly Ball, "Why Trump's 'Forgotten Man' Still Supports Him," *Time*, February 15, 2018, http://time.com/5159859/why-trumps-forgotten-man-still-supports-him/.

16   "America Employed," Express Employment Professionals, August 29, 2018, https://www.expresspros.com/Newsroom/America-Employed/Blue-Collar-Workers-Career-and-Life-Satisfaction-High-Trust-in-Elected-Officials-Low.aspx.

17   John Binder, "Majority of Blue Collar Workers: We're Better Off Under Trump than Obama," *Breitbart*, September 5, 2018, https://www.breitbart.com/politics/2018/09/03/majority-of-blue-collar-workers-were-better-off-under-trump-than-obama.

18   Danielle Kurtzleben, "Is 'Rural Resentment' Driving Voters To Donald Trump?," NPR, August 18, 2016, https://www.npr.org/2016/08/18/490240652/is-rural-resentment-driving-voters-to-donald-trump.

19   Helena Bottemiller Evich, "Revenge of the Rural Voter," *Politico*, November 13, 2016, https://www.politico.com/story/2016/11/hillary-clinton-rural-voters-trump-231266.

20   "Trump Campaign Announces Agricultural Advisory Committee," Ohio AgriBusiness Association, 2019, http://www.oaba.net/aws/OABA/pt/sd/news_article/126454/_PARENT/layout_details/false.

21   Joel Ebert and Joey Garrison, "President Trump in Nashville: 'Farm Country is God's Country,'" *Tennessean*, January 8, 2018, https://www.tennessean.com/story/news/politics/2018/01/08/trump-tout-republican-tax-bills-benefits-farmers-during-nashville-speech/1013389001/.

22   Scott Horsley, "Trump plants seeds of rural revival with friendly farm audience," Minnesota Public Radio, January 8, 2018, https://www.mprnews.org/story/2018/01/08/npr-trump-plants-seeds-of-rural-revival-with-friendly-farm-audience

23   Joel Ebert and Joey Garrison, "President Trump in Nashville: 'Farm Country is God's Country," *Tennessean*, January 8, 2018, https://www.tennessean.com/story/news/politics/2018/01/08/trump-tout-republican-tax-bills-benefits-farmers-during-nashville-speech/1013389001/.

24   "President Donald J. Trump is Working to Rebuild Rural America," White House, January 8, 2018, https://www.whitehouse.gov/briefings-statements/president-donald-j-trump-working-rebuild-rural-america/.

25   Ken Silverstein, "Trump's Relationship With American Farmers Is Soiled Because Of Biofuels Stance And Trade War," *Forbes*, September 10, 2018, https://www.forbes.com/sites/kensilverstein/2018/09/10/trumps-relationship-with-american-farmers-is-soiled-because-of-biofuels-stance-and-trade-war/.

26   Donald J. Trump, Twitter, November 15, 2012, 11:23 A.M., https://twitter.com/realdonaldtrump/status/269113467104010240?lang=en.

27 Anthony Licata, "Q&A: Donald Trump on Guns, Hunting, and Conservation," *Field & Stream*, January 21, 2016, https://www.fieldandstream.com/articles/hunting/2016/01/qa-donald-trump-on-guns-hunting-and-conservation.

28 Alexa Lardieri, "Trump Reverses Ban on Elephant Trophy Imports," *U.S. News*, November 16, 2017, https://www.usnews.com/news/politics/articles/2017-11-16/trump-reverses-ban-on-elephant-trophy-imports.

29 Erica Martinson, "Trump administration proposes reverses of Obama-era hunting rule in Alaska national Parks," *Anchorage Daily News*, May 21, 2018, https://www.adn.com/alaska-news/wildlife/2018/05/21/trump-administration-proposes-reversal-of-obama-era-hunting-rule-in-alaskas-national-parks/.

30 "Senate Confirms Interior Secretary David Bernhardt," Safari Club, May 11, 2019, https://www.safariclub.org/press/senate-confirms-interior-secretary-david-bernhardt.

31 Alexandra Deabler, "Donald Trump Jr. slams PETA on Twitter over mocking 'trophy-hunting' Halloween costume," Fox News, September 23, 2018, https://www.foxnews.com/lifestyle/donald-trump-jr-slams-peta-on-twitter-over-mocking-trophy-hunting-halloween-costume.

32 Frank Miniter, "What the left does not understand about hunters," Fox News, October 27, 2018, https://www.foxnews.com/opinion/what-the-left-does-not-understand-about-hunters.

33 "HN19003—Utah Elk Hunt for One with Donald Trump Jr.," Hunter Nation, Fall 2019, https://hunternation.org/product/hn19003-utah-elk-hunt-with-donald-trump-jr/.

11: PERMISSION TO HATE

1 Leonard Greene, "Trump called for death penalty after Central Park jogger attack, and still has no sympathy for accused despite convictions overturned," *New York Daily News*, July 19, 2018, https://www.nydailynews.com/new-york/ny-news-trump-death-penalty-central-park-five-20180713-story.html.

2 Michael Wilson, "Trump Draws Criticism for Ad He Ran After Jogger Attack," *New York Times*, October 23, 2002, https://www.nytimes.com/2002/10/23/nyregion/trump-draws-criticism-for-ad-he-ran-after-jogger-attack.html.

3 Donald J. Trump, "Donald Trump: Central Park Five Settlement Is a 'Disgrace,'" *New York Daily News*, June 21, 2014, https://www.nydailynews.com/new-york/nyc-crime/donald-trump-central-park-settlement-disgrace-article-1.1838467.

4 Steven Holmes, "Member of 'Central Park 5' blasts Trump," CNN, October 7, 2016, https://www.cnn.com/2016/10/06/politics/reality-check-donald-trump-central-park-5/.

5 Lisa Mascaro, "A growing number of prominent Republicans withdraw support or condemn Trump—here's who is speaking up," *Los Angeles Times*, October 8, 2016, https://www.latimes.com/politics/la-na-pol-trump-react-20161007-snap-htmlstory.html.

6 John O'Donnell and James Rutherford, *Trumped!: The Inside Story of the Real Donald Trump—His Cunning Rise and Spectacular Fall* (New York: CrossRoad Press, 2016).

7 Mark Bowden, "The Art of the Donald: The Trumpster Stages the Comeback of a Lifetime," *Playboy*, May 1997, https://www.playboy.com/read/the-art-of-the-donald.

8. Jill Colvin, "Trump says he saw people celebrating 9/11 in Jersey City," Fox10 Phoenix, November 23, 2015, http://www.fox10phoenix.com/news/us-world-news/trump-says-he-saw-people-celebrating-911-in-jersey-city-nj.
9. Christina Wilkie, "Trump: 9/11 memorial is where heroes 'stopped the forces of terror,'" CNBC, September 11, 2018, https://www.cnbc.com/2018/09/11/trump-911-memorial-is-where-heroes-stopped-the-forces-of-terror.html.
10. Theodore Schleifer, "Trump: Judge with Mexican heritage has an 'inherent conflict of interest,'" CNN, June 2, 2016, https://www.cnn.com/2016/06/02/politics/donald-trump-judge-mexican-heritage-conflict-of-interest/index.html.
11. Scott Thistle, "Trump's statements about Somali immigrants in Maine draw rebuke," *Portland Press Herald*, August 5, 2016, https://www.pressherald.com/2016/08/05/trump-statements-on-maine-somali-immigrants-draws-sharp-rebuke/.
12. Rachel Barenblat, "Yes, Ranting Against 'Globalism' Is Anti-Semitic," *Forward*, October 24, 2018, https://forward.com/scribe/412627/yes-ranting-against-globalism-is-anti-semitic/.
13. Harry Cheadle, "'These Aren't People. These Are Animals,'" *Vice*, May 17, 2018, https://www.vice.com/en_us/article/nekb3k/these-arent-people-these-are-animals.
14. Donald J. Trump, Twitter, January 22, 2016, 10:51 A.M., https://twitter.com/realdonaldtrump/status/690562515500032000?lang=en.
15. Samantha Schmidt, "Trump retweets alt-right conspiracy theorist on Chicago homicides in wake of Charlottesville criticism," *Chicago Tribune*, August 15, 2017, https://www.chicagotribune.com/nation-world/ct-trump-retweets-alt-right-media-figure-20170814-story.html.
16. Donald J. Trump, Twitter, June 5, 2013, 4:05 A.M., https://twitter.com/realdonaldtrump/status/342190428675796992?lang=en.
17. Donald J. Trump, Twitter, August 22, 2018, 10:28 P.M., https://twitter.com/realdonaldtrump/status/1032454567152246785?lang=en.
18. Marc Olsen, "From his gold resort, Trump aims some sharp tweets at a mayor in Puerto Rico," *Los Angeles Times*, September 30, 2017, https://www.latimes.com/politics/washington/la-na-essential-washington-updates-trump-doing-battle-again-this-time-1506772353-htmlstory.html.
19. Donald J. Trump, Twitter, August 22, 2018, 10:28 P.M., https://twitter.com/realdonaldtrump/status/1032454567152246785?lang=en.
20. South African Government, Twitter, August 2018, 2:00 A.M., https://twitter.com/governmentza/status/1032507810460909568?lang=en.
21. Clare Foran, "Donald Trump and the Rise of Anti-Muslim Violence," *The Atlantic*, September 22, 2016, https://www.theatlantic.com/politics/archive/2016/09/trump-muslims-islamophobia-hate-crime/500840/.
22. Ibid.
23. Karsten Müller and Carlo Schwarz, "Making America Hate Again? Twitter and Hate Crime Under Trump," SSRN, May 16, 2018, https://papers.ssrn.com/sol3/papers.cfm?abstract_id=3149103.
24. Alejandro Beutel, "How Trump's nativist tweets overlap with anti-Muslim and anti-Latino hate crimes," Southern Poverty Law Center, May 18, 2018,

https://www.splcenter.org/hatewatch/2018/05/18/how-trump's-nativist-tweets-overlap-anti-muslim-and-anti-latino-hate-crimes.

25   Ayal Feinberg, Regina Branton, and Valerie Martinez-Ebers, "Counties that hosted a 2016 Trump rally saw a 226 percent increase in hate crimes," *Washington Post*, March 22, 2018, https://www.washingtonpost.com/politics/2019/03/22/trumps-rhetoric-does-inspire-more-hate-crimes/?noredirect=on&utm_term=.830da84351e6.

26   Meghan Keneally, "A look back at Trump comments perceived by some as encouraging violence," ABC News, October 19, 2018, https://abcnews.go.com/Politics/back-trump-comments-perceived-encouraging-violence/story?id=48415766.

27   Harriet Sinclair, "Trump Told White Supremacists to Attack Protesters, So They Did," *Newsweek*, August 14, 2017, https://www.newsweek.com/trump-told-white-supremacists-attack-protesters-so-they-did-650622.

28   Kelly J. Baker, "Make America White Again?," *The Atlantic*, March 12, 2016, https://www.theatlantic.com/politics/archive/2016/03/donald-trump-kkk/473190/.

29   Eric Hoffer, *The True Believer: Thoughts on the Nature of Mass Movements* (New York: Harper, 2002).

30   Kathleen M. Blee, *Women of the Klan: Racism and Gender in the 1920s* (Berkeley: University of California Press, 2008), p. 21.

31   Jeremy Berke, "Former KKK leader David Duke: Voting against Donald Trump is 'treason to your heritage'," *Business Insider*, February 25, 2016, https://www.businessinsider.com/david-duke-donald-trump-treason-heritage-2016-2.

32   "Trump disavows support from KKK ex-grand wizard David Duke," *Times of Israel*, February 28, 2016, https://www.timesofisrael.com/trump-disavows-support-from-kkk-grand-wizard-david-duke/.

33   Christina Coleburn, "Donald Trump on Racist Endorsement: 'I Don't Know Anything About David Duke,'" NBC News, February 29, 2016, https://www.nbcnews.com/politics/2016-election/donald-trump-racist-endorsement-i-don-t-know-anything-about-n527576.

34   Glenn Kessler, "Donald Trump and David Duke: For the Record," *Jewish World Review*, March 2, 2016, http://www.jewishworldreview.com/0316/fact_checker030216.php3.

35   Ibid.

36   Libby Nelson, "'Why we voted for Donald Trump': David Duke explains the white supremacist Charlottesville protests," *Vox*, August 12, 2017, https://www.vox.com/2017/8/12/16138358/charlottesville-protests-david-duke-kkk.

37   Sam Kestenbaum, "Is Trump an Anti-Semite? Ask David Duke, He Should Know," *Forward*, February 21, 2017, https://forward.com/fast-forward/363750/is-trump-an-anti-semite-ask-david-duke-he-should-know/.

38   Rachel Pendergraft, Twitter, https://twitter.com/rachelpen?lang=en.

39   Peter Holley, "KKK's official newspaper supports Donald Trump for president," *Washington Post*, November 2, 2016, https://www.washingtonpost.com/news/post

-politics/wp/2016/11/01/the-kkks-official-newspaper-has-endorsed-donald-trump-for-president/?utm_term=.8cd3c1149dce.
40. Ibid.
41. "About," National Policy Institute, 2017, https://nationalpolicy.institute/whoarewe/.
42. "'Hail Trump!': Richard Spencer Speech Excerpts," *The Atlantic*, video, 03:07, November 21, 2016, https://www.youtube.com/watch?v=1o6-bi3jlxk.
43. "Hate crime suspect attacks employee at Middle Eastern restaurant with pipe," Fox 4 KC, March 11, 2017, https://fox4kc.com/2017/03/11/hate-crime-suspect-attacks-employee-at-middle-eastern-restaurant-with-pipe/.
44. "Hate Crimes," Sikh American Legal Defense and Education Fund, 2019, http://saldef.org/archive/legal-defense-advocacy/hate-crimes/#.XN8PA7bMzix.
45. Manveena Suri and Huizhong Wu, "Sikhs: Religious minority target of hate crimes," CNN, March 7, 2017, https://www.cnn.com/2017/03/06/asia/sikh-hate-crimes-us-muslims/index.html.
46. "Anti-Semitic Incidents Remained at Near-Historic Levels in 2018; Assaults Against Jews More Than Doubled," Anti-Defamation League, 2019, https://www.adl.org/news/press-releases/anti-semitic-incidents-remained-at-near-historic-levels-in-2018-assaults.
47. "New FBI Statistics Show Alarming Increase in Number of Reported Hate Crimes," Human Rights Campaign, November 13, 2018, https://www.hrc.org/blog/new-fbi-statistics-show-alarming-increase-in-number-of-reported-hate-crimes.
48. "A National Epidemic: Fatal Anti-Transgender Violence in America in 2018," Human Rights Campaign, 2018, https://assets2.hrc.org/files/assets/resourcesAntiTransViolence-2018Report-Final.pdf
49. "Advocates See 'Disturbing' Rise in Hate Crimes Targeting Asian Americans," Asian American Advancing Justice, August 14, 2017, https://www.advancingjustice-aajc.org/news/advocates-see-disturbing-rise-hate-crimes-targeting-asian-americans.
50. Ibid.
51. Tony Rizzo, "'Get out of my country,' he said before shooting. He pleads guilty to hate crime," *Kansas City Star*, May 22, 2018, https://www.kansascity.com/news/local/crime/article211576754.html.
52. Mike Carter and Evan Bush, "FBI opens federal civil-rights investigation into shooting of Sikh man in Kent," *Seattle Times*, March 6, 2017, https://www.seattletimes.com/seattle-news/crime/sikh-man-shot-in-kent-recovering-at-home-wants-to-keep-to-himself/.
53. Lillianna Byington, Brittany Brown, and Andrew Capps, "Black Americans are still victims of hate crimes more than any other group," *Texas Tribune*, August 16, 2018, https://www.texastribune.org/2018/08/16/african-americans/.
54. Michael Cabanatuan, "'Disturbing' rise in hate crimes in California," *San Francisco Chronicle*, July 9, 2018, https://www.sfchronicle.com/crime/article/Hate-crimes-on-the-upswing-in-California-13061474.php.
55. Acee Agoyo, "Anti-Indian hate crimes rose dramatically in first year of Trump

presidency," *Indianz*, November 13, 2018, https://www.indianz.com/News/2018/11/13/antiindian-hate-crimes-rose-dramatically.asp.

56 Mary Hudetz, "Navajo commission aims to raise awareness of hate crimes," Associated Press, June 21, 2018, https://www.apnews.com/5fa3c199f2e1420f90dd0ad85c8bd2d6.

57 Anna V. Smith, "Why don't anti-Indian groups count as hate groups?," *High Country News*, October 8, 2018, https://www.hcn.org/issues/50.20/tribal-affairs-why-dont-anti-indian-groups-count-as-hate-groups.

58 "The Year in Hate: Trump buoyed white supremacists in 2017, sparking backlash among black nationalist groups," Southern Poverty Law Center, February 21, 2018, https://www.splcenter.org/news/2018/02/21/year-hate-trump-buoyed-white-supremacists-2017-sparking-backlash-among-black-nationalist.

59 Victoria Bekiempis, "Terrorism After 9/11: Dealing with Lone Wolves," *Newsweek*, September 13, 2015. Accessed March 27, 2016. http://www.newsweek.com/september-11-lone-wolf-terrorist-terrorism-nypd-isis-isil-371216.

60 "Patriot Front," Southern Poverty Law Center, 2019, https://www.splcenter.org/fighting-hate/extremist-files/group/patriot-front.

61 "Caravan paranoia is tearing the border militia movement apart," Southern Poverty Law Center, November 15, 2018, https://www.splcenter.org/hatewatch/2018/11/15/caravan-paranoia-tearing-border-militia-movement-apart.

62 Kate Prengel, "United Constitutional Patriots: 5 Fast Facts You Need to Know," *Heavy*, April 22, 2019, https://heavy.com/news/2019/04/united-constitutional-patriots/.

63 Simon Romero, "Militia in New Mexico Detains Asylum Seekers at Gunpoint," *New York Times*, April 18, 2019, https://www.nytimes.com/2019/04/18/us/new-mexico-militia.html.

64 "New Black Panther Party," Southern Poverty Law Center, 2019, https://www.splcenter.org/fighting-hate/extremist-files/group/new-black-panther-party.

65 "Farrakhan Praises Trump for Destroying His Enemies—the FBI and Justice Department," *Haaretz*, May 28, 2018, https://www.haaretz.com/us-news/farrakhan-praises-trump-for-destroying-his-enemies-1.6130805.

66 Gabrielle Levy, "Trump: We Are Not Racists," *U.S. News*, August 25, 2016, https://www.usnews.com/news/articles/2016-08-25/trump-we-are-not-racists

67 "Donald Trump: 'I am not a racist'," *The Guardian*, Video, 00:15, January 15, 2018, https://www.youtube.com/watch?v=zR5EuwvxsMc.

68 Tim Haines, "Ben Carson: I've Interacted with Racist People, Trump Is Not One of Them," *Real Clear Politics*, March 19, 2019, https://www.realclearpolitics.com/video/2019/03/19/ben_carson_ive_interacted_with_racist_people_trump_is_not_one_of_them.html.

69 Toluse Olorunnipa, "Sanders Says Trump Isn't Racist, Citing 'The Apprentice,'" *Bloomberg*, January 16, 2018, https://www.bloomberg.com/news/articles/2018-01-16/sanders-defends-trump-as-not-racist-citing-apprentice-tv-role.

70 Rick Klein, "Trump said 'blame on both sides' in Charlottesville, now the anniversary

puts him on the spot," ABC News, August 12, 2018, https://abcnews.go.com/Politics/trump-blame-sides-charlottesville-now-anniversary-puts-spot/story?id=57141612.

71 "Trump Blames Pittsburgh Synagogue Shooting on Lack Of Security—Not Lax Gun Laws," *Foward*, October 2018, https://forward.com/fast-forward/412805/trump-blames-pittsburgh-synagogue-shooting-on-lack-of-security-not-lax-gun/.

72 "Trump signs law expanding hate crime protections to religious institutions," *Jewish Telegraphic Agency*, October 3, 2018, https://www.jta.org/2018/10/03/united-states/trump-signs-law-expanding-hate-crime-protections-religious-institutions.

73 Lorenzo Ferrigno, "Donald Trump: Boston beating is 'terrible'," CNN, August 21, 2015, https://www.cnn.com/2015/08/20/politics/donald-trump-immigration-boston-beating/index.html.

74 Wilfred Reilly, *Hate Crime Hoax: How the Left is Selling a Fake Race War* (Washington, DC: Regnery Publishing, 2019).

75 "Hate Hoax Map," *American Renaissance*, 2019, https://www.amren.com/archives/reports/hate-crime-hoax-map/.

76 Ibid.

77 Robert Stacy McCain, "A Real Epidemic of Fake Hate," *American Spectator*, April 1, 2019, https://spectator.org/a-real-epidemic-of-fake-hate/.

78 Nicole Goodkind, "Donald Trump Jr. Falsely Claims Majority of Hate Crimes Are Hoaxes," *Newsweek*, February 25, 2019, https://www.newsweek.com/donald-trump-jr-hate-crimes-hoaxes-fox-friends-jussie-smollett-1343168.

79 David Jackson and Aamer Madhani, "President Trump: Jussie Smollett case 'embarrassment' to the nation, FBI will investigate," *USA Today*, March 28, 2019, https://www.usatoday.com/story/news/politics/2019/03/28/donald-trump-says-fbi-look-into-jussie-smollett-case/3296713002/.

80 Rachel Pendergraft, "Hate Crime Legislation," The Knights Party, 2018, https://kkk.bz/hate-crime-legislation/.

81 Ibid.

82 Westley Parker, "Anti-Trump Hate Map," *American Renaissance*, 2019, https://www.amren.com/archives/reports/anti-trump-hate-map/.

83 Maria Perez, "Donald Trump MAGA Hat Attacks, Intolerance: List of Reported Incidents Against People Wearing President's Caps," *Newsweek*, March 11, 2019, https://www.newsweek.com/criminal-acts-trump-maga-hats-1357179.

84 Rachel Pendergraft, "True Hate Crimes and the Media," The Knights Party, 2018, https://kkk.bz/true-hate-crimes-and-the-media/.

85 Masha Gessen, "Why the Tree of Life Shooter Was Fixated on the Hebrew Immigrant Aid Society," *New Yorker*, October 27, 2018, https://www.newyorker.com/news/our-columnists/why-the-tree-of-life-shooter-was-fixated-on-the-hebrew-immigrant-aid-society.

86 "Hate-Crazed Synagogue Shooter Tells Police: Jews 'Committing Genocide,'" *Forward*, October 29, 2018, https://forward.com/fast-forward/412977/hate-crazed-synagogue-shooter-tells-police-jews-committing-genocide/.

87 "Deadly Shooting at Pittsburgh Synagogue," Anti-Defamation League, October 27, 2018, https://www.adl.org/blog/deadly-shooting-at-pittsburgh-synagogue.
88 David Duke, Twitter, August 12, 2017, 11:03 A.M., https://twitter.com/drdavidduke/status/896431991821926401?lang=en.
89 Ben Schreckinger, "Trump's Culture Warriors Go Home," *Politico*, November/December 2018, https://www.politico.com/magazine/story/2018/10/29/trump-cernovich-milo-yiannopoulos-richard-spencer-alt-right-2018-221916.
90 Identity Evropa Ma, Twitter, https://twitter.com/massachusettsie?lang=en.
91 Anna Schecter, "White nationalist leader is plotting to 'take over the GOP,'" NBC News, October 17, 2018, https://www.nbcnews.com/politics/immigration/white-nationalist-leader-plotting-take-over-gop-n920826.
92 "Are white nationalists turning on Trump?," Southern Poverty Law Center, November 27, 2018, https://www.splcenter.org/hatewatch/2018/11/27/are-white-nationalists-turning-trump.

12: THE UNEXPECTED FOLLOWERS

1 Steve Benen, "Trump thinks he knows what women are thinking (polls show otherwise)," MSNBC, September 27, 2018, http://www.msnbc.com/rachel-maddow-show/trump-thinks-he-knows-what-women-are-thinking-polls-show-otherwise.
2 "An examination of the 2016 electorate, based on validated voters," Pew Research Center, August 9, 2018, https://www.people-press.org/2018/08/09/an-examination-of-the-2016-electorate-based-on-validated-voters/.
3 Desiree Zapata Miller, "Why Women like Me Support Donald Trump," *Charlotte Observer*, November 3, 2018, https://www.charlotteobserver.com/opinion/op-ed/article220954225.html.
4 Caitríona Perry, *In America: Tales from Trump Country* (Dublin: Gill & Macmillan Ltd., 2018).
5 Ibid.
6 Julie Bykowicz, "3 women to launch super PAC to support Donald Trump," Fox 23 News, June 9, 2016, https://www.fox23.com/news/3-women-to-launch-super-pac-to-support-donald-trump-1/332008763.
7 "About the Women Vote Trump Project," Women Vote Smart, 2019, http://womenvotesmartpac.com/our-story/.
8 "Women Voted Smart. Women Voted Trump," Women Vote Smart, 2019, http://womenvotesmartpac.com.
9 Ibid.
10 Jason Riley, "Among Black Voters, Trump's Popularity Inches Upward," *Wall Street Journal*, November 6, 2018, https://www.wsj.com/articles/among-black-voters-trumps-popularity-inches-upward-1541547594.
11 Clare Foran, "Meet the YouTube Stars Trying to Convert Democrats to Team Trump," *The Atlantic*, January 29, 2016, https://www.theatlantic.com/politics/archive/2016/01/donald-trump-democrats/433503/.
12 "About Diamond and Silk," Diamond and Silk, Inc., 2017, https://www.diamondandsilkinc.com/about-us.

13 Dan Mangan, "Michael Cohen: Trump said 'Black people are too stupid to vote for me,'" CNBC, November 2, 2018, https://www.cnbc.com/2018/11/02/michael-cohen-trump-said-black-people-are-too-stupid-to-vote-for-me.html.
14 Dahleen Glanton, "We all can learn something from Donald Trump's token black friend," *Chicago Tribune*, March 4, 2019, https://www.chicagotribune.com/news/columnists/glanton/ct-met-dahleen-glanton-donald-trump-token-friend-20190301-story.html.
15 Ibid.
16 "Black Trump supporters aren't 'tokens': Readers sound off," *USA Today*, March 17, 2019, https://www.usatoday.com/story/opinion/readers/2019/03/17/donald-trumps-african-american-supporters-arent-tokens-readers/3165804002/.
17 Nora Gámez Torres, "Trump says he won 84 percent of the Cuban-American vote. Fake news?," *Miami Herald*, August 4, 2017, https://www.miamiherald.com/news/nation-world/world/americas/cuba/article165450707.html.
18 Joshua, Alvarez, "Trump Disrupts Cuban-American Politics," *The Atlantic*, March 17, 2016, https://www.theatlantic.com/politics/archive/2016/03/trump-disrupts-cuban-american-politics/474165/.
19 "Remarks by President Trump in Roundtable with Hispanic Pastors," White House, January 25, 2019, https://www.whitehouse.gov/briefings-statements/remarks-president-trump-roundtable-hispanic-pastors/.
20 "Gays for Trump," Facebook Group, 2019, etc., https://www.facebook.com/groups/gaysfortrump/.
21 Ibid.
22 Chris Moody and Alexander Rosen, "Gays for Trump? Activist plans new effort," CNN, June 15, 2016, https://www.cnn.com/2016/06/15/politics/gays-for-donald-trump/index.html.
23 Paul Moakley, "Inside Gays for Trump's Deploraball Dance Party," *Time*, January 21, 2017, http://time.com/4642202/trump-inauguration-gay-deploraball/.
24 "'I'm a Muslim who voted for Donald Trump', BBC, video, 00:16, January 14, 2018, https://www.bbc.com/news/av/world-us-canada-42677735/i-m-a-muslim-who-voted-for-donald-trump.
25 Asra Q. Nomani, "I'm a Muslim, a woman and an immigrant. I voted for Trump," *Washington Post*, November 10, 2016, https://www.washingtonpost.com/news/global-opinions/wp/2016/11/10/im-a-muslim-a-woman-and-an-immigrant-i-voted-for-trump/?utm_term=.d4e02bd56d31.
26 Aiden Pink, "Trump, Pence Speeches at Republican Jewish Coalition Event Show Group's Rise," *Forward*, April 5, 2019, https://forward.com/news/national/422126/trump-pence-republican-jewish-coalition/.
27 "Donald Trump says Jews are leaving the Democrats. Are they?," *Jewish Telegraphic Agency*, March 12, 2019, https://www.jta.org/2019/03/12/politics/donald-trump-says-jews-are-leaving-the-democrats-are-they.
28 Ibid.
29 "CIRCLE 2016 Millennial Poll: Full Analysis," Circle, October 27, 2016, http://civicyouth.org/circle-2016-millennial-poll-full-analysis/.

30 "Meet the millennials who support Trump," MSNBC, March 14, 2016, https://www.msnbc.com/msnbc-quick-cuts/watch/meet-the-millennials-who-support-trump-644528195854.
31 Ibid.
32 "Trump: I could shoot somebody and not lose voters," CNN, Video, 00:48, January 23, 2016, https://www.youtube.com/watch?v=iTACH1eVIaA.

13: THE MENTAL HEALTH OF A NATION

1 "Managing stress related to political change," American Psychological Association, February 2017, https://www.apa.org/helpcenter/stress-political-change.
2 "Stress in America Generation Z," American Psychological Association, October 2018, https://www.apa.org/news/press/releases/stress/2018/stress-gen-z.pdf.
3 L. T. Hoyt, K. H. Zeiders, et al., "Young adults' psychological and physiological reactions to the 2016 U.S. presidential election," National Institutes of Health, March 26, 2018, https://www.ncbi.nlm.nih.gov/pubmed/29606376.
4 Clare Lombardo, "Virginia Study Finds Increased Schooled Bullying in Areas That Voted for Trump," NPR, January 9, 2019, https://www.npr.org/2019/01/09/683177489/virginia-study-finds-increased-school-bullying-in-areas-that-voted-for-trump.
5 "How Bullying Affects the Brain," *Neuroscience News*, December 12, 2018, https://neurosciencenews.com/brain-bullying-10331/.
6 John F. Harris, "Trump May Not Be Crazy, But the Rest of Us Are Getting There Fast," *Politico*, October 12, 2018, https://www.politico.com/magazine/story/2018/10/12/donald-trump-anxiety-disorder-pscyhologists-221305.
7 Matt Kwong, "In a divided U.S., therapists treating anxiety are hearing the same name over and over: Donald Trump," CBC, July 28, 2018, https://www.cbc.ca/news/world/trump-anxiety-disorder-mental-health-political-divide-us-1.4762487.
8 Melissa DeJonckheere, Andre Fisher, and Tammy Chang, "How has the presidential election affected young Americans?," National Institutes of Health, February 13, 2018, https://www.ncbi.nlm.nih.gov/pmc/articles/PMC5809872/.
9 Kirsten A. Gonzalez, Joanna L. Ramirez, and M. Paz Galupo, "Increase in GLBTQ minority stress following the 2016 US presidential election," American Psychological Association, February 28, 2018, https://psycnet.apa.org/record/2018-16944-008.
10 Tara Santora, "Trump's transgender memo could damage trans mental health, experts say," *Scienceline*, November 13, 2018, https://scienceline.org/2018/11/trumps-transgender-memo-could-damage-trans-mental-health-experts-say/.
11 General Flynn, Twitter, February 26, 2016, 8:14 P.M., https://twitter.com/genflynn/status/703387702998278144?lang=en.
12 G. Samari, H. E. Alcalá, and M. Z. Sharif, "Islamophobia, Health, and Public: A Systematic Literature Review," US National Library of Medicine, National Institutes of Health, June 2018, https://www.ncbi.nlm.nih.gov/pubmed/29672152.
13 Donald J. Trump and Kate Bohner, *Trump: The Art of the Comeback* (New York: Times Books, 1997).

ENDNOTES

14 "Trump supporter attacks BBC cameraman at El Paso rally," BBC, February 12, 2019, https://www.bbc.com/news/world-us-canada-47208909.

15 Dakin Andone and Gisela Crespo, "Suspect's van—plastered with Trump, Pence stickers—a focus of bomb investigation," CNN, October 27, 2018, https://www.cnn.com/2018/10/26/politics/cesar-sayoc-white-van-stickers/index.html.

16 "RAW/UNEDITED: 'Fahrenheit 11/9' outtake of Cesar Sayoc at 'Trump 2020' Rally in February 2017," MMFlint, video, 03:38, October 28, 2018, https://www.youtube.com/watch?v=opM6YIx3gA8.

17 Donald J. Trump, Twitter, January 18, 2019, 5:22 A.M., https://twitter.com/realdonaldtrump/status/1086252588088082432.

18 Anna Giaritelli, "Border rancher: 'We've found prayer rugs out here. It's unreal,'" *Washington Examiner*, January 16, 2019, https://www.washingtonexaminer.com/news/border-rancher-weve-found-prayer-rugs-out-here-its-unreal.

19 Colby Itkowitz, "'Nut Job,' 'Wacko,' 'Basket Case': How Donald Trump's Put-Downs May Impact Mental Stigma," National Alliance on Mental Illness, 2018, https://namimc.org/nut-job-wacko-basket-case-how-donald-trumps-put-downs-may-impact-mental-health-stigma/.

20 Jen Christensen, "Trump's language on school shooter's mental health could be harmful, experts say," CNN Health, February 22, 2018, https://www-m.cnn.com/2018/02/22/health/trump-mental-illness-comments-bn/index.html?r=https%3A%2F%2Fwww.google.com%2F.

14: THE LEFT'S REACTION

1 Zachary Newkirk, "Donald Trump's Donations to Democrats, Club for Growth's Busy Day and More in Capital Eye Opener: February 17," Open Secrets, February 17, 2011, https://www.opensecrets.org/news/2011/02/donald-trumps-donations-to-democrats/.

2 Eli Okun, "Awkward: How Trump's past donations could haunt 2020 Dems," *Politico*, March 5, 2019, https://www.politico.com/story/2019/03/05/2020-presidential-dems-trump-money-1202938.

3 Michael Rothfeld and Mark Maremont, "Donald Trump Said Hillary Clinton Would 'Make a Good President' in 2008," *Wall Street Journal*, July 11, 2016, https://www.wsj.com/articles/donald-trump-said-hillary-clinton-would-make-a-good-president-in-2008-1468281714.

4 Andrew Kaczynski, "Trump in 2008: Hillary Clinton will 'go down at a minimum as a great senator,'" CNN, October 19, 2016, https://www.cnn.com/2016/10/19/politics/trump-ny1-clintons/index.html.

5 Dan Balz, "Yes, the Republican Party has changed since 2016. You think the Democratic Party hasn't?," *Washington Post*, March 9, 2019, https://www.washingtonpost.com/politics/yes-the-republican-party-has-changed-since-2016-you-think-the-democratic-party-hasnt/2019/03/09/b3a8f376-41da-11e9-9361-301ffb5bd5e6_story.html?utm_term=.ba60974192b5.

6 Andrew Malcolm, "How Donald Trump is Changing the Democratic Party," *San Francisco Chronicle*, January 10, 2019, https://www.sfchronicle.com/news/article/How-Donald-Trump-is-changing-the-Democratic-Party-13522138.php?pid=39D0T.

7 Perry Bacon Jr., "The Six Wings of the Democratic Party," *FiveThirtyEight*, March 11, 2019, https://fivethirtyeight.com/features/the-six-wings-of-the-democratic-party/.

8 William A. Galston, "The liberal faction of the Democratic party is growing, new polling shows," Brookings, January 11, 2019, https://www.brookings.edu/blog/fixgov/2019/01/11/the-liberal-faction-of-the-democratic-party-is-growing-new-polling-shows/.

9 Dan Mangan and Kevin Breuninger, "House Speaker Nancy Pelosi says Trump 'unfit' to be president, but 'I'm not for impeachment'," CNBC, March 12, 2019, https://www.cnbc.com/2019/03/11/house-speaker-nancy-pelosi-says-im-not-for-impeachment-of-trump.html.

10 Clare Foran, Manu Raju, and Lauren Fox, "Dems pushing impeachment undeterred by Pelosi saying Trump 'not worth it'," CNN, March 12, 2019, https://www.cnn.com/2019/03/12/politics/pelosi-trump-impeachment-house-democrats/index.html.

11 "Resources," Need to Impeach, 2019, https://www.needtoimpeach.com/barr-vs-mueller/.

12 Miles Parks, "Poll: Most Democrats Back Impeachment Hearings, A Move That's Unpopular Overall," NPR, May 1, 2019, https://www.npr.org/2019/05/01/718710736/poll-most-democrats-back-impeachment-hearings-a-move-thats-unpopular-overall.

13 Robert McCartney, "Blackface, sexual assault scandals seem to have done only limited harm to Virginia's reputation," *Washington Post*, March 3, 2019, https://www.washingtonpost.com/local/blackface-sexual-assault-scandals-dont-appear-to-have-tarnished-virginias-image/2019/03/03/c8b5b1fc-3bb1-11e9-a2cd-307b06d0257b_story.html.

14 Zack Beauchamp, "Tulsi Gabbard, the controversial, long-shot Democratic 2020 candidate, explained," *Vox*, January 17, 2019, https://www.vox.com/policy-and-politics/2019/1/16/18182114/tulsi-gabbard-2020-president-campaign-explained.

15 Ashley Rae Goldenberg, "Rashida Tlaib Follows Anti-Semitic Instagram Page," Capital Research Center, March 8, 2019, https://capitalresearch.org/article/rashida-tlaib-follows-anti-semitic-instagram-page/.

15: FOREIGN AFFAIRS

1 Donald J. Trump, *Time to Get Tough: Make America Great Again!* (Washington, DC: Regnery Publishing, 2015).

2 Donald J. Trump, Twitter, October 11, 2012, 3:57 P.M., https://twitter.com/realdonaldtrump/status/256483626026426368.

3 Donald J. Trump, *Crippled America: How to Make America Great Again* (New York: Simon & Schuster, 2011).

4   Vivian Salama and Peter Nicholas, "Talk to Trump, Skip the Diplomats: World Leaders' New U.S. Tactic," *Wall Street Journal*, March 14, 2019, https://www.wsj.com/articles/world-leaders-new-tactic-to-read-u-s-policy-skip-the-diplomats-and-talk-to-trump-11552581757.
5   "EU's Tusk says no 'Common position' on Russia with Trump," AFP, video, 00:32, May 25, 2017, https://www.youtube.com/watch?v=xKw3NR2q8Mw.
6   Lesley Stahl, "President Trump on Christine Blasey Ford, his relationships with Vladimir Putin and Kim Jong Un and more," *60 Minutes*, October 15, 2018, https://www.cbsnews.com/news/donald-trump-full-interview-60-minutes-transcript-lesley-stahl-2018-10-14/.
7   Ibid.
8   Aaron Blake, "Rex Tillerson on Trump: 'Undisciplined, doesn't like to read' and tries to do illegal things," *Washington Post*, December 7, 2018, https://www.washingtonpost.com/politics/2018/12/07/rex-tillerson-trump-undisciplined-doesnt-like-read-tries-do-illegal-things/.
9   Lewis Sanders IV, "Donald Trump on Germany: Top quotes," *Deutsche Welle*, June 19, 2018, https://www.dw.com/en/donald-trump-on-germany-top-quotes/g-39000457.
10 Ibid.
11 Ibid.
12 "France is still France whatever Donald Trump has said," *The Local*, July 12, 2017, https://www.thelocal.fr/20170712/trump-president-france-is-still-france-whatever-donald-trump-might-say.
13 Madeleine Albright, *Fascism: A Warning* (New York: Harper, 2018).
14 Kristen Bialik, "How the world views the U.S. and its president in 9 charts," Pew Research Center, October 9, 2018, https://www.pewresearch.org/fact-tank/2018/10/09/how-the-world-views-the-u-s-and-its-president-in-9-charts/.
15 Donald J. Trump, Twitter, January 11, 2017, 7:31 A.M., https://twitter.com/realdonaldtrump/status/819159806489591809.
16 Donald J. Trump and Tony Schwartz, *Trump: The Art of the Deal* (New York: Random House, 1987).
17 Howard Kurtz, "Gorbachev on the road to new Soviet frontiers," *Washington Post*, December 4, 1988, https://www.washingtonpost.com/archive/politics/1988/12/04/gorbachev-on-the-road-to-new-soviet-frontiers/1f5bc965-2d25-40b3-acad-ad4ae09613a2/.
18 Mark Singer, "Trump Solo," *New Yorker*, May 12, 1997, https://www.newyorker.com/magazine/1997/05/19/trump-solo.
19 "US 'Miss Universe' billionaire plans Russian Trump Tower," *RT*, November 9, 2013, https://www.rt.com/business/trump-plan-skyscraper-russia-479/.
20 Lesley Stahl, "President Trump on Christine Blasey Ford, his relationships with Vladimir Putin and Kim Jong Un and more," *60 Minutes*, October 15, 2018, https://www.cbsnews.com/news/donald-trump-full-interview-60-minutes-transcript-lesley-stahl-2018-10-14/.
21 "Larry King Live-Interview with Donald Trump," CNN, October 15, 2007, http://edition.cnn.com/TRANSCRIPTS/0710/15/lkl.01.html.

ENDNOTES

22 Donald J. Trump, *Time to Get Tough: Make America Great Again!* (Washington, DC: Regnery Publishing, 2015).

23 Donald J. Trump, Twitter, June 18, 2013, 11:17 P.M., https://twitter.com/realdonaldtrump/status/347191326112112640?lang=en.

24 "Trump: 'I think I'd get along very well with Vladimir Putin,'" Reuters, video, 01:21, July 30, 2015, https://www.reuters.com/video/2015/07/30/trump-i-think-id-get-along-very-well-wit?videoId=365130681.

25 Steve Benen, "Trump celebrates Russia's Putin as a real 'leader'," MSNBC, December 18, 2015, http://www.msnbc.com/rachel-maddow-show/trump-celebrates-russias-putin-real-leader.

26 Bruce Riedel, "Trump's 'take the oil' madness," Brookings, September 16, 2016, https://www.brookings.edu/blog/markaz/2016/09/16/trumps-take-the-oil-madness/.

27 Donald J. Trump, *Time to Get Tough: Make America Great Again!* (Washington, DC: Regnery Publishing, 2015).

28 Christopher Woody, "H. R. McMaster reportedly called Trump out for asking about taking Iraq's oil," *Business Insider*, November 26, 2018, https://www.businessinsider.com/hr-mcmaster-criticized-trump-for-asking-about-taking-iraqs-oil-2018-11.

29 Donald J. Trump, Twitter, December 19, 2018, 9:29 A.M., https://twitter.com/realdonaldtrump/status/1075397797929775105?lang=e.

30 Tom LoBianco, "Donald Trump on terrorists: 'Take out their families'," CNN, December 3, 2015, https://www.cnn.com/2015/12/02/politics/donald-trump-terrorists-families/index.html.

31 "Saudi Arabia offers Abbas $10bn to accept US peace plan," Middle East Monitor, May 1, 2019, https://www.middleeastmonitor.com/20190501-saudi-arabia-offers-abbas-10bn-to-accept-us-peace-plan/.

32 Donald J. Trump, *Time to Get Tough: Make America Great Again!* (Washington, DC: Regnery Publishing, 2015).

33 "Statement from President Donald J. Trump on standing with Saudi Arabia," White House, November 20, 2018, https://www.whitehouse.gov/briefings-statements/statement-president-donald-j-trump-standing-saudi-arabia/.

34 Zachary Warmbrodt, "Trump: 'I don't know' if Saudi prince lied," *Politico*, November 11, 2018, https://www.politico.com/story/2018/11/18/trump-saudi-murder-khashoggi-1001699.

35 "Trump: 'Saudi Arabia buys a lot, I don't want to lose them'," Al Jazeera, April 28, 2019, https://www.aljazeera.com/news/2019/04/trump-saudi-arabia-buys-lot-donlose-190428094048617.html.

36 "President Donald J. Trump is Ending United States Participation in an Unacceptable Iran Deal," White House, May 8, 2018, https://www.whitehouse.gov/briefings-statements/president-donald-j-trump-ending-united-states-participation-unacceptable-iran-deal/.

37 "Statement from the President on the Designation of the Islamic Revolutionary Guard Corps as a Foreign Terrorist Organization," White House, April 8, 2019,

https://www.whitehouse.gov/briefings-statements/statement-president-designation-islamic-revolutionary-guard-corps-foreign-terrorist-organization/.

38 Ibram X. Kendi, "The Day 'Shithole' Entered the Presidential Lexicon," *The Atlantic*, January 13, 2019, https://www.theatlantic.com/politics/archive/2019/01/shithole-countries/580054.

39 Cara Anna, "'Reprehensible and racist:' Trump's remarks outrage Africans," Associated Press, January 12, 2018, https://apnews.com/578096f9eb504b65903df31127dc11b3.

40 "'Sh*thole countries' respond to Trump's rhetoric," CBS News, January 12, 2018, https://www.cbsnews.com/news/donald-trump-shthole-countries-response-from-haiti-africa-el-salvador/.

41 Donald J. Trump and Dave Shiflett, *The America We Deserve* (Kent, OH: Renaissance Books, 2000).

42 Donald J. Trump, *Time to Get Tough: Make America Great Again!* (Washington DC: Regnery Publishing, 2015).

43 Michelle Ye Hee Lee, "How many Trump products were made overseas? Here's the complete list," *Washington Post*, August 26, 2016, https://www.washingtonpost.com/news/fact-checker/wp/2016/08/26/how-many-trump-products-were-made-overseas-heres-the-complete-list/?noredirect=on&utm_term=.7c5911f205e.

44 "US denies change to 'one China' policy after Taiwanese President Tsai Ing-wen's speech in California," *South China Morning Post*, August 15, 2018, https://www.scmp.com/news/china/diplomacy-defence/article/2159735/us-denies-change-one-china-policy-after-taiwanese.

45 Miles Parks, "Trump Invites Controversial Philippines Leader To White House," NPR, April 30, 2017, https://www.npr.org/sections/thetwo-way/2017/04/30/526268975/trump-invites-controversial-philippines-leader-to-white-house.

46 "Duterte says Trump speaks his 'language'," *Phnom Penh Post*, September 4, 2018, https://www.phnompenhpost.com/international/duterte-says-trump-speaks-his-language.

47 "Trump in 1999: Negotiate with North Korea," CNN, video, 01:31, August 9, 2017, https://www.youtube.com/watch?v=p7nrU4cEWRk.

48 "What Trump said about North Korean nukes in 1999," CNN, video, 03:24, https://www.youtube.com/watch?v=1-1WE-ivtO4.

49 Donald J. Trump and Dave Shiflett, *The America We Deserve* (Kent, OH: Renaissance Books, 2000).

50 Robert R. King, "President Trump Raises Otto Warmbier Human Rights Case in Hanoi," Center for Strategic and International Studies, March 5, 2019, https://www.csis.org/analysis/president-trump-raises-otto-warmbier-human-rights-case-hanoi.

51 Adam K. Raymond, "'Everyone Thinks So, But I Would Never Say It': Trump on Whether He Deserves Nobel," *New York Magazine*, May 9, 2018, http://nymag.com/intelligencer/2018/05/trump-on-whether-he-deserves-nobel-everyone-thinks-so.html.

52 "Abe nominated Trump for the Nobel at behest of Washington," *Asahi Shimbun*, February 17, 2019, http://www.asahi.com/ajw/articles/AJ201902170021.html.

53 John Bacon, "President Donald Trump on Kim Jong Un: 'We fell in love' over 'beautiful letters'," ABC 10, September 30, 2018, https://www.abc10.com/article/news/nation-now/president-donald-trump-on-kim-jong-un-we-fell-in-love-over-beautiful-letters/465-14c599db-9142-4f1a-a44f-6ed2b647568e fbclid=IwAR0j7ScEQrbDRex6JjmMP9i1FoPbWKJYz7uqFjTka13XTIdt_eDk5-54Th4.
54 "Donald Trump on talks with Kim Jong-un: 'Sometimes you have to walk'" BBC, February 28, 2019, https://www.bbc.com/news/av/world-asia-47399329/donald-trump-on-talks-with-kim-jong-un-sometimes-you-have-to-walk.
55 Noh Ji-won, "Choe Son-hui openly criticizes Pompeo and Bolton," *Hankyoreh*, May 1, 2019, http://english.hani.co.kr/arti/english_edition/e_northkorea/892282.html.
56 Joshua Berlinger, "Vladimir Putin and Kim Jong Un hold first summit," CNN, May 7, 2019, https://www.cnn.com/asia/live-news/kim-jong-un-vladimir-putin-summit-intl/index.html.
57 "Vox Populi, Vox Peanut Gallery?," EGF, 2019, https://egfound.org/stories/independent-america/worlds-apart.

16: WHAT DOES THE FUTURE HOLD?
1 Joshua A. Geltzer, "What if Trump refuses to accept defeat in 2020?," CNN, February 23, 2019, https://www.cnn.com/2019/02/23/opinions/trump-contest-2020-election-loss-geltzer/index.html.

INDEX

A
al-Abadi, Haider, 206
Abbas, Mahmoud, 207, 208
Abdelkader, Engy, 141
abortion, 88, 115–116
Abse, D. Wilfred, xvi
absolutism, xix–xxii, 140
Access Hollywood tape, 74, 110
Acosta, Jim, 100
actor-specific behavioral modeling, xii
Adams, Cindy, 42
admiration, 35, 39, 80–81
adolescents, 180
Affordable Care Act, 5, 73, 130, 167
Africa, 210
African Americans, 151, 157, 161–162, 168–170
African Union, 210
Agenda, 21, 152
aggression, 8–9
Agriculture Advisory Council, 130
Albright, Madeleine, 198
Ali, Muhammad, 98
alt-right, 81–82, *see also* right-wing extremists
America First policy, 124–126, 193, 220
American decline, 91–92
American Farm Bureau Federation, 130–131
American Identity Movement, 164

American Psychiatric Association, 179, 180
American Psychological Association, 179
American Renaissance, 157–158, 160–162
Americans for Prosperity, 86, 127
American Spectator, 158
America We Deserve, The (Trump), 97–98, 113, 210–211, 213–214
Angelou, Maya, 51–52
anger, 145
anti-Arab hate crimes, 149
anti-immigrant rhetoric, 109–110, 125–126, 151, 185
anti-politician voters, 113–114
anti-Semitism, 53, 137–139, 146, 148–150, 155, 162, 174, 191
anti-Trump conservatives, 105–106, *see also* Never Trump movement
anxiety, 180–182
appearance, 64–65
Apprentice, The, 34, 38–39, 48, 50, 52, 80, 156
Arabs, 149, *see also* Muslims
arrogance, 69–71
Art of the Comeback, The (Trump), 7–8, 41–43, 57–58, 182–183, 188
Art of the Deal, The (Trump), 34, 63, 121–122, 199
Asian Americans, 149, 150–151
al-Assad, Bashar, 25–26, 206, 207
al-Assad, Bassel, 25–26

INDEX

Atatürk, Mustafa Kemal, xxvi, xxvii
attention, need for, 80
Ayres, Whit, 127

B
Babaz, Paul, 133
Baker, Kelly, 142
baldness, 64–65
Baldwin, Stanley, 24
bankruptcies, 31
Bannon, Steve, 92–94
Barr, Andy, 173
Barrack, Tom, 54
Barron, Chris, 172
basic assumption states, xxv
Bates, Don, Jr., 114
Baylis, Kerrie, 37
Beam, Louis, 153
Beame, Abraham, 32
Be Best campaign, 44
Begin, Menachem, x, xiii
Benvie, Jim, 155
Berger, Victor L., 110
Bernhardt, David, 132–133
Bernstein, Blaze, 150
Best, Ricky John, 149
Biaggi, Mario, 32
Biblical references, xx
Biden, Joe, 188, 191, 192
Billado, Mariah, 36
Binder, John, 128
bin Laden, Osama, xx, xxvii
bin Salman, Mohammad, 208–209
Bion, Wilfred, xxv, 229n5
bipolar disorder, 11
birtherism, 89–90
black nationalist organizations, 155
black voter turnout, 168
Blitzer, Wolf, 213
Blumenthal, Richard, 7, 73
board game, 34
boasting, 69–71
Bolling, Eric, 111–112

Bolton, John, 197
Booker, Cory, 70, 188
border separation of families, 7, 45, 83
border wall, 55–56, 75, 108–110, 125
Bossie, David, 92
Boston Tea Party, 84–85
Botswana, 210
Bowden, Mark, 138
Bowers, Robert Gregory, 162
Boykin, Peter, 173
Branch Davidians, xxvi
Breitbart News, 92, 93, 94, 109, 128
broadband internet, 130
Brodie, Fawn, 62
Brody, David, 88
Brooks, David, 11, 65
Brown, Brittany, 175
Brzezinski, Mika, 7, 73
Buchanan, Patrick, 145
Buck, Ken, 112
Budapest Memorandum, 204
"Build the Wall," 108–110, 125
bullying, 180
Burnett, Mark, 39
Bush, Billy, 74, 117
Bush, George H. W., 68, 129
Bush, George W., 5–6, 67, 68
Bush, Jeb, 93, 96, 98, 185
business career, 30–33, 55–61, 113–114
Bychowski, Gustav, xx
Bytner, Lisa, 41

C
campaign finance, 71
Campbell, W. Keith, 22
caravan paranoia, 154, 185
career diplomats, 194
Carlson, Tucker, 140
Carnegie Corporation Commission on Preventing Deadly Conflict, xii
Carrier Corporation, 125
Carson, Ben, 109, 156
Casey, Patrick, 163, 164

INDEX

casinos, 31, 32
Castro, Fidel, xix
Celebrity Apprentice, The, 39
celebrity status, 33–39, 80
Central Park Jogger case, 135–137
Cernovich, Mike, 163
certainty, xix, xxi, 175
Cerven, Roger, 131
Chamberlain, Neville, 100
charisma, xvi, xxi
charismatic authority, xv, xvi
charismatic leader-follower relationships, xv–xxvii, 79–83, 229n5; as form of mass hypnosis, xxii; group behavior patterns and, xxv–xxvi; narcissistic transferences and, xviii–xix; societal crisis and, xxiii–xxiv; use of rhetoric and, 127
charismatic leaders, 229n5; definition of, xvi; destructive vs. reparative, xxvi–xxvii, 83, 140; as mirror-hungry personality, xix
charismatic religious cults, xxiv–xxvi
Charlottesville, Virginia protests, 15, 82, 139, 144, 152–153, 156, 223
Chechnya, 203
Cheney, Dick, 101
children: development of, xxiv, 228n2; firstborn, 21; impact of Trump on, 180; role of mothers in shaping, 17–23, 80; separation of immigrant, 7, 45; of Trump, 45–53
China, 126, 130–131, 151, 198, 208, 210–212, 220
Choate, 47
Christianity, 108, 115, 146, 154, 159–160
Christie, Chris, 117
Churchill, Winston, xxiii, xxvii, 83, 100
Citizen Kane, 10–11
Citizens Equal Rights Alliance (CERA), 152
Citizens for a Sound Economy (CSE), 85–86, 127
civil war, 222–223

Clarke, Edward Young, 143
Claver-Carone, Mauricio, 170
Clay, Henry, 68
climate change, 53, 91, 126–128
Clinton, Bill, 5, 44, 67, 73, 74, 107, 188, 189
Clinton, Chelsea, 73–74
Clinton, Hillary, 10, 48–49, 74, 104, 107, 139, 165, 172, 174, 183, 187, 188
Clinton Foundation, 188
Club for Growth Action, 106
CNN, 7, 34, 46, 61, 66, 83, 96, 100, 137, 144, 172, 184, 213
coal industry, 83, 126
Cohen, Michael, 169
Cohn, Roy, 15, 31–33, 57–58
collective self, xxv–xxvi
collective suicides, xxvi
college students, 175
comeback tips, 7–8, 58–59, 182–183
Comey, James, 73, 74, 101
Commodore Hotel, 32
Common Cause, 111
Congress, 61, 112
conscience: no constraint of, 7; Swiss cheese, 74–75
Conservative Political Action Conference (CPAC), 102, 119, 197
conspiracy theories, 49, 89–90, 140, 152, 154, 157–160, 184, 185
construction, 71
Convention Against Torture, 29
Cooper, Anderson, 46
Corker, Bob, 106
Cornell, Dewey, 180
Coulter, Ann, 120
countersuits, 31–32
coups, 184
courts, 69
Cramer, Katherine, 128
crime, 109, 125–126, 139, *see also* hate crimes
Crimea, 203, 204, 205

265

Crippled America: How to Make America Great Again (Trump), 8, 16, 26–28, 45, 66–67, 117, 194
Cruz, Nikolas, 185
Cruz, Ted, 92, 117, 185
Cuban Americans, 170–171
Curiel, Gonzalo, 138
curiosity, lack of, 66, 68
currency manipulation, 91, 211

D
Davis, Dee, 128
Dean, Trevor, 130
debt, 70
decision-making process, 61, 62, 71
"deep state," 184
Democratic Party: 2016 election and, 188–189; 2020 elections and, 189–192; attacks on, 7; controversies in, 190–191; midterm elections and, 189; structure of, 188–189; Trump and, 71, 96–97, 187–188
deplorables, 172
depression, 180–182
derogatory language, 135, 138, 140, 141, 143–144, 185, *see also* rhetoric
destructive charismatic leaders, xxvi–xxvii, 83, 140
Deutch, Ted, 56
Diagnostic and Statistical Manual V (DSM), 11
Diamond and Silk, 168–169, 170
disillusion, xxiii
Ditch and Switch Now movement, 168–169
divine guidance, xx
divorces, 41–42, 47, 74
Dixon, Tasha, 36
Dobias, Theodore R., 27, 28
Doctor Patient Medical Association, 167
Donald J. Trump Collection, 72–73
Donald Trump's Real Estate Tycoon, 35
doubt, xxi–xxii, 72, 175

Douglass, Frederick, 68
"Drain the Swamp," 110–112
drones, 69
Dubinin, Yuri, 199
Duke, David, 81, 82, 144–147, 163
Duterte, Rodrigo, 212–213
Dyer, Allen, 227n3

E
economic fears, 109, 124, 166
economy, 71
Edward VIII, 24
Eichler, Ned, 32
either/or categorization, xix–xxii
Elam, Debbie, 166
elites, 112
emotional reactions, 72–74
empathy, 4–7
enemies, 183
environmentalism, 126–128
Environmental Protection Agency (EPA), 53, 126
Erdogan, Recep Tayyip, 195, 209
Erikson, Erik, xvi
Eskenazi, Maxine, 68
Esposito, Luigi, 109
Eubanks, William, 41
Europe, 195–199, 220
evangelicals, 88, 115–116, 171
externalization, 124
extramarital affair, 41, 42, 74

F
Facebook, 3
Fagan, Garrett, 81
Faircloth, Jean, 20
Fairfax, Justin, 191
fake news, 8, 73, 183
family divisions, 182
family separation policy, 7, 45, 83
family values, 74
farmers, 129–131
Farrakhan, Louis, 155

fathers, idolized, 26–27
FBI hate crime statistics, 148
Fea, John, 115
fear, xxv, 115
female supporters, 165–168
Fields, James Alex, Jr., 156
Finley, Laura, 109
Fiol, Juan, 170
firstborn child, 21
First Lady, 44–45
Flavor Aid suicide, xvi, xxvi
Fletcher, Micah David-Cole, 149
Flynn, Michael, 93, 181
Foley, Elizabeth Price, 87–88
followers: group behavior of, xxv–xxvi; as ideal-hungry personalities, xxii–xxiii, xxiv, xxvii; psychological qualities of, xvi–xvii; right-wing extremists, 143–148; temporarily overwhelmed, xxii–xxiii, 83; unexpected, 165–175, *see also* Trump supporters
foreign policy, 69, 193–220
"Formula of Knowledge," 67
Forti, Carl, 89
fossil fuel industry, 127
Fournier, Ryan, 175
Fox News, 92
France, 197–198
FreedomWorks, 86
Freud, Sigmund, xvi, 21
friends: divisions between, 182; of Trump, 54
Fuchs, Joseph, 66
Fulani, Lenora, 145

G

G20 Summit, 53
Gabbard, Tulsi, 191
Galanter, Marc, xxiv
Gandhi, Mohandas, xxvi, xxvii, 83
Gandhi, Rajiv, 25
Gandhi, Sanjay, 25
Garin, Geoff, 188–189
Garten, Alan, 106

Gaylord, Winfield R., 110
Gays for Trump, 172–173
Geltzer, Joshua, 221, 222
Geneva Conventions, 29, 205, 207
George, Alexander, xii
George V, 24
George VI, 24
Germany, 197
Gervais, Bryan, 91–92
Gianforte, Greg, 81
Gillibrand, Kirsten, 188, 192
Gilmore, Jim, 130
Gingrich, Newt, 100, 117, 122
globalists, 138, 162
globalization, 123, 124–125
global warming, 91, 126–128
God, xx
Goebbels, Joseph, 62
Golan Heights, 208
golden age, 107
Gold Star parents, 6, 105
Goldwater, Barry, 62
Goldwater Rule, xi, xii, 11, 227n3
Good, Chris, 87
good vs. evil, xix–xxii
Gore, Al, 126
Gourguechon, Prudence, 22
Graham, Lindsey, 101–102, 185
grammar, 68
grandiose omnipotence, xix, 80
grandiose self, xviii, 4, 228
grandiosity, 3, 4, 9–10, 35, 72, 79
Great Wall of China, 56
Green, Al, 190
Green, Joshua, 93
Greenacre, Phyllis, xxi
Greenberg, Jonathan, 62–63
group behavior, repetitive patterns of, xxv–xxvi
group mind, xxv, xxvi
Guilfoyle, Kimberly, 119
gun rights, 117–119, 134, 154, 174–175
gut instinct, 59

INDEX

H
Hacham, Mike, 173
hair, 64–65
Hall, Daniel G., 55
hand size, 65
Hannity, Sean, 8, 52, 187
Hardaway, Lynnette, 168–169
hard-line supporters, 73–74, 79–83
Harris, Kamala, 188, 192
Hart, Peter, 89
Harvey, Tonya "Kita," 150
Haslam, Bill, 130
hate crimes: anti-Trump, 160–162; hoax theories, 157–160; rhetoric and, 140–144; during Trump presidency, 135, 148–152; Trump rallies and, 141–142; Trump's response to, 155–157; Twitter and, 141; against whites, 159–160
hateful rhetoric, 135–148
hate groups, 152–155, 163–164
Hawke, Robert, 20
Hawkins, Kristan, 108
Haydon, Vanessa, 48
health insurance, 5, 73
Hebrew Immigrant Aid Society (HIAS), 162
Herring, Mark R., 191
Hewitt, Hugh, 66–67
Heyer, Heather, 156
Hezbollah, 67
hijabs, 149
The Hill School, 47
Hitchcock, Alfred, 8
Hitler, Adolf, xx, xxi, xxii, xxv, xxvi, xxvii, 62, 83, 212, 229n3
hoax theories, 157–160, *see also* conspiracy theories
Hochfelsen, Jerry, 90
Hoffa, James P., 98
Hoffer, Eric, 142–143
Hogan, Larry, 106
Hollande, François, 197–198
Honberg, Ron, 185–186

Hopkins, Larry Mitchell, 154
Horn, Peter, 132
Horton, Johnny, Jr., 154–155
House Un-American Activities Committee, 31
housing discrimination, 31–32, 135
Hoyt, Lindsay, 180
Huang, Francis, 180
Huckabee, Mike, 88, 100, 104, 222
hunting, 131–134
Hurricane Betsy, 7
Hurricane Harvey, 6–7
Hurricane Maria, 139–140
Hussein, Saddam, xx, 39
Hyde, Tim, 86
hypnosis, mass, xxii

I
Iacocca, Lee, 90
ideal-hungry personality, xvii, xviii, xxi, 82–83; followers and, xxii–xxiii, xxvii; narcissistically wounded, xxiv
idealization, xxiii
Identity Evropa, 163–164
illegal immigration, 91, 109, 125–126, 157, 185
immigrant children, separation of, 7, 45, 83
immigration policy, 44–45, 91, 92, 108–110, 125–126, 139, 163–164
impeachment, 184, 189–190
inaugural address, 91–92, 223
inauguration turnout, 10
information processing, 71–72
infrastructure, 70, 99
Ing-wen, Tsai, 211
injured self, xvii–xviii, 79–80
inner doubt, xxi–xxii
insecurity, 7, 9–10, 64–65, 72, 80, 81
intelligence, 68–69, 71
intelligence briefings, 68, 71
International Wildlife Conservation Council, 132
investigations, 32
Iran, 206, 209

268

INDEX

Iran Deal, 209
Iraq, 205–206
Irizarry, Dillon, 153
Isaacson, Jason, 156
ISIS, 69, 71, 206–207
Islamic extremism, 172, 173
Islamic Revolutionary Guard, 209
Islamic State, 69, 71, 206–207
Islamophobia, 181–182
Israel, 207–208
issue appeal, 115–119
Itzkowitz, Norman, xxvi

J

Jackson, Andrew, 68
Jang Song Thaek, 215, 219
Japan, 217
Jeffress, Robert, 115
Jeong, Sarah, 100
Jerusalem, 207–208
Jewish community, 149–150, 162, 173–174
Jindal, Bobby, 101
Jingping, Xi, 212
job creation, 99
Johnson, Greg, 164
Johnson, Jenna, 6
Johnson, Lyndon, 7, 183
Joint Comprehensive Plan of Action (JCPOA), 209
Jones, Jim, xxv
journalists: attacks on, 6, 7, 184; on Trump's mental stability, xi–xii, 11, 65, *see also* media
judgment, 65–66

K

Kalondo, Ebba, 210
Kamen, Al, 98
Kasich, John, 106
Keefe, Patrick Radden, 38–39
Kelly, John, 62
Kelly, Megyn, 73
Kendall, Jason, 149
Kennedy, Joe, 25
Kennedy, John F., 25
Kerry, John, 187
Kew-Forest elementary school, 23
Khan, Humayun, 6, 105
Khan, Khizr, 6
Khashoggi, Jamal, 208–209
Khomeini, Ayatollah, xx, xxiii, xxv, xxvii
Khrushchev, Nikita, xiii
Ki, Jong-chul, 218
Kim Il-sung, 215
Kim Jong-il, 215, 219
Kim Jong-nam, 216, 218
Kim Jong-un, 4, 8, 195, 212–219, 224
Kim Kyong-hui, 219
King, Larry, 136, 200
King, Martin Luther, xxvi, xxvii, 83
Klan Springs Eternal (KSE), 157
knowledge, 66–72
Koch, Charles, 85, 127
Koch, David, 85, 127
Kohut, Heinz, xvii, xxi, 41
Korean War, 218
Kovaleski, Serge, 6
Kremer, Amy, 166, 167
Kuchibhotla, Srinivas, 151
Ku Klux Klan, 15, 81–82, 144, 146–147, 153, 161–162, 191
Kushner, Jared, 46, 49, 52–53, 94, 142–143

L

Lambert, John, 175
Lamont, Michèle, 123
Land, Richard, 116
Lasch, Christopher, 35
Latinos, 141, 151, 170–171
lawsuits: racial discrimination, 31–32; Trump's knowledge of, 70
leaders: role of mothers in shaping, 17–23, 80, *see also* charismatic leaders
leadership style, of Trump, 33, 57–62
Lebanon, 67
Lebed, Aleksander, 199–200

269

Le Club, 31
Left, reaction to Trump by, 187–192
Leibovich, Mark, 102
Levin, Brian, 140–141, 161
Lewandowski, Corey, 93
Lewinsky, Monica, 44
LGBTQ community, 53, 150, 160, 172–173, 181
LGBTQ issues, 88
Licata, Anthony, 117–118, 131
lies, 62–63
life course, xiii, xiv
life events, xiii
Lim, Shi, 37
lobbying, 111
loyalty, 7, 54
luck, 59
lure of the arena, 81

M

MacArthur, Douglas, 19–20, 80
MacDonald, Kevin, 163
Machado, Alicia, 73
Macron, Emmanuel, 198
Macy's, 72
"Made in America" campaign, 52
MAGA hats, 108, 161
Make America Great Again (MAGA), 80, 91, 98, 107–108
Malcolm, Andrew, 189
malignant narcissism, 4, 7–10
Manafort, Paul, 49, 93
Mandela, Nelson, xxvii
Manhattan real estate, 23, 31
manufacturing jobs, 125, 126, 127
Maples, Marla, 42–43, 74
Martin, Jenny Beth, 94
Mascaro, Lisa, 92
Mason, Meredith, 114
mass hypnosis, xxii
Mattis, James, 61–62, 66, 71, 196, 206
Mayer, Jane, 29
McAuliffe, Terry, 223

McCain, John, 5–6, 73, 91, 102, 126–127, 137
McCain, Robert Stacy, 158–159
McCarthy, Joseph, 31
McConnell, Mitch, 102
McIntosh, David, 106
McMaster, H. R., 62, 206
McNamara, Robert, 33
Meadow, Mark, 169–170
media: Russian investigation by, 8; as scapegoat, 8; as Trump's enemy, 183–184, 222
Medvedev, Dmitry, 202
"me generation," 3
Meili, Trisha, 135–136
Melker, Scott, 47–48
mental health issues, 179–186
Merkel, Angela, 197
Mexicans, 138, 170
Mexico, 72–73, 75
Middle East, 205–210
midterm elections, 189, 222
military service, 28–29
militias, 154–155
millennials, 174–175
Miller, Desiree Zapata, 166
Mines, Keith, 223
minimum wage, 130
Miniter, Frank, 133
minority groups: derogatory language against, 138; hate crimes and, 148–152; for Trump, 168–174, 175
mirror-hungry personality, xvii-xviii, xix, xxi-xxii, xxvii, 79, 80–81
Miss Teen USA pageant, 36
Miss Universe pageant, 35–37, 200, 201
Miss USA pageant, 36
monarchy, 56
money, 70
Moon, Sun Myung, xxv
Moore, Dale, 130
Moore, Ryan, 107–108
moral prohibitions, 74–75

INDEX

Morning Joe, 7, 69, 90, 194, 201
Morris, Irwin, 91–92
Morrison, Toni, 51
mothers, role of, 17–23, 80
movies, 34, 35
Mueller investigation, 49, 54, 56, 183
Mueller Report, 101, 104, 190
Muir, David, 28
Muller, Karsten, 141
Muslim Reform Movement, 173
Muslims, 6, 140–141, 149, 173, 181–182
Muslim travel ban, 181, 206

N

Namkai-Meche, Taliesin Myrddin, 149
narcissism: charismatic leader-follower relationships and, xv–xxvii; of Trump, 33, 34, 55–56
narcissistically wounded individuals, xxiv, xxv–xxvi
narcissistic personality, 3–11
Narcissistic Personality Disorder (NPD), 3–4
narcissistic rage, 72
narcissistic transferences, xvii, xviii–xix
Narcissus, 55
Nasrallah, Hassan, 67
National Policy Institute, 147
National Rifle Association (NRA), 118–119, 132, 174–175
National Security Council, 93
National Socialist Legion (NSL), 153–154
Nation of Islam, 155
Native Americans, 152
NATO alliance, 66, 196, 197, 220
neo-Nazis, 15, 82, 144, 147, 153
Nesbit, Jeff, 85
Netanyahu, Benjamin, 207
Netanyahu, Bibi, 25
Netanyahu, Yonatan, 25
Never Trump movement, 105–106, 170
New American, The, 157
New Black Panther Party, 155
New York Military Academy, 26–29, 72

New York Times, x, 7, 11, 32, 34, 64, 73, 95, 99, 102, 108, 181
Nielsen, Kirstjen, 171
Nieto, Enrique Peña, 170
9/11 terrorist attacks, 66, 181
Nineteenth Amendment, 224
Nixon, Richard, 62, 216
Nobel Peace Prize, 217
Nobel Prize Complex, 4
No Climate Tax initiative, 127
Nolan, Jim, 141
Nomani, Asra Q., 173
non-followers, 105–106
normal narcissism, 3–4
Northam, Ralph, 191
North American Free Trade Agreement (NAFTA), 125
North Korea, 151, 195, 197, 213–219
nostalgia, 115
"Not a Politician," 113–114
nuclear weapons, xii, 107, 204, 209, 213, 214, 215, 216, 219
Nussbaum, Emily, 38

O

Obama, Barack, 5–6, 21, 67, 73, 74, 86, 89–91, 126, 173, 194
Obamacare, 5, 73, 130, 167
O'Donnell, John, 137–138
O'Donnell, Rosie, 9
oil, 205–206, 208
Omar, Ilhan, 191
One China Policy, 211–212
O'Reilly, Bill, 207
organized crime, 15, 31, 32
Our Principles PAC, 99, 105–106
outsourcing, 125
overestimation of success, 34
overvaluation, 21
Owen-Smith, Ashli, 181

P

Packer, Katie, 99, 105–106

INDEX

Page, Lisa, 184
paid family leave, 53
Palestinian Authority, 207–208
Palmieri & Co., 32
Panning, Jennifer, 180
paranoia, xxi, xxii, 58, 154, 157, 182–185
paranoid orientation, 7–8
Paris climate agreement, 53, 126
Park Guen-hye, 219
Parkland, Florida shooting, 185
party affiliation, 96–97
passion, 58
pathological narcissism, 3–4, 7–10
Patriot Front (PF), 153–154
Patton, Lynn, 169–170
Paul, Scott, 127–128
Pelosi, Nancy, 189–190
Pence, Mike, 116–117, 171, 172–173
Pendergraft, Rachel, 81–82, 146, 159–162
Penn Central, 32
People for the Ethical Treatment of Animals (PETA), 133
Peoples Temple, xvi, xxvi
Perot, Ross, 97
Perry, Caitríona, 166
Perry, Rick, 129
personality study, xiii, xiv
Philippines, 212–213
Playboy, 35, 38, 97, 138
polarization, xix–xxii, 140
policy decisions, 65–66
political contributions, 97, 187–188
political correctness, 109–110
political divisions, 182, 223
political paranoia, 183
political personality profiles, xii–xiv;
    Donald Trump, 64–75; Donald Trump Jr., 46–49; Eric Trump, 49–50; Ivanka Trump, 50–53; Kim Jong-un, 218–219; Melania Trump, 43–45; Mike Pence, 116–117; Steve Bannon, 94; Vladimir Putin, 201–205
political polls, 10, 88, 90, 222

Pompeo, Mike, 68, 197, 217
popular vote, 10
populism, 123
Porto, Bob, 87
Posobiec, Jack, 139
Post, Jerrold, vii–xiv
prenuptial agreements, 59
presidential biographies, 67–68
presidential campaigns: 2000, 44, 98, 145; 2016, 48–49, 50, 52, 81, 93, 96, 143
presidential election of 2016, 10, 56, 98–99, 180, 188–189, 221–222
presidential election of 2020, 106, 191–192, 221–224
projection, 222
pro-life issue, 115–116
Propecia, 64–65
Protecting Religiously Affiliated Institutions Act, 156
pseudo-charisma, xx
psychiatrists, 11
psychobiography, xiii, xiv
psychological impact, 179–186
psychopathic personality, 11
publicity, 57
Puder, John, 110
Puerto Rico, 139–140
Purinton, Adam, 151
Putin, Vladimir, 9, 195, 200–205, 217–218, 224

Q

Qin (emperor), 57
Quinn, Annalisa, 51
Quivers, Robin, 44

R

racial discrimination, 31–32, 135
racism, 123, 135–138, 155–156, 169–170, 210
Rai, Deep, 151
rallies, xxii, 6, 63, 80–81, 83, 94–95, 141–142, 223

INDEX

reading habits, 66–69
Reagan, Ronald, 107, 110, 120
real estate development, 23, 30, 32–33
recognition, need for, 80
Reform Party, 44, 97, 98, 138, 145
refugees, 49, 138, 197
Reilly, Wilfred, 157
religious cults, xxiv, xxv
religious minorities, 173–174, 181–182
religious rhetoric, xx
religious symbols, 149
renewable energy, 70
reparative charismatic leaders, xxvi-xxvii, 83, 140
Republican Jewish Coalition (RJC), 173–174
Republican Party: during 2016 election, 98–99; divisions in, 96–120; Trump and, 96–98, 120, 189
Republican politicians, 99–105
Republicans, 83
retweets, 139
revenge, 8–9, 57–58, 59–60
Reyes, Matias, 136
rhetoric: anti-immigrant, 109–110, 125–126, 151, 185; of hate, 135–148, 151; power of, 140–144; religious, xx; of Trump, 107–114, 123–124, 127, 135–144, 151
Rhoad, Erica, 132
Richardson, Rochelle, 168–169
right-wing extremists, 143–148, 153, 162–164
Robb, Thomas, 146
Robespierre, Maximilien, xx
Rockefeller, John D., 13
romantic relationships, 182
Romney, Mitt, 99, 103–104, 194, 198
Rona Barrett Looks at Today's Super Rich, 64
Roosevelt, Eleanor, 18–19
Roosevelt, Franklin Delano, 18–19
Roosevelt, Sara, 18–19
Rose, Richard, 151

Ross, Ronnie, 152
Rousseau, Thomas, 153
Rubio, Marco, 73, 101, 127, 170
rural areas, 128–134, 174
Russert, Tim, 138, 213
Russia, 195, 198, 199–201, 208, 217–218
Russia investigation, 8, 9–10, 73, 184
Ryan, Paul, 93, 102

S

Safari Club International (SCI), 132, 133
Samari, Goleen, 181–182
Sanders, Bernie, 49, 185, 191, 192
Sanders, Sarah Huckabee, 63, 100–101, 156
Santelli, Rick, 84
Satan, xx
Saudi Arabia, 208–209
Sayoc, Cesar Altieri, Jr., 183–184
scapegoating, 7, 8, 124
Scherb, Aaron, 111
school shootings, 185
Schroth, Rob, 113
Schumer, Chuck, 56, 187–188
Schwartz, Tony, 34
Schwarz, Carlo, 141
Second Amendment, 117–119
second sons, 24–27
self-doubt, 35, 81
self-esteem, 41
self-object relationships, xxvii, 40–54
self-preservation, xxvi
Serkes, Kathryn, 166–167
Sessions, Jeff, 33, 54, 73
setbacks, 35
Shabazz, Samir, 155
Shepard, Matthew, 160
Shiflett, Dave, 97
Sikh Coalition, 149
Sikhs, 149, 151
SilencerCo., 118
Simmons, William Joseph, 143
Simpson, Wallis, 24

Sirleaf, Ellen Johnson, 51
Skitka, Linda, 182
Slater, Robert, 48
slights, sensitivity to, 10
Smith, Ty, 175
Smollett, Jussie, 159
social issues, 88
social media, 3, 69
societal crisis, temporarily overwhelmed followers and, xxiii-xxiv
Soros, George, 49, 154
South Africa, 140, 210
South Korea, 219
Soviet Union, 199, 203, *see also* Russia
Spellbinders, The (Willner), xvi-xvii
Spencer, Richard, 82, 139, 147, 163
Spicer, Sean, 101
"Spirit of America" rallies, 94–95
splitting, xix-xxii, 124
"spoils of war" rhetoric, 205–206
Stahl, Lesley, 195–196, 200
steel dossier, 201
Stefano, Jennifer, 95
Stephanopoulos, George, 6
Stern, Howard, 36–37, 43, 44, 46
Stewart, Corey, 120
stimulus package, 84, 87
Stone, Ann, 166, 167
Stone, Roger, 107, 167
stress, 179–180
Strzok, Peter, 184
Students for Life, 175
Students for Trump (S4T), 175
success: expectation of, 80; overestimation of, 34; Trump's tips for, 58–59
Sullivan, Harry Stack, 9
Swain, Carol, 169–170
Swiss cheese conscience, 74–75
sycophants, 7
Syria, 206–207; troop withdrawal from, 61, 65–66, 71, 198, 207
Syrian refugees, 49

T

Tackett, Ann, 166
Taiwan, 211
Take Back Our Republic, 110
Tarasoff principle, 227n2
tariffs, 125, 128, 195
Tartakoff, Helen, 4
taxes, 70
Tea Party: history of, 84–86, 127; supporters, 86–88; Trump and, 88–92, 94–95
teavangelicals, 88
technology, 71
television shows, 34, 35, 38–39
terrorism, xxv, 138, 181–182, 191, 197, 198, 207
terrorist organizations, 67, 209
Think Big and Kick Ass (Trump), 9, 59–60, 67
Thomas, Dylan, 221
Tillerson, Rex, 197
Time to Get Tough (Trump), 193, 200–201, 206, 208, 211
Tlaib, Rashida, 169–170, 190, 191
tobacco companies, 85–86
Tolentino, Jia, 51
Tomasello, Willie, 15
Torricelli, Bob, 98
torture, 29
trade policies, 70, 124–125, 130–131, 195, 210–212, 220
transference, 227n2
transgender individuals, 150, 181
transgender policy, 53, 65
Trans-Pacific Partnership, 125
Tree of Life synagogue shooting, 162
Trump, Barron, 46
Trump, Donald: 2020 elections and, 106, 191–192, 221–224; Africa and, 210; aggression by, 8–9; attacks by, 7; Bannon and, 92–94; business career of, 30–33, 55–61, 113–114; as celebrity, 33–39, 80; on Charlottesville protests,

INDEX

15, 82, 139, 144, 152–153, 156, 223; children of, 45–53; China and, 210–212; on *Citizen Kane*, 10–11; Democratic Party and, 71, 96–97, 187–188; early years of, 16–17; emotional reactions of, 72–74; Europe and, 195–199; family background of, 12–24, 26–27, 80, 122–123; as father's successor, 23–24, 31, 80; foreign policy of, 193–220; friends of, 54; hate crimes and, 141–142, 155–157; impact of, 179–186; insecurity of, 9–10; Kim Jong-un and, 4, 212–214, 216–218, 224; as King, 55–56; lack of empathy in, 4–7; leadership style, 57–62; Left's reaction to, 187–192; lying by, 62–63; McCain and, 5–6, 73, 91, 102, 126–127, 137; on mental health issues, 185–186; Middle East and, 205–210; at military academy, 26–29; mirror-hungry personality of, 79–80; mother of, 15, 20–23; narcissism of, 7–10, 33, 34, 55–56; North Korea and, 213–219; opinion on mental stability of, xi–xii; paranoia of, 7–8; Philippines and, 212–213; political personality of, 64–75; political psychology of, xiii–xiv; as president, 57–63; psychiatric diagnoses of, 11; racism of, 155–156, 169–170, 210; relationship with father, 16–17, 22, 23–24; Republican Party and, 96–98, 120; Republican politicians and, 99–105; rhetoric of, 107–114, 123–124, 127, 135–144, 151; Russia and, 199–201; sensitivity to slight of, 10; Swiss cheese conscience of, 74–75; Tea Party and, 88–92, 94–95; as troublemaker, 23, 26–27; wives of, 40–45

Trump, Donald Jr., 45, 46–49, 118, 119, 131–134, 159, 188

Trump, Elizabeth, 14

Trump, Eric, 45, 46, 47, 49–50, 118, 132, 156

Trump, Fred III, 5

Trump, Fred, Jr., 5, 16, 21–24, 26, 56

Trump, Fred, Sr., 5, 16–17, 21–24, 26–27, 31, 55

Trump, Friedrich, xiv, 12–16

Trump, Ivana, 10, 40–41, 42, 47, 74

Trump, Ivanka, 45, 46, 47, 50–53, 94

Trump, Mary, 15, 20–23

Trump, Melania, 41, 43–45, 52

Trump, Tiffany, 45, 46

Trump, William, 5

Trump Airlines, 30

Trump Anxiety Disorder, 180

Trump Card: Playing to Win in Work and Life, The (Trump), 51

Trump Entertainment Resorts, Inc., 31

Trump: How to Get Rich (Trump), 65

Trump Marina, 31

Trump Organization, 62

Trump Plaza, 31

Trump supporters, 106; 2020 elections and, 224; alt-right, 81–82; disillusioned, 163–164; evangelicals, 88, 115–116, 171; foreign policy and, 220; gay, 172–173; hard-line, 73–74, 79–83; hate crimes against, 160–162; issues appealing to, 115–119; Jewish, 173–174; millennials, 174–175; minorities, 168–174, 175; Muslim, 173; paranoia of, 182–185; relationship between Trump and, 79–83; rhetorical appeal to, 107–114; in rural areas, 128–134; women, 165–168, 175; working class, 121–124

Trump Taj Mahal, 31

Trump: The Game, 34

Trump University, 30–31, 138

Trump Village, 16

trust, 22

turbans, 149

Turkey, 195

Tusk, Donald, 195

TV ratings, 69

Twenge, Jean, 22

Twenty-Fifth Amendment, 71

INDEX

Twitter, 139, 141
Twitter storms, 65–66, 72–74, 192, 194
Tyler, Elizabeth, 143

U
Ukraine, 203, 204, 205
Ulman, Richard Barrett, xvi
uncertainty, 35
undocumented immigrants, 91, 109, 125–126, 157, 185
Unification Church, xxiv
United Constitutional Patriots, 154–155
United Nations Arms Trade Treaty, 119
United States: allies of, 195–199, 208, 220; world opinion of, 199
Unite the Right rally, 144, 152–153, 156, *see also* Charlottesville, Virginia protests
U.S. embassy, in Israel, 207–208
U.S. government system, 70
U.S. military, 53, 65, 104–105
USS *McCain*, 6

V
Vanguard America (VA), 153–154
vanity, 64
Venezuela, 9–10, 197, 224
Veselnitskaya, Natalia, 49
victim blaming, 156
video game, 35
Vietnam War, 28, 33
violence: encouragement of, 81, 83, 142; school shootings, 185, *see also* hate crimes
visa system, 70
vocabulary, 68
Volkan, Vamik, xxvi
Votel, Joseph, 61, 65, 71
voter fraud, 221–222

W
Waldron, Joshua, 118
Wall Street Journal, 88, 90, 101, 103, 195

war dead program, 218
Warmbier, Otto, 216
Warner, John, 104–105
Warren, Elizabeth, 73, 191
Warren, Michael W., 136
Washington Post, 6, 7, 34, 63, 68, 73, 89, 92, 98, 103, 146
Waters of the United States rule, 130
Weber, Max, xv, xvi, xxiii
Welch, Jack, 98
Weld, Bill, 106
Wharton Business School, 45–46
"white genocide," 140, 153, 159, 164
white nationalists, 153–154, 164
white supremacists, 82, 139, 140, 144–148, 153, 156, 157–158, 161–162
Wildenmann, Rudolf, xx
Willner, Ann Ruth, xvi–xvii, xx
Wilson, Woodrow, 17–18
Winfrey, Oprah, 42, 51, 97–98
wives, 40–45
Wolff, Michael, 130
women: mental heath issues and, 181; as Trump supporters, 165–168, 175
Women Vote Trump, 166–168
Women Who Work (Trump), 51
working class, 121–126, 127–128
wounded self, xvii, xviii, 79–80
Wright, Robin, 222–223

X
Xi Jinping, 223

Y
Yamoah, Adwoa, 37
Yang, John, 150–151
Yates, Elizabeth A., 92

Z
Zelizer, Julian, 68

CPSIA information can be obtained
at www.ICGtesting.com
Printed in the USA
LVHW04230705 0121
675792LV00014B/2765